The Bazaar

The Bazaar

MARKETS AND MERCHANTS OF THE ISLAMIC WORLD

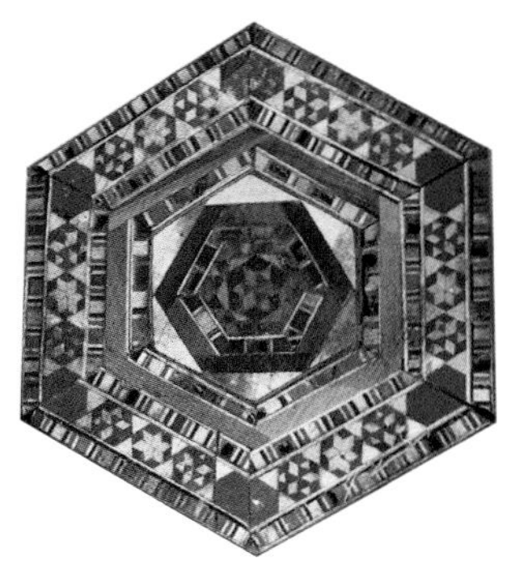

Walter M. Weiss

Photographs by
Kurt-Michael Westermann

Plans by E.T. Balic

THAMES AND HUDSON

Pages 8 to 21: 'In the Empire of the Senses'
Berber palace in the old kasbah, Ouarzazate, southern Morocco
Weekly market, Agadez, Niger
The Ghadaia oasis, Mzab, Algeria
Street intersection in the middle of the bazaar, Aleppo, Syria
Tea house in the camel market, Imbaba, Cairo, Egypt
Part of the main street, Talaa Seghira, Fez, Morocco
Fabric printers in the souk, Aleppo, Syria

Page 22: Khane Firaun, 'Pharaoh's treasury', Petra, Jordan

The calligraphy at the beginning of each chapter is reproduced, with permission, from *Sufi, Expressions of the Mystic Quest* by Laleh Bakhtiar (Thames and Hudson, London, 1976)

Translated from the German *Der Basar: Mittelpunkt des Lebens in der islamischen Welt* by Lorna Dale

For the transliteration of non-Roman alphabets, see the note on page 251

First published in the United States of America in hardcover in 1998 by Thames and Hudson Inc., 500 Fifth Avenue, New York, New York 10110

Library of Congress Catalog Card Number 97-61954
ISBN 0-500-01839-1

Printed and bound in Italy

CONTENTS

God is the east and the west;
whichever way you turn, there is God's countenance.
Truly, God is all-embracing and all-knowing.

KORAN, 11.115

Foreword

An encounter I had in the City of the Dead outside Cairo made a deep impression on me. The *khamsin*, the notorious desert wind, had covered everything in a mantle of grey dust. The smoke from the smouldering rubbish tips stung the eyes. The air was burning hot. The alleyways between the densely populated graves and wooden shacks were deserted, littered with rubbish, utterly desolate. A young woman in a colourful threadbare *galabiyya* appeared, struggling along with two cans of water. As she passed, to my surprise she greeted me with a laugh – and what a laugh! She was telling me with her eyes that the grinding poverty all around us did not touch her deep inside. Daily life was not a burden for her because her strength came from elsewhere. You would never hear a laugh like that in a poor quarter of a European city.

Since that unforgettable meeting in the early eighties I have made some thirty trips to Islamic countries and seen their finest mosques, palaces and landscapes. But – and I am aware when I write this of the inherent contradictions in the conventional romanticized image of the 'spiritual' Orient – wherever I go I am charmed by the cheerful realism of the people and their unshakeable trust in God. Antoine de Saint-Exupéry said: 'There are main road people and footpath people. The main road people bore me. I am bored on the asphalt road between the milestones. These people have set their sights on a particular goal: profit, success. Along the path there are hazel bushes instead of milestones and you can amble along and crack the hazelnuts. You are there for the sake of being there.' In the bazaars there are no milestones.

The mass media tend to oversimplify; they see everything in black and white. In their search for 'bogeymen' they have found plenty of material in the Arab world in recent years. As so often since the time of the Crusades, East and West see each other, in different ways, as a threat. But in both East and West it is the aggressive propagandists and not the quiet thinkers who attract attention, and so in the collective imagination of the West every Muslim becomes a feared and unpredictable fanatic.

Fortunately for us all, a new generation of orientialists and Islamic experts is now emerging, replacing the tired old clichés with fresh ideas. Surprisingly, however, only a few writers have looked at the phenomenon of the bazaar (and even then from a purely academic point of view). Until now, it has been difficult to find a book that gave the interested layman a clear and coherent picture of all the aspects of this traditional and unique achievement of Islamic culture.

In this book we – author and photographer – had two objectives. Firstly, we have tried to explain and communicate – to show that a bazaar is much more than just a picturesque maze of workshops and shops in which tourists pick up souvenirs and get lost. It is a city within a city, with its own economy and way of life and a spiritual background from which western society has a great deal to learn, especially now when it is having to redefine concepts like work, time and solidarity.

Secondly, we have tried to take stock of the situation. However untouched many of the bazaars might seem at first sight, their traditional features – old buildings and trades, customs and values and aesthetic perceptions – are increasingly threatened by western technology and industry.

As a sheikh from Tangier remarked when Europeans, having just occupied his home town, introduced electric lights: 'If these people prayed five times a day, they would not worry about such childish things.'

Walter M. Weiss

THE ENDLESS CARAVAN

A BRIEF HISTORY OF TRADE

The major routes

The camel

Incense, amber silk and gold

In the traditional and complex form in which it is still found in many Middle Eastern countries, the bazaar is – as will be explained – a unique achievement of Islamic culture. But the fundamental impulse which inspired it, to trade and barter for profit, is of course as old as the human race. The first civilizations on the banks of the Euphrates, the Tigris and the Nile already had active trading links, supplying each other with all kinds of valuable weapons and metals, precious stones, fabrics and foodstuffs, transported by camel or donkey. Rare spices and perfumes soon began to arrive from India and South Arabia, ivory from the heart of Africa, and wood and furs from the regions north of the Caspian Sea. By then the Assyrians were already building and mapping out a proper road network, with wells alongside.

In the early days, large-scale farming was rare in the Orient because of the climate, the threat from the nomads and the low social status of farmers. The deserts and steppes remained trackless wastes, with only an occasional caravanserai between the oases and towns. The picture shows a desert post between Kerman and Bam in eastern Iran.

The ancient Persian Achaemenians were expert in communications. They were in contact with practically all the peoples in the known world. Their main coin, the gold *darikon,* was recognized as currency even in the remotest parts of the empire and they were the first to standardize customs duties and taxes. Their kings even had plans for a route round Africa and a canal between the Mediterranean and the Red Sea. But the most remarkable evidence of their logistic skills was their invention of the postal system. Around 550 BC Cyrus the Great had rest houses built approximately 25 kilometres (15½ miles) apart along the new 2,800-kilometre (1,740-mile) 'king's road' from Susa through Armenia, Cappadocia, Phrygia and Lydia to Sardes in the Aegean. Horses and couriers could be changed at any time of the day and night. Herodotus wrote enthusiastically that 'messages travel across country almost quicker than cranes can fly'. These first 111 caravanserais also had another use; they offered travellers shelter against robbers and the rigours of the weather at night. They were also bases for the military patrols which escorted the caravans during the day.

Qasr el-Hir ash-Sharqi (above), in the middle of the desert half-way between Palmyra and the Euphrates, is one of the biggest defensive posts along the Silk Road. Its walls enclosed a huge artificially irrigated garden as well as the large khan. *Below: camels on the way to Dubai racecourse.*

Asia Minor and the Levant were probably linked to distant China by a direct trading route even before Alexander the Great set out east in 334 BC with his army. But it was not until the 1st century BC that this route was given its legendary name, when a hitherto unknown material became popular with the Romans. The Silk Road ran from the Chinese capitals Luoyang and Chang'an in two arcs south and north of the Taklamakan desert to Kashgar and on to Samarkand and Bukhara. There one section branched off north to the Caspian Sea. This was used to transport goods via the Volga or Don to the Amber Road and on to the Baltic and the White Sea (where the Arabs later obtained furs, slaves, falcons, weapons and, above all, the much-prized amber). The main route went further

The main long-distance trade routes of Asia, Europe and Africa already intersected in Syria in ancient times. The oasis of Palmyra was a central crossing point (below: remains of the colonnaded street, with the Arab fort behind). Its economic importance grew in the second century BC as the Nabataean empire declined and was at its height under the legendary empress Zenobia around the year AD 270.

The region was no less important in world trade during the Islamic period. There were huge caravanserais like the splendidly restored one underneath the citadel of Apamea (above) all along the routes between Aleppo and Damascus or between the Euphrates and the Mediterranean.

west to Merv, Nishapur and Hamadan (from which one road led north to the Black Sea port of Trabzon, another south to Isfahan and Hormuz) and finally to Baghdad and Palmyra, the former seat of the empress Zenobia, where the Silk Road forked for the last time. The northern branch ended in Antioch; the southern – beyond Damascus, Tyre and Gaza – in Cairo.

Not only was the 14,000-kilometre (8,700-mile) road a trading route, it was also a cultural link. For instance, mirrors, paints, medicines and camphor (later so important in the manufacture of gunpowder and for mothproofing) were brought from east to west; so too were porcelain and paper, the magnetic compass and printing. Gold, glass and precious stones were taken in the opposite direction, as well as religion. Nestorian Christians and followers of the now long-defunct Manichaean religion

were particularly successful as missionaries in the wilds of Asia.

By far the most important product, however, was silk. Europeans paid the highest prices for it. Traders were prepared to go to great lengths to obtain it. A Chinese princess is said to have smuggled a cocoon out of the country in her hair around AD 500 (other sources say that Christian monks were the culprits). Nonetheless, the Chinese guarded the secret of silk-making for centuries and it worked to their advantage. Europeans – the Moors in Spain and the Normans in Sicily – did not manage to breed silkworms commercially until the 11th century.

Obviously, however, the aim of the rulers in securing the long-distance routes militarily was not so much to stop this early form of industrial espionage as to put an end to the widespread banditry which made every journey a hazardous undertaking. That was the reason for the fortresses built along the caravan routes in the middle of the 1st century BC by the Sogdians in Central Asia and for the heavily fortified Buddhist monasteries farther to the east. The border forts built by the Romans in the Syrian desert and their counterparts in western China were designed to protect not only their territory but also traders passing through. The international trading agreements which the Parthian king Mithridates II signed with the Chinese Han dynasty around 115 BC also aimed to improve security. In Roman times, many towns had private and official information points for traders. They prepared travel guides with useful advice on lodgings, distances and facilities for changing horses and buying food.

In the early days, shipping played a minor role in world trade, although ships were certainly built in the time of the Pharaohs and ancient Babylonians. In the 3rd millennium BC the Egyptians were already bringing their building timber from Lebanon by water. Around 2000 BC the Cretans were sailing the eastern Mediterranean and the Phoenicians sailed the whole of the Mediterranean not long after that. But on the seas between East Africa, Arabia, China and India, sailors were still reluctant to lose sight of the coast.

It was not until around 200 BC, when the Greek merchant Hippalus discovered how the monsoon winds worked and showed how they could be used to sail from Arabia diagonally across the ocean to India and back, that transcontinental shipping began to develop in the east. By the start of the Christian era – by which time the feared waters of the Red Sea had been further explored and navigation techniques significantly improved – the Roman merchant navy already had 120 ships regularly plying between Egypt and the subcontinent. In the other direction, the Chinese sailed as far as the Euphrates.

On the other hand, the Atlantic remained a blank space on the traders' nautical charts throughout antiquity. The Phoenicians were believed to have sailed between the Pillars of Hercules as far as the Canaries and the Azores in 600 BC; but the Genoese and Portuguese who ventured along the coast of West Africa at the end of the Middle Ages were unable to find any sizeable harbours. The reason was that the main trading centres were in the interior, on rivers like the Niger and the Congo. Goods were traded with the northern peoples across the Sahara and not by sea.

The Arabian Peninsula was a centre of world trade even in pre-antiquity. Perfumes such as myrrh and incense, which were essential in the religious rites of the Egyptians and Babylonians, grew on its south coast and in the north of present-day Somalia. The subjects of the Queen of Sheba and their neighbours in the adjoining tributary states profited from this natural wealth. They organized the supplies on trading routes from South Arabia across the mountains of Yemen and through the Hejaz to the Mediterranean and also acted as middlemen for goods from India. Around 300 BC, a unique caravan state developed in the north of Arabia. The Nabataeans, a desert people, had flocked to the area between Aqaba and the Dead Sea in the local migration following the Babylonian captivity of the Jews. At first, they lived mainly by robbing caravans, but they soon began to run the long-distance transport themselves from their capital, Petra. They set up a security cordon with guard posts and guarded wells and built goods depots where the roads intersected. They took over the incense from the southern Arabians in the Hegra oasis. From there their camel convoys took it in thirty to forty daily marches either along the incense route to the posts of Gaza or Rhinocolura (later el-Arish) or further into the interior, via Wadi Sirhan to Bosra and Damascus.

The Nabataean state was at its most extensive around the time of Christ's birth. It was an unusually peaceful state geared solely to profit from trade, with no real borders, no taxation or social unrest and very few slaves. Its strength was that it consistently managed to keep a distance between the producers and consumers of the goods it transported. The success of this strategy first came under threat after the year 106, when the Romans designated the north of the peninsula 'Provincia Arabia' and increased shipping on the Red Sea. But eventually the Nabataeans lost the monopoly only through the incursion of new nomadic tribes, who at first merely demanded a protection tax, but gradually took over land transport in Arabia.

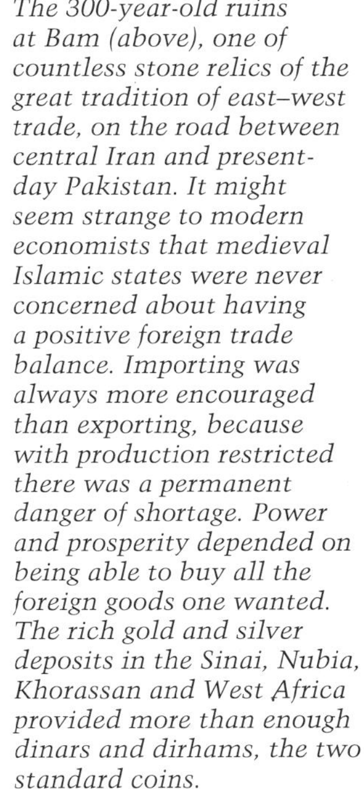

The 300-year-old ruins at Bam (above), one of countless stone relics of the great tradition of east–west trade, on the road between central Iran and present-day Pakistan. It might seem strange to modern economists that medieval Islamic states were never concerned about having a positive foreign trade balance. Importing was always more encouraged than exporting, because with production restricted there was a permanent danger of shortage. Power and prosperity depended on being able to buy all the foreign goods one wanted. The rich gold and silver deposits in the Sinai, Nubia, Khorassan and West Africa provided more than enough dinars and dirhams, the two standard coins.

The port of Mocha at the southern end of the Red Sea is a striking example of the rapid rise – and fall – of a trading centre. When coffee became popular in Europe in the 17th century, much of it came from plantations in the mountains of Yemen and was exported via Mocha until coffee began to be grown on other continents. Above: remains of a mosque and an Ottoman trader's house. Kasbahs like those still found in the south of Morocco were precursors to the city markets. Below: the Ait-Benhaddou settlement near Ouarzazate.

One such tribe, the Qoraishites, had settled in a barren valley half way between Yemen and the Mediterranean and set up a small trading republic through which a number of caravan routes passed. The place was known as Mecca and it soon developed into a local capital with regular goods fairs and festivals. Every year, the most celebrated poets competed for the laureateship there. The main attraction of the town was the religious site of the Kaaba, a cube-shaped stone building surrounded by idols, with a black meteorite built into its walls. Every year, thousands of people walked reverently around it on the annual pilgrimage.

In this heathen Mecca a son was born – it is believed in 571 – to the family which had the prerogative of distributing the holy water from the Zemzem well to the pilgrims. For many years he was known as Abul-Qasim. Later he was called Mohammed, 'the praiseworthy'.

Before God revealed a holy book to him in his sleep (from the year 610) and he became the founder of a great religion, Mohammed was himself a trader. When he was about 25, he married Khadija, a merchant's widow considerably older than he was, and travelled to Syria with a caravan as her agent – an experience which, as will be explained later in this book, gave trade a particular status in Islam.

After Mohammed's death in 632, the new world power expanded at an unprecedented rate. Islam's followers were already conquering Mesopotamia by 633 and two years later they took Damascus. In 642 they captured Persia and Egypt. In 711 they crossed the Straits of Gibraltar. In 732 their armies were in western France. Scarcely twenty years later they inflicted a heavy defeat on the Chinese deep in Central Asia.

It is often said that the Arab advance severely restricted international trade. Some trade routes were certainly cut off for a short period, but by the middle of the 8th century trade – especially between the Levant, Arabia and the Far East – was more flourishing than ever. Barriers such as those between the Byzantine and Sassanian Empires had fallen. The spread of Arabic as the new *lingua franca* simplified trade relations. Soon Muslim merchants were settling in India, Malaysia and Indonesia (bringing Islam peacefully to those regions). Mohammed had imposed a duty on his followers to make the pilgrimage to Mecca, the *hajj*, and this too was a boost to trade. Damascus and Cairo supplied the holy cities of the Hejaz with goods in special caravans which later, in the heyday of the Ottoman Empire, contained tens of thousands of animals. The faithful also used to take goods with them and sell them to raise money for their journey.

As early as the 10th century, the Arabs were improving on many of the ancient trade practices. They used cashless payment methods, bills of exchange and cheques (our word comes from the Arabic) and they were also familiar with letters of credit, which could be cashed anywhere in the empire like travellers' cheques. There was no banking system in the modern sense and rich merchants exploited their capital through trade, acting as moneylenders, moneychangers and financiers. Their trade was highly speculative, since it often took months to transport the goods, during which time prices at their destination might have fallen, and in order to minimize the risks they set up joint trading companies for fixed periods. They also established a network of intercontinental contacts at a very early stage by appointing local agents in foreign cities to handle customs formalities and make payments on written instructions.

The Arabs had begun to use camels rather than carts for transport. Camels were more useful because they adapted to any terrain and were better able to cross obstacles such as fords or passes, making surfaced roads like those built by the Persians and Romans superfluous. However, the rest houses and stores which Cyrus built along the long-distance routes, which we now call by the later Turkish name caravanserais, were far from superfluous. In fact, their numbers increased as trade developed.

When the celebrated world traveller ibn-Battuta set out from Cairo for Damascus in 1326, he noted in his diary: 'At the end of each day's journey there is a rest house known as a *khan* on this stretch of road, where travellers can stay with their animals. The *khans* are surrounded by high walls and have a single entrance. Their courtyards are lined with stables and sleeping niches. They have public wells and shops where people can buy what they need for themselves and their animals.' What ibn-Battuta did not mention was that, long before then, many *khans* had shops and stores, mills, bakeries and tea houses, even baths and mosques. The most impressive date from the time of the Seljuks and can still be seen today on the plateaux of Central Anatolia, some well maintained, some in ruins.

Although the Muslim merchants travelled remarkable distances to the east, south and even west, they were not familiar with Europe. Syrian pirates regularly attacked the Greek coast in the early days of Islam; Sicily was under Arab rule for over two hundred years; and North Africans and Moors settled in southern Italy and the south of Spain, even occasionally advancing as far as the Swiss Alpine valleys; but it was some time before the oriental merchants became aware of the main Mediterranean ports in France and northern Italy. In Venice, for instance, it was the Ottomans who first set up a *fondaco*, a trading company.

Muslims were for many years suspicious of the land route to the north-west. To them the Carpathians and the Alps were a barrier between the inhabited world and the realms of darkness.

The Western Europeans, on the other hand, were very active in the east. The early Crusaders and pilgrims to Jerusalem rediscovered the ancient routes along the Danube and through the Balkans to Asia Minor, and even before that Charlemagne had sent a diplomatic delegation to Harun ar-Rashid. At that time foreign trade between Western Europe and the south and east was mainly organized by the Jews, firstly because, for religious reasons, Christians were reluctant to travel to the 'enemy territory' of the Muslims, especially in the early centuries, and secondly because, with their enforced mobility, the Jews were generally more polyglot and more seasoned travellers. Wherever they found themselves, between the Atlantic and the Indian Ocean, they could always count on the help of fellow Jews locally. A legendary group of Jewish merchants, the *rahdaniya* (Persian for 'people who know the roads'), travelled back and forth regularly between Western Europe and China across the Red Sea and the Persian Gulf or through southern Russia and Central Asia.

From the 12th century onwards, Italian seafarers from Amalfi, Genoa, Pisa and, above all, Venice dominated east–west trade. In their settlements in the Levant and along the Black Sea coast, they loaded their ships with all the exotic goods so much prized by the European aristocracy – luxury fabrics, carpets, mirrors, porcelain, medicines and spices (especially pepper), used to liven up the monotonous winter diet of salted meat. However, if they wanted to travel farther east, through Syria and Persia or Egypt, their way was blocked by the Turks and Arabs. The trade monopoly on the routes to China and India was much too lucrative.

Archaeologists uncovered the oldest remains of a pre-Islamic bazaar in Dura-Europos on the bank of the Euphrates in the east of what is now Syria. The ruins (above) are about 2,300 years old. The Seleucids established this trading post between the centres on the Mediterranean and in Mesopotamia. Their successors, the Parthians, used it as a border fortification against the Roman Empire. Even then long-distance trading was in well-organized large caravans. Few people travelled individually, not least for safety reasons.

It was not until 1250 that the barrier was lifted, thanks to the Mongols, whose influence on the world has otherwise been regarded as disastrous. Under Genghis and Kublai Khan they inflicted unutterable misery on a great part of Asia and Eastern Europe, but paradoxically they helped the development of foreign trade. Their huge empire, at times stretching from the Carpathians to Korea, formed the largest free-trade area that had ever existed. The Khans proved to be tolerant to every religion and a number of European missionaries and diplomats were invited to their court. They also encouraged traders, regardless of where they came from or of their religious beliefs, to travel widely by reducing taxes and customs duties, giving them letters of safe conduct and imposing severe penalties for highway robbery. It was with their help that Marco Polo travelled from Venice to Cathay (China) and back along the Silk Road.

European and Arab trade with the Far East flourished for a century until the Mongol rulers sank into decadence. The Chinese rebelled and founded their own Ming dynasty in 1368, cutting themselves off from the rest of the world. In 1405 Tamerlane died and his empire collapsed. The barriers went up again in the east. When the Portuguese seafarer Vasco da Gama discovered the sea route to India for King Manuel I of Portugal in the 15th century, the East finally lost its dominant position in transcontinental trade.

Considering how well-versed the Arabs were in the art of navigation at the time, it is surprising that they were not the first to discover the Cape of Good Hope passage. Nevertheless, Arab seafarers were actively trading in its ports long before the Islamic soldiers reached India by the land route. It was mainly the Persians, Iraqis and Omanis in their dhows who established a close network of routes between all the main bases in the Gulf and the Indian Ocean in the 9th and 10th centuries – from Basra and Siraf, Aden and Hormuz to Zanzibar, Ceylon (Sri Lanka) and Malaysia. Arab cosmographers like al-Idrisi (who drew the famous map of the world for the Norman king of Sicily, Roger II) were the first to refute Ptolemy's claim that the Indian Ocean was an inland sea. At the time, their European counterparts, hidebound by Catholic dogma, had not even heard of Ptolemy's revolutionary theories. The nautical manual written around 1490 by ibn-Majid (who after his death became patron of all Muslim seamen) is still valid in many areas even today. It is no accident that Sindbad, one of the main heroes of the tales from *A Thousand and One Nights*, is a seafarer.

So why did the Arabs not conquer the seas at the beginning of modern times?

One reason is superstition. Just as the Portuguese were afraid to push on to the west coast of Africa south of the Canaries because they believed it would lead to disaster, for the Arabs to the east the Mozambique Channel was the point of no return. It is written twice in the Koran that God separated the two seas by a barrier which no man could cross. Apart from that, the Arabs had general reservations about sea travel.

But there were also practical reasons, not least the geography of their homeland. The Arabian Peninsula has no navigable rivers or natural harbours and the hinterland is not populated. The razor-sharp coral reefs along its coasts are hazardous to shipping. Nor does it have any of the raw materials necessary for shipbuilding: wood or resin or flax for canvas sails. Another reason was the technology. The Arabs had introduced the triangular 'Latin' sail to the Mediterranean and invented the stern rudder, but, unlike the Europeans and Chinese, they joined their ships' planks together with ropes made of coconut fibre and not with nails (there was a legend that a magnetic mountain under the sea draws nails out of the wood). This made

The Arabs have always been traditionally sceptical about seafaring. Even the fearless general Amr ibn-al-As, who conquered Palestine and Egypt, said: 'There is little trust and great fear. Man at sea is like an insect on a splinter of wood – always in danger of being swallowed up by the waves and always frightened to death.' On rivers there were no such misgivings. The Nile, for instance, has been used for traffic from time immemorial. Above: feluccas off Cairo. Below: Sudanese waiting in the harbour of ash-Shallal, near Aswan, for the ferry to Wadi Halfa.

them much less durable, especially if there was a storm at sea.

Another possible reason is that they saw no cause to travel because they had, in a way, already arrived. The first people Vasco da Gama met when he landed on the Malabar Coast are known to have been traders from Tunis. Their fellow-Muslims had long since reached Korea on Chinese ships. And one of the greatest ironies of world history is that it was ibn-Majid himself who unwittingly showed the Portuguese captain the way on his voyage from Malindi to Calicut, accelerating, if not actually causing, the defeat of the Arab traders by their European rivals.

In the desert sands the Arabs were indisputably the master navigators. Long before the emergence of Islam, the Bedouin had become familiar with the constellations as they travelled to their grazing grounds at night and they could identify more than 250 stars. When they conquered North Africa in the name of Allah, they found traces of the Garamantes and Romans even in the middle of the Sahara. Their leader, Oqba ibn-Nafi, reached the road that led through Cyrenaica and Fezzan to the area around Lake Chad in 666. Islamic traders were soon venturing even further into the desert than the soldiers. They came to the borders of the legendary kingdom of Mali with its inexhaustible supplies of slaves and gold from the far west, from Marrakesh, and later from Fez and Sijilmassa via Taghaza and Timbuktu. Another route started from Tunis or the island of Djerba and went via Ghadames, past the Hoggar and Air Mountains to Gao on the Niger or via Agadez to Kano. A third route was from the Dakhla and Kharga oases in Egypt westwards to Ghat. The main north–south axis ran from Tripoli in the old kingdom of Kanem and Bornu to the banks of Lake Chad. From here the Arabs imported ivory, ostrich feathers, slaves, soda and alum for tanning and dying skins. Iron, paper and Arab horses, and later also guns and steel, went in the opposite direction.

These trans-Saharan caravans of up to 25,000 camels, covering distances of several thousand kilometres, finally came to an end at the beginning of the 20th century. There were many reasons, all connected with the growing influence of the European powers in North and West Africa. The abolition of slavery deprived traders of their main commodity. The artificial boundaries between the new states – Algeria, Libya, Mali, Niger and Chad – and the bureaucracy they created ruined the caravans' business. The modern traffic infrastructure was another factor. The ports along the west coast were enlarged and railway lines and lorry tracks built into the hinterland as far as the Sahel. New financial practices, such as cash transactions and paid work, also destroyed the old barter system.

However, a few caravans have survived in the Sahara to this day – despite war and colonization, robberies and rebellions. The best known is the *tarhalamt*, the Tuareg salt caravan from Bilma to the Fakhi saltworks in the north-east of what is now Niger. It is part of a complex system of caravans supplying markets in the Agadez–Kano–Bilma/Fakhi triangle. The central transfer point for this seasonal movement of goods is the area around the Kawar oasis east of the Ténéré desert. The system was seriously endangered by the catastrophic drought there in the late 1960s and when rainfall was at a record low at the beginning of the 1980s salt caravans were stopped and the government replaced them with lorries. An age-old tradition had finally died out, or so it seemed. But in 1986 the old mode of transport was revived, as though it had simply been brought to a temporary halt by the climate.

Once again, the camel had triumphed.

Even in the Middle Ages, before the advent of lorries, foreign trade was in a sense dependent on oil. Marco Polo mentioned 'black gold' as a cure for skin diseases in camels. Even earlier, in the 10th century, Arab writers described caravans taking oil all over Asia from Baku, the Caspian Sea port. The famous Turkish historian Evliya Celebi wrote in 1666: 'In Baku there are many infertile places. When a man or an animal sets foot there and stands still for a while, his foot begins to burn. The caravan leaders dig holes in the ground, put pots into them and the food is ready straight away. God's wisdom is wonderful!'

God's greatest gift

The technical specifications for this living four-legged HGV are impressive, showing how aware its creator was of economics and the environment. It can travel at 20 kilometres (12 miles) an hour over considerable distances; with a load, its speed is 4 to 5 kilometres (about 3 miles) an hour. It can cover 150 kilometres (almost 100 miles) in a day. Maximum load: 200 kilograms (440 pounds). Consumption: very low. Fuel capacity: up to 135 litres (30 gallons) of water. It is very economical to run; even in summer it only has to stop at a watering hole every two weeks. In between, all it needs to run perfectly is a couple of branches from woody plants, a few bushels of grass or even, in the middle of the desert, some dry straw. It lasts 25 to 30 years. Its main disadvantage is the low reproduction rate. The females only give birth up to ten

With the advance of the car and the railway, the age of the great long-distance caravans is over. The last two regularly crossing the Sahara are the assalai *between Taoudeni and Timbuktu in Mali and the* tarhalamt *between the oases of Bilma and Fakhi in Niger, both carrying mainly salt.*

times in their lifetime. Their young do not mature sexually until they are three or four.

There are two standard types. The two-humped Bactrian (*Camelus ferus*) from the mountainous areas of Central Asia and Western China has an ungainly but sturdy body and a shaggy coat. The thinner and faster one-humped dromedary (*Camelus dromedarius*), commonly also called a camel, comes from North Africa and Arabia. There are also several special breeds, such as the curiously ill-proportioned Iforas camel from the central Sahara (usually very light in colour), its normal-sized front half contrasting oddly with its stunted back half; or the pale-eyed deaf piebalds bred by a Tuareg tribe in the Air Mountains, which are particularly placid and docile.

All of them have several features in common. In hot dry weather their body temperature can rise to 46°C (115°F) to delay loss of fluid through sweating. At the same time, the carbamide content of their urine increases to two and a half times the normal level for mammals, reducing the need to urinate. Their nasal passages are so twisted that the air cools by 10°C (18°F) after they breathe it in and dries out as they exhale, conserving valuable water. When they drink (camels can drink 100 litres [22 gallons] or more in a few minutes), the water is stored in the tissue cells and the blood, not in the stomach. Their oval red blood corpuscles can expand by 240 times their volume. If they live off their water reserves, they can literally shrink and lose up to a quarter of their body weight without coming to any harm. They have extremely long eyelashes to protect them against the glare of the sun, and the soles of their feet are so broad and callused that they do not feel the heat of the sand. Their kidneys can easily absorb an excess of sodium chloride, so they are well protected against the often poor, brackish well water.

However, there is one feature for which there is no logical explanation and that is the comparatively small size of the male's reproductive organ. The Bedouin have an anecdote to explain this. After all the occupants of the Ark had moved into their quarters, Noah asked the males to hand over their organs for the duration of the voyage. With space so short, there was not going to be room for offspring. When the flood subsided, the animals went ashore and everything was returned to them, but in the confusion the donkey was given what had previously belonged to the camel. This might be why the male camel is so jealous and aggressive in the mating season that most are castrated at an early age as a precaution; but perhaps the disastrous error may also account for their highly unpredictable temperament. Camels never recognize their owner as their master. They run away whenever they can and have to be chased after. They are just as unwilling to be caught by their owners as by strangers, making them easy to steal. They are extremely unforgiving and vindictive – hence the belief, still widespread today, that they are descended from demonic supernatural *jinns*, whose shape they sometimes take on.

Long journeys are arduous for both men and animals. They usually start at first light and make camp again late at night. The caravaneers generally travel on foot, only riding during the hottest part of the day. They rarely stop, eating and drinking on the move. The caravan leaders find their bearings from mountains, dunes, cairns or, on well-travelled routes, the tracks left by other convoys of camels.

In general, the 'ships of the desert' are mentally and physically more delicate than their reputation suggests. They are very susceptible to polluted water or indigestible plants and often fall victim to mysterious diseases. After exhausting journeys, they take a long time to recover. If they are driven too hard, instead of refusing to work when they need to rest, they carry on until they drop dead. The reproductive act is fraught with difficulties because of the clumsiness of both partners and the male's physical inadequacy. Births are risky; the young can be injured as they fall or be inadvertently trampled by their mothers. Even milking them – a task performed only by men – is a delicate balancing act. Not only is the herdsman standing on one leg, resting his head on the animal's flank and balancing the pail on his thigh, but the camel keeps trying to bite him.

So it is no wonder that the Bedouin resort to all kinds of ruses to deal with these unmanageable beasts. They spoil their favourites with titbits and encourage them with rhythmic singing to keep them trotting on long marches. Without them the Bedouin would not be able to survive in the desert and they are devoted to the animals, decorating their reins and saddles with loving care.

The Arabic language has more than 160 words for the camel. The word *jamal* can

The famous annual pilgrim caravan from Cairo or Damascus to Mecca had its origins in the time of the Abbasids. Under the Ottomans it was a highly organized operation with tens of thousands of men and animals, including – as well as the faithful – warriors, traders and kadis, *water carriers and desert guides. Its departure and return were always the occasion for great festivities revolving around the flags of the Prophet and the state palanquin, the Sultan's baldachin-shaped symbol of majesty. These symbolized legitimate rule over the holy city. The camel market in Imbaba (where the pictures on this page were taken) is an indirect reminder of the tradition of the Cairo pilgrim caravan.*

mean either a camel or a beautiful woman, depending on the stress. If an Arab wants to be especially complimentary to his wife, he will call her his 'faithful camel'. A widow lamenting her dead husband will say, 'Oh, my camel!' Bedouin are buried in the skin of their favourite animal to be near it in the afterlife. Dreaming of a camel is a good omen. In mythology the stars are 'grazing camels which have found eternal peace with Allah'.

Soon after the first camels were domesticated – probably in the 3rd millennium BC – they became the focus of important ceremonies. As soon as a herd grew to a thousand animals, an eye was removed from a selected male. If the number doubled, the animal lost both its eyes. This was believed to protect against the evil eye and against sickness and robbers. It was considered good manners for well-to-do hosts to welcome guests with a ritually slaughtered camel. This was also the customary sacrifice in the month of the pilgrimage to Mecca in pre-Islamic times. Since the camel is especially favoured by God, eating its flesh is like a profession of faith. The Prophet once said, 'A man who does not eat my camels is not one of my people.'

This veneration is not at all surprising, considering that the desert peoples rely on the camel for everything: its meat (although the meat from older animals can be fairly tough); its milk, which is low in fat, rich in minerals and vitamins and a highly effective prophylactic against eye diseases; its skin, used to make strong leather belts, bags and sandals; and its coat, used for tents and soft, warm blankets. Its dung is dried for fuel and its urine is the only sterile liquid available for washing newborn babies and wounds. Camels are also a capital investment; they can be used to buy brides and to atone for crimes. Without the camel there would be no social contacts or power structures in the desert. By finding hidden wells, they have saved many Bedouin from dying of thirst. When a camel dies, several litres of valuable water can be extracted from its stomach and hump.

This multitude of uses explains why baby camels are treated with such care. They are allowed to stay in the tent for a few nights, to accustom them to human company. The ones that will be used for riding are carefully selected after a few months and trained a year or two later.

This deep relationship with the camel survives even in communities that have abandoned the nomadic life and embraced modern conveniences in the boom towns like Dubai or Abu Dhabi. At the big Friday camel races there, it is obvious that the cool and urbane exteriors mask archaic passions. Admittedly, the huge Bedouin tent beneath which sheikhs and ministers with their Raybans and Rolexes follow the races on television screens is actually made of concrete; the

camels are pampered creatures of luxury brought in from Qatar, Saudi Arabia and Oman on articulated lorries, and not working beasts of burden; and the riders are lightweight boys of six or seven tied to the humps, and not warriors. But the setting, with hundreds of camels and men stretched out asleep on the sand, is a timeless picture of a huge caravan camp. The hysterical groans and bellows of the camels at the start and the no less hysterical cries of the trainers are like the sounds of battle. Even the enthusiasm with which the stable owners talk about their favourites harks back to the time when camels were the only important earthly possession besides women and hunting falcons.

But there is no emotion involved when the animal becomes just a commodity – a means of transport or a source of meat. A dramatic example of this is the camel market, the Suq el-Gimal, at Imbaba in west Cairo, the biggest of its kind in the Middle East. Even tourists are sometimes drawn to this terrifying and heartless place by its exoticism. Several hundred camels are sold there every day, most of them scabby and emaciated, their will long since broken by whippings and beatings. Even so, one will sometimes rebel against its fate and, as best it can with its front legs hobbled, break away across the square in a desperate panic. The dark-skinned Sudanese traders in their white robes and their Egyptian customers briefly stop bargaining or jump to one side in alarm while the helpers catch the camel, cursing loudly and brandishing their long sticks.

It is not surprising that the animals are upset. By the time they arrive here, they have already travelled for forty days from central Sudan 1,500 kilometres (almost 1,000 miles) across the desert to the village of Daraw near Aswan, where they are sold to middlemen, loaded on to lorries or trucks and taken on a twelve-hour journey to Imbaba. And they have endured all this to end up at the slaughterhouse and be turned into *shawarma*, the Egyptian version of *döner kebab*, or to be chopped up to make *bastirma*.

In his famous History of Africa *the Arab historian Leo Africanus (1495–1550) devoted a whole chapter to the camel, remarking that without it the Arabs would not have been able to live freely in the desert. The importance of the camel is reflected in the story told by the Bedouin about its creation. When God created the first human beings from clay, two small pieces fell to the ground. From them grew the date palm and the camel – both inseparably bound up with man because of their common origin. Above: in the Empty Quarter (Rub al-Khali), the great central desert of Saudi Arabia. Below: the somewhat chaotic start of the Dubai Grand Prix.*

HOLY PLACE AND MARKET PLACE

HOW THE BAZAAR WORKS

Philosophy of life
Society
Buildings and layout
The elixir of life

Rational feeling

At first, it can be slightly terrifying. As you enter the bazaar, your senses are assaulted by thousands of smells – blood and balm and spices and dung. If you stand in the rays of sunshine that penetrate the vaults here and there, your eyes are dazzled with a sea of colours. You can taste dust on your tongue. Your ears are battered by the hoarse shouts of the porters and the guttural cries of the beggars. People come closer to you than they do in western cities, follow you with their eyes, try to catch hold of you, make contact.

But the longer you stroll through the labyrinth, the more you will be carried along by the flow. You will never tire, never get enough of it, and the chances are that your attention will soon be caught by some exquisite object. The shopkeeper will try and tempt you, talk you round. If you don't want to bargain with him, he will tell you his life story and ply you with cups of tea.

Even more than the sensory stimuli, newcomers are intoxicated by the unique all-embracing atmosphere of the bazaar.

'It seemed to me that for the first time I had come across a community in which people's relationships were based not on chance similarities of race and economic interests but on deeper and more lasting foundations: a common view of the world and an attitude to life which removed any barriers of isolation.

'Everyone seemed to feel like laughing ... so that one might almost think they did not take the grinding poverty of their country and its political problems too seriously. It seemed as if their intense and explosive excitement could at any time give way to total serenity without any visible transition, as if nothing had happened and all was well.'

In the traditional hierarchy of Islamic society very little distinction is made between craftsmen and artists. Both enjoy the same high respect and often the same privileges. The guilds used to hold splendid public parades to show off their artistic skills and economic power. The Turkish historian Evliya Celebi described a parade in Istanbul in 1638, watched by the Sultan and his household, in which 735 groups in 57 sections took part. Opposite: the Bazaar-e-Vakil in Shiraz.

Page 36: Entrance to the Imam Reza mosque, Mashhad, eastern Iran.

This was the experience of the Austrian Jewish journalist Leopold Weiss (who later became the highly respected Islamic scholar Muhammad Asad) when he first visited the East in the 1920s. This freedom of emotion and unshakeable cheerfulness, 'rational feeling' as he called it, can still be found in many parts of the Islamic world. It gives the picturesque markets a magic which no European can possibly resist.

The phenomenon has its roots in Islam. Before God revealed himself to the Arabs through Mohammed at the beginning of the 7th century, they lived by archaic tribal law, 'a state of barbarism', according to ibn-Khaldun (1332–1406), 'which they liked, because it ensured them freedom from any authority'. Nothing was more natural to the Bedouin than to rob their neighbours whenever they had the chance. They were not worried about laws, not even to deter others from wrongdoing. There was no political power or civilization to protect property. It was Mohammed who unified these wild desert tribes in a state, the *umma* – the community of believers who were under Allah's rule and protection and obeyed his laws unconditionally.

Religions govern man's relationship both with God and with his fellow men. Of the three prophets venerated by Muslims – Moses, Jesus and Mohammed – it was undoubtedly Mohammed who was most concerned with human relations. He ended the blood feuds that had been an almost daily occurrence up to then by introducing the principle of proportionality into retaliation and advising the acceptance of blood money instead of revenge. He urged his followers to show solidarity by making charitable donations. Instead of the previous non-binding relationships between the sexes, he enshrined polygamous marriage in the law, with harsh penalties for transgression, and reformed the law of inheritance, significantly enhancing the status of women. Women were now treated as individuals and they and their children enjoyed a certain measure of security.

The two sources of these religious precepts, the Koran and the Sunna, the posthumously collected sayings and deeds of the religion's founder, not only regulate fundamental spiritual and social questions, they also attach importance to numerous aspects of daily life which, at first sight, may seem trivial. For instance, how one should cook and eat, how to sit while doing so and how to clean one's teeth afterwards. This is what is so difficult to understand for westerners brought up in the Christian faith with the concept of original sin. Since Islam makes no distinction between the 'low' physical and the 'high' spiritual, or indeed between the profane and the sacred, politics and religion are ultimately inseparable.

Muslims are encouraged to enjoy earthly pleasures, but are exhorted always to remember that life on earth is merely a transitional stage in a longer journey – a kind of caravanserai on the road to God. That is why many actions, from meals to sexual intercourse, have to be preceded by a blessing, the *basmala*: *bismi llahi r-rahmani r-rahim*, which translates as, 'In the name of Allah, the compassionate, the merciful.'

The Koran teaches that individual and social welfare in this world is desirable, but that well-being in the next world is the real ultimate goal. Man must therefore learn to control his desires (even though they are not in themselves forbidden). In this he is governed by the *sharia*, the Islamic law. As well as the detailed rules it contains (the ban on the consumption of wine, blood and pork or the exhortation to acquire knowledge and spread the faith being the best known), it also lays down obligations known as the Five Pillars of Islam: to testify to the unity of God (*shahada*), to pray five times a day (*salat*), to abstain temporarily from eating and drinking (*saum*), to give alms (*zakat*) and to make the pilgrimage (*hajj*) to Mecca. All

There are two widespread misconceptions in the West about the Iranian chador. *Firstly, it covers the body from head to foot but not the eyes, nose and mouth. The tradition of the face veil, as worn by the Afghan woman in the picture above, started at the Sassanian court and was rejected by Ayatollah Khomeini as a feudal custom, having already been banned by Shah Reza Pahlavi in the 1930s. Secondly, wearing the* chador *(it literally means 'tent') is an old Iranian custom, particularly in the rural areas, and not something imposed by the rulers in Tehran. All that is required is that the arms and legs should be properly covered and the shape of the body not emphasized in a sexually provocative way. A western-style headscarf and long dress or coat are quite sufficient.*

these rules have a crucial influence on life in the bazaar, especially since many of them concern practical aspects of trade, industry and finance.

Many religions have a relatively liberal approach to striving for earthly gain. For that reason, but probably also because in the recent past North Africa and the Middle East have fallen behind Europe in their development, Islam is widely believed to be opposed in principle to economic progress. In fact, the reverse is true. Mystics have certainly advocated asceticism and idleness throughout the course of history, but the Koran and Sunna unequivocally approve of believers providing for themselves and their families and obtaining personal advantage from their work. Material as well as sexual desires are essentially accepted as God-given. After all, Mohammed was himself a businessman for many years.

Islam, unlike communism, tolerates a society in which some people are rich and some poor. But profit can never be an end in itself, as it is in the capitalist system. Business and morality are closely linked. The more a man has, the greater are his responsibilities. The Prophet said that a man should earn his wealth in an honest manner and give part of it to the needy.

Theft, greed and exploitation, ostentation, hoarding, speculation, creating monopolies, prostitution, gambling, astrology, drug dealing and fortune-telling – as well as begging, unless in dire need – are sinful and therefore frowned upon. Even such practices as options, loans and mortgages, guarantees and bankruptcy are strictly regulated on ethical grounds.

The Koran is particularly strict in its prohibition on interest. This is understandable, considering that it was previously the practice in Mecca for debts (or payments in kind) to be doubled, together with the interest, when they could not be paid by the due date. Admittedly, people have always resorted to all kinds of legal ruses to evade the ban: making bogus sales, fixing the profit margin for a transaction beforehand or putting more than the sum received on debt certificates. In many places, minorities – Jews, Christians or Hindus – handled financial transactions. Even now, legal experts disagree as to whether the word *riba*

in the Holy Book actually means any kind of interest or just usury *per se*. For some time now, the majority of financial managers in the modern Islamic states have taken the liberal view and run banks on western lines. But, in a return to the original principles of Islam, a number of establishments have been set up since the 1970s (the biggest and best known being the Islamic Development Bank) at which the lender receives a proportionate share of the firm's profit and loss instead of interest.

Another important rule calls for the payment of an annual alms tax, the *zakat*. This benefits the poor and needy and also debtors, tax collectors, travellers and unbelievers, encouraging them to convert to Islam. It is collected and administered by the government according to a highly complex scale. In the case of agricultural crops and fruit, for example, the amount payable is 10 per cent of the value, but with artificial irrigation the rate is only 5 per cent. For precious metals and commodities, the figure is 2½ per cent – but only if they are kept for at least a year. Calculating the proportion for camels, goats and sheep is almost a science in itself. Often the amount of the *zakat* is left to the honesty of the owner.

Bazaars are generally male preserves, but apart from the fact that the number of women has increased rapidly over the last generation, there is one notable exception: the Berber women's markets in the Rif mountains of northern Morocco. They sell goods mainly produced by women (clothes and ceramics, for instance) or taboo for the opposite sex (such as cosmetics and contraceptives and special aphrodisiacs). A woman is elected market overseer, amina, *by the council of notables. Men are banned from entering, on pain of severe punishment. The system is believed to have originated in wartime, allowing women, who were not involved in the tribal feuds, to continue trading while the main markets were closed. Opposite below: at the clothing market in Marrakesh. Above: the Madhat Pasha souq in Damascus.*

Even more complicated to administer, but morally more commendable, is the *sadaqa*, the voluntary pious donation. This includes practical contributions such as emergency assistance, favours and praise or mediating between the parties in a dispute. The intention of the giver always carries more weight than the favour being shown to the recipient.

However, the tradition of *bakshish* (a contribution not requiring anything in return), which is so famous/infamous amongst tourists, is only partly to do with the religious rules on donations. It has its roots in the custom amongst pre-Islamic nomads of paying each other rewards for loyalty or specific hostilities or demanding tribute. Later, in the Middle Ages, it was continued by non-local rulers, who bought

Contrary to popular belief in the West, bargaining, whether it be in the fish market in Sharjah in the United Arab Emirates or in the Imbaba camel market in Cairo, is a ritual with its own language and gestures, intended to build up confidence between seller and buyer.

the loyalty of their subjects with money and gifts. Strictly speaking, western visitors could not be asked for *bakshish* when the Koran commended it as a form of alms, because then it would be purely a matter for Muslims.

What does all this have to do with bazaars? A great deal, because it explains the moral principles which enable all *suwwaqa*, all market people – whether they be rich merchants or poor farmers, moneylenders, story tellers or day labourers – to live together in harmony. Traditional bazaar society has in some respects been corrupted by modern life, but piety, honesty and solidarity are still fundamental values for most of its members. Most business people (*basaris*) still make agreements verbally, with a handshake, rather than through written contracts and lawyers. Even in the gold market, you still see traders leaving their shops open when they go to the mosque to pray and just putting a symbolic cord across them. It is quite unthinkable that anyone would steal from others in these circumstances. Even messengers, often youngsters known only by sight, are entrusted with valuables without a receipt. Some bazaars have guards, in the Maghreb or Sanaa for instance, but only for protection against intruders and then only at night.

It is also not done to entice customers away from the adjoining shops. In fact, if a neighbouring shopkeeper is away for a short time, it is customary to act for him and, if necessary, sell his (competing) goods. To take personal advantage of such an opportunity would be seen as *aib*, a disgrace. Admittedly, this system of mutual aid has its dangers. There is an unwritten law that a balance always has to be maintained between help given and help sought. Anyone who asks his neighbours for favours too often, whether it be in the workplace, shop or home, is in danger of losing respect. The close link between mutual trust and reputation is also evident in the ritual of bargaining. In the West it is always seen as typical of the bazaar mentality, but very little thought is given to its complexity and deeper meaning.

These rhetorical exchanges go on between shopkeepers and prospective customers in the bazaar every day. The basic phrases are always more or less the same. The shopkeeper usually talks to the other person like a member of the family, calling him or her brother, mother, father or uncle to suggest intimacy. By mentioning that the shop has been recommended by a mutual acquaintance, the prospective buyer intimates that he could become a regular customer.

If he moves on to specifics and asks the price, he is given a politely non-committal reply. The aim is purely to create a friendly atmosphere. It is only after long hesitation that the salesman names his price, which is invariably refused. In the meantime, he – an expert on human nature – has deduced the customer's status from his name and accent,

clothes and various remarks. He soothes the 'indignant' customer by saying that other people of the same calibre – which, of course, he exaggerates flatteringly – have bought the same thing. For tourists, a pile of postcards from America or a visitors' book with tributes from satisfied customers is always brought out at this point. When the deal is concluded, he emphasizes his own selflessness by protesting that he has made nothing or has even made a loss.

Outsiders assume that the ritual is an intrinsic part of the culture. After all, people in the Orient are known to be fond of flowery language and dramatic gestures. But it is not as simple as that. Bargaining is not unknown in the western industrialized countries, when the value is not determined in advance – for wages, real estate or antiques, for instance, or for anything secondhand. Many items – like basic foodstuffs and cheap consumer goods – are sold at fixed prices in the bazaar. Furthermore, bargaining can be damaging to a person's reputation. Dignitaries would rather pay exorbitant prices than lower themselves to a duel of words. The less exalted gain respect if they simply refuse to take part.

This form of trading is largely due to social and economic conditions. In the bazaar economy, very little objective information is available. There are no mass media reporting on supply and demand, quality and prices, no market-research or consumer-protection bodies. In the traditional retail trade, trademarks are unknown and weights and measures are not fully standardized. The illiteracy rate is very high almost everywhere (over 50 per cent in Morocco and Egypt, 62 per cent in Yemen). As a result, a system based on the oral exchange of information has been preserved.

First of all, the buyer 'checks out' the current prices by asking various shopkeepers without obligation. When he finds the most favourable quote, he begins to bargain. The shopkeeper's aim is to acquire a regular customer. The customer's aim is to establish a lasting contact with a reliable dealer, so that he can save time in future by avoiding lengthy negotiation.

The ways in which they do this are highly inventive. In Yemen, for example, they use gestures to prevent anyone else overhearing. Both hands are covered with a cloth. They communicate by moving their fingers, each finger symbolizing a number, and express refusal or agreement with their eyes. Iranian carpet dealers usually mention how much they have – allegedly – paid for an item, establishing a minimum price in advance. In the Levant they like to act out a little comedy. After asking a price, the shopkeeper then lets his son name a lower price in his absence. Later he tells him off in front of the customer for being too soft. This gives the impression that the second price is actually a good one.

Sometimes buyers send their wives to bargain, in the (usually justified) hope that gallantry will make the shopkeeper more generous. The time of day is important too. In the early afternoon, the shopkeeper's enthusiasm for verbal sparring is blunted by the heat and often also by hashish or *qat*. But the best chance of a bargain is just before evening prayer. According to an old convention, the last customer has to be given a discount. Once a deal has finally been concluded, the shopkeeper still has one last trump card:

The general attitude to life in the market is based on high ethical standards, centering around the concept of jiwar. *It also comes from the Bedouin's sense of community, which could not survive in the desert without solidarity. Neighbours are required to offer each other help and protection. On a visit to Istanbul 150 years ago, Maurice Michaud, a member of the French Academy, wanted to buy a briefcase. He was impressed when he was advised to buy it from the shopkeeper next door because the briefcases there were much better. Above: friends greeting each other in the medina in Marrakesh. Below: a banana seller in the old city in Cairo.*

Normally women cannot show themselves on the street unless they have to go shopping. Apart from this, the only other contact they are allowed with men is with close relatives. But women too are becoming more and more involved in trade, either to earn their living independently or, as in this picture of the bread seller in the bazaar at Hajjah in the Yemeni mountains, to supplement the family income.

he suggests that the customer might pay another time, indicating trust in his creditworthiness. It is a gesture that seldom fails.

The Prophet was amazed that, in spite of the long-drawn-out process, the daily prices were exactly in line with supply and demand. He is quoted as saying that in the souq no one less than God sets the prices himself.

Opinions as well as goods are traded in the bazaar. It is a stock exchange for reputations with strict rules and sanctions. Since the influence of women is normally confined to the house and its immediate surroundings, the stock exchange is dominated by male morality. The most important stock is a man's honour. The price is high when a man's household has a good name with the neighbours. Any appearance in public therefore, whether it be bargaining or praying, in the workplace, at the baths or meeting friends at the end of the day, has only one aim: to defend one's personal reputation. If a man's honour is devalued in any way, for instance as a result of malicious jokes or rumours, social exclusion threatens – that is, being barred from the men's groups.

The bazaar was, and to some extent still is, a major influence in politics. It is hard to believe, seeing the wholesalers – most of them secretly rolling in money – sitting in their offices with just a pocket calculator, a tattered notebook and an old-fashioned bakelite telephone. But understatement for fear of the tax authorities (and not keeping books) is one thing; holding the reins of power behind the scenes is another. Rulers might come and go, but the bazaar people are, and always have been, an influential elite. Normally, all that is needed to safeguard their interests is a word to the legal experts, who then inform the authorities at one of their regular consultations. If it seems that a strong protest is necessary – although this is very rare – they demonstrate by closing down their shops. Then the bazaar is in a state of confusion, with excited debate going on all over the place, rumours rife and violence in the air.

The 1979 coup in Iran showed the power of strikes in the bazaar. Back in the fifties, the Shah had allowed his favourites to wrest control of wheat imports and exports from the wholesalers. In the early seventies, he helped them set up a modern industry to replace the outmoded structures of traditional trade. The people in the bazaar, seeing their livelihood threatened by this western-style progress, threw in their lot with the mullahs and ayatollahs and became the main supporters of the Islamic revolution. Before Ayatollah Khomeini returned from exile, the bazaar in Tehran was closed for five months.

Serious crime is rare in the bazaar. Firstly, because most have sacred burial places in them and to disturb the peace of a consecrated site would bring punishment from on high. Secondly, because for centuries bazaars have been used as a neutral meeting place for opposing groups. There is a very good reason why people are still forbidden to carry weapons in many bazaars. The market people are well aware of the dangers of a *nefra* – a single incident spreading to epidemic proportions, stirring up feeling, leading to mass disturbances and the destruction of their business. A *nefra* (Arabic for 'fleeing in panic'), after a murder for instance, means that the market has to be closed for a year for 'purification' – although actually this only applies to the smaller souqs in the provinces. For that reason alone, everyone tries to live in harmony.

'We meet people from every walk of life, from the caliph to the barber, from the poor fisherman to the rich merchant. They lift us up and sweep us along on a tide of humanity; we are amidst spirits, magicians, demons, and yet we feel completely at home.' This feeling of security comes from the idea of *kismet*, an incomprehensible but infinitely wise plan underlying every misfortune or good fortune. Europeans used to talk about Oriental fatalism, with an unmistakable tinge of contempt. Even today, people on business trips complain about the 'passivity' they encounter in the Middle East – a fundamental misunderstanding.

Islam literally means 'submission to the will of God'. Submission is not passivity, but a willingness to live in harmony with creation instead of trying to subjugate and reorganize it, a completely different, carefree relationship with all living things.

When asked if he was ever lonely on his journeys, the British explorer and eminent Arabist Wilfred Thesiger replied that, in towns where he did not know anyone, he simply went into the bazaar and struck up a conversation with a shopkeeper. Tea would be brought, other people would join them, and he would be invited for lunch or an evening meal.

The freedom of the eastern mind, particularly evident in the proverbial hospitality, is expressed in other ways as well. For instance, old people are revered in the Islamic world, not feared and shunned, as they often are in the West. Most families have three or four generations living together. Nearly every shop has a framed picture of the late grandfather or great-grandfather on the wall.

Work is not a punishment for man's fall from Paradise, as it is in the Bible, but an enriching part of everyday life. So on Friday, the Muslim sabbath, no one in the bazaar indulges in feverish leisure activities to make up for having to work during the week.

People in the Middle East have a different relationship with time, too: even before the end of the 1st millennium, cities like Baghdad and Damascus had magnificent and accurate sundials and water clocks. But in the bazaar no one thought it necessary to divide time up, and they still feel the same way. People take a break because they are tired or hungry or feel like a chat, not because the clock tells them to. The only person who is regularly allowed to interrupt things is the *muezzin* with his penetrating call to prayer, '*Allahu akbar*', 'God is great'.

It is many years since people used the bazaars as heavily guarded strong rooms and safes for their savings and valuables, but it is still possible to find treasures in the better-class souvenir and antique shops. Above: a jewelry and fabric shop in Rissani, southern Morocco.

Imams, kadis and market overseers

Jesus said, 'Render to Caesar the things that are Caesar's, and to God the things that are God's.' For Westerners with a Christian view of the world, this was the definitive pronouncement on responsibility for this world and the next. Even in late antiquity and the Middle Ages, the emperor was in many empires considered to be God's governor on earth. Since the beginning of modern times, Europe (and later most of the rest of the world) has taken the view that the state and religion are, theoretically at least, two separate entities.

When looking at the social structure of the bazaar – the relationship between the different sections of society, their organizations and economic bases – it has to be remembered that the traditional power structure in Islam is fundamentally different from that of the West. All three political powers – legislation, enforcement and jurisprudence – were vested in the head of the Muslim community, but he also had all the functions of a religious leader. As ibn-Khaldun explained, his role was to 'protect the religion and to guide the world through it'. This axiom has been applied in various ways throughout history, but its basic tenets remained valid until European constitutions were established in the second half of the 19th century and its repercussions are still being felt even now.

In fact, the first caliphs combined all public functions, temporal and spiritual. They were regents, judges and military commanders, led the religious worship and held the *khutba*, the Friday prayers. But the new empire was growing so fast that more and more responsibilities had to be delegated to officials. By the time Islam split into an Omayyad branch (with its capital in Córdoba) and an Abbasid branch (in Baghdad) in the middle of the 8th century, the title of caliph was already more symbolic than indicative of real power.

Mohammed exhorted his followers to seek for knowledge: 'One hour of contemplation is better than two hours of worship.' Opposite: a scholar reciting the Koran in the Topkapi Palace in Istanbul. Below: studying in the prayer hall of the el-Hakim Mosque in Cairo.

The role of prayer leader was one of the most important new offices. He had – and still has – to conduct communal prayers, facing towards Mecca, preceded by ritual bowing and prostration and recital of the appropriate phrases. He also leads the burial ceremonies, in which one of his tasks is to tell the dead the answers they should give to Munkar and Nakir, the angels guarding the tomb. His Arabic title, *al-imam*, has a double meaning, and even for Muslims is a little confusing. To Shiites, imams are the favoured descendants of Ali, whom they regard as the only legitimate heir to Mohammed. It is believed, particularly in Iran, that the twelfth imam (the seventh according to the Ismailis) has been borne away into invisibility and will one day return as leader of mankind. In Sunni Islam, on the other hand, the name was originally a synonym for caliph, but it incorporated the office of prayer leader. Later imams were usually experts with theological and legal training who also had other public functions. Nowadays, even reputable laymen without any special training often act as prayer leaders, especially in the smaller prayer houses.

The *muezzins* (criers) are equally indispensable to the running of the mosque. Since the days when Mohammed's dark-skinned companion Bilal first held this position in Medina, the *muezzin* has been responsible for giving the call to prayer (*azan*) from the minaret five times a day – before sunrise, at midday, in

Although the Koran and the Sunna emphasize the importance of acquisition through one's own work and striving, property is always bound up with social obligations. The poor are entitled to share in the wealth of the rich. This means more than just giving alms and generous donations; it is the responsibility of the community to fight poverty and starvation. Above: an informal council of elders outside the Great Mosque in Sanaa.

the middle of the afternoon, at sunset and one-and-a-half hours later. For some time now they have been using loudspeakers and recently also cassettes, sold by the Azhar mosque in Cairo.

The *mufti* is still the highest authority on religious and legal matters in many countries. With his comprehensive knowledge of the Koran and the Hadith, the handed-down sayings of the Prophet, he gives the faithful binding guidance on how to lead a devout life and provides a legal opinion, the *fatwa*, in major disputes. The emirs were leaders of the army, the viziers were the ministers. The head of the government as a whole – although only in the Ottoman Empire – was the grand vizier. He was also keeper of the seals and the sultan's representative. The office of judge was held by the *kadi*. The *shurta* was a kind of military police force with extensive prosecution and enforcement powers and the *mazalim* courts were parallel courts directly answerable to the ruler. Not only did the *kadi* act as a judge, he also administered royal and private foundations and was the guardian of foundling children and under-age orphans, the mentally ill and the profligate.

The main responsibility for the management of the bazaar lay with the *muhtasib* (Turkish: *ihtisab agasi*), who was directly accountable to the *kadi*. He supervised the market and checked weights and measures, the purity of the coinage, the quality of the goods and, in particular, compliance with the building regulations – although there were very few of these. In emergencies he had to prevent profiteering and panic-buying and, if necessary, set official maximum prices. He could also impose penalties and award quality marks. The market supervisor also had general responsibility for public order. For instance, he ensured that the faithful observed the hours of prayer, that Christians and Jews complied with discriminatory laws, such as clothing regulations and bans on demonstrations, and that relations between men and women were moral and decent (which did not necessarily prevent him from sharing in the proceeds of prostitution). At the same time he had to be familiar with the market situation and the *sharia*, the religious law. He also had to be a shrewd pragmatist, since the main objective was to resolve any disputes internally wherever possible, without having to refer them to the *kadi*.

Modern historians are always surprised at the small number of officials who were involved in administering large Islamic cities, even into the 20th century. There were the *kadi* and a few district governors, the *muhtasib* and a few representatives for each trade, a limited number of notaries, overseers, court clerks and official witnesses – compared to its present inflated size, the bureaucratic apparatus was extremely modest.

How, then, did people manage to live together with so little friction, as they still do in the older quarters of the cities? First of all, as has already been explained, the rules of everyday life were so deeply ingrained in every individual that they were observed with very little pressure from outside. As ibn-Khaldun said, religion provides a form of internal control. Furthermore, the old Bedouin tribal and clan ideas still survive in the towns. People living in a district (Arabic: *hara*; Turkish: *mahalla*) are usually related in some way to each other, or at least belong to the same ethnic group or religion. Like the trade associations, of which more below, they are a largely self-supporting community. It is only when the group's interests come into conflict with those of the public at large or of their neighbours that the state authorities are involved. As a result, there was very little need for local councils and consequently the Islamic city was never regarded as a political entity, nor did it ever develop into a legal entity. With no coinage or customs duty or tax privileges, it did not have its own budget (its infrastructure was financed privately or else by the state). Nor did it have any fortification or market rights, official city court or institutionalized state parliament. An informal 'council of notables' met as necessary – an open forum in which the community elite, their spiritual leaders, the influential merchants and representatives of the various trades discussed current issues. Sometimes the ruler also attended.

What bound all city dwellers together was the consciousness of belonging to the Muslim community as a whole, the *umma*, and having the same rights – at least before the law. Any man – any free man, at least – could settle where he wanted and learn, teach and exercise his trade without restriction. There was no discrimination on the basis of race or skin colour and national barriers were unknown. The humanistic spirit called for tolerance towards people of different religions. Admittedly, the other 'Peoples of the Book' – that is, Christians and Jews – were from time to time treated as second-class citizens; for instance, they had to wear special clothes and were not allowed to ride, appear as witnesses or work in government posts. But generally they were not forcibly converted (although this could well have had something to do with the poll tax they had to pay for the right to practise their religion).

Even the position of slaves was in some respects better in the Islamic world than, for instance, in ancient Rome or, at a later date, across the Atlantic. Freeing them was seen as pleasing in the sight of God and was strongly recommended. Slaves could use their savings more or less as they wished; they could even run businesses and buy their freedom from their masters. They did not as a rule work on the land, but were used mainly as guards or in the house. The house slaves were usually treated as members of the family and, although legally they were excluded from holding political or religious office, they often had more power than many freemen, since masters could transfer their authority to their living property more or less as they wished.

Islamic cities have never had corporative institutional rules like those in medieval or absolutist Europe, or even class distinctions in the modern sense. However, there were – and still are – clearly defined sections of society. On one side were the authorities: the army, official secretaries (*kuttab*) and, in the main cities, the rulers. They appointed the chief dignitaries – the *mufti*, the *kadi*, the *muhtasib* – and so had indirect control over life in the city. On the other side were the bourgeoisie – the rich merchants and *ulama* (legal scholars), and also the retailers and craftsmen. After them came the amorphous masses: the poor, beggars, street pedlars, parking attendants, unofficial tourist guides and porters.

The rulers lived their lives in the palaces and citadels, the rest of the population in the residential districts and the bazaar. There was very little contact between the two worlds.

Apart from these broad groups, there is of course an even more informal hierarchy based on ethnic grounds. At the top are the

Meeting of two worlds in Mashhad, eastern Iran. A group of Shiite mullahs deep in theological debate (below). Behind them, the entrance to the holy tomb of the revered eighth imam, Reza. In the same courtyard (overleaf above) a pilgrim woman in a chador, *deep in prayer. Above: the* muezzin *of the Omayyad Mosque in Aleppo in conversation.*

Beggars are a frequent sight in the streets of the bazaar (below). Muslims have a duty to give alms to the needy, but a distinction is made between the *zakat* and the *sadaqa*. The *zakat* is an alms tax, one of the Five Pillars of Islam. The *sadaqa* is a voluntary donation.

shurfa, who can trace their origins back to the Prophet's family and are therefore regarded as nobles. Also very highly regarded are the *hafiz*, the 'keepers', who can recite the Koran by heart, and the *hajji*, who have been on the pilgrimage to Mecca, the *hajj*. At the other end of the scale are those in religiously suspect occupations: prostitutes and cuppers (bloodletters) for instance and, in the past, slave castrators and also pigeon breeders (because they could watch women covertly from the rooftops).

Since pre-Islamic times, shopkeepers and craftsmen have enjoyed a privileged position, partly because of the religion's mercantile roots. Mecca and Medina/Yathrib were trading centres long before the Koran 'came into the heart of the Prophet' in a cave on Mount Hira in the year 612. The long caravan journeys he had gone on in his youth had made a profound impression on Mohammed. Geographical location was another important factor. It was inevitable that the Middle East, situated as it is between two continents, should become a trading centre. It should also not be forgotten that, until the industrial revolution, craft goods were amongst a community's main sources of income and its only movable property. Many conquerors therefore looked on gifted artists as desirable booty, especially as a way of improving their image.

Although shopkeepers and craftsmen generally enjoyed a high social status, there were marked economic differences within the group. Transport, supplies and trade had always been privately organized in Islam (the state distribution systems in Fatimid Cairo or Ottoman Istanbul, with their monopolies and factories, were merely the exceptions that prove the rule) and an elite group of importers and exporters established itself at the very beginning. So enterprising were they that they quickly became very prosperous. They then began to specialize in particular fields: buying goods from various countries through agents, going on trips themselves to negotiate with suppliers, or helping visitors who did not speak the local language and were unfamiliar with local customs and prices to sell their goods. As in the Christian world, up to the end of the Middle Ages no distinction was made between traders and bankers; traders supervised coinage, accepted investments and granted loans independently of the official moneychangers and state finance officials, which obviously increased their wealth.

The position of the small market traders and craftsmen has always been quite different. Under the traditional economic and social system which still remains common today, a relatively small number of moneylenders and international businessmen, together with the ruler's family, control a large part of the means of production. As Eugen Wirth explains in *'Zum Problem des Basars'*, this financially powerful local elite usually supplies both the equipment (smelting ovens, lathes, looms and so on) and the raw materials (yarn, wooden bars, metal plates, etc.). The same few people also own many of the shops and workshops in the bazaar and often estates around the city. Farmers and businessmen are usually up to their ears in debt to them.

Although the main object of these 'capitalists' is to make as much profit as possible, their role is slightly different from that of the traditional feudal lords. The rights are freely traded and not based on an inherited or conferred title. In principle, anyone can become a member of the elite. Even the criticism that it is a parasitic system is not strictly true. Admittedly, few owners think of reinvesting profits to maintain or even increase production, but the added value is often invested in religious foundations (Arabic: *waqf*, also known as *habus* in the Maghreb).

These are institutions built with private money for a purpose that is pleasing to God. They fall into two categories. The family foundations, before they gradually came under state control in most countries in the 20th century, were usually commercial properties whose profits were used by the founder's descendants. They were a neat way of circumventing the Koranic law of inheritance, by excluding individual heirs, designating non-legal heirs and protecting the property against fragmentation. The profits only went to the public after the last heir had died.

The numerous religious or charitable foundations, on the other hand, always had charitable aims. Some were used to build or maintain hospitals, baths, schools or mosques, libraries, wells or cemeteries. Others were set up to help the poor, the old or the sick, schoolchildren, debtors or travellers. Others again paid for circumcisions for boys, dowries for girls or feed and water for animals.

The system of protection in bazaar society also provides a measure of security. The basic concepts are *jiwar*, *jar* and *wala*. *Jiwar*, a verbal agreement between two equals, is based on the pre-Islamic principle of mutual support originating with the Bedouin, without which it was impossible to survive in the desert. Neighbours are expected to show solidarity in any situation. *Jar* is the relationship between patron and protégé which allows underprivileged citizens to share in the wealth of more prosperous families. *Wala* is the pact of protection and loyalty which the retailers or craftsmen usually enter into with their particular trade association.

A great deal has been written about the Islamic trade associations, much of it contradictory. One theory is that they originated directly from the Byzantine corporations. Another is that they were set up in the 9th century by the Qarmatians, a Shiite secret society, to bring down the Abbasids. Certainly trade organizations existed in some form even before the end of the 1st millennium, when there was an expansion of trade in the Middle East. They offered their members protection against state despotism and social security, guaranteed them medical treatment, old-age pensions and help in emergencies, and paid certain taxes on their behalf. All their members had to pay into a fund which was used, for instance, to pay for funerals, loans to set up businesses, alms for beggars and wages for night watchmen and fire wardens. In wartime, they had to provide equipment and often also troops.

Later there was an enormous increase in the number of guilds. In the 17th century, for instance, Cairo had more than 300 and Istanbul as many as 1,000. A hundred years ago, Damascus still had 347. Every trade, however small, had its own association. The large associations, such as the tailors, shoemakers or builders, were subdivided into dozens of smaller categories. The masters of each guild chose an especially respected, usually wealthy, man as their leader, the *amin*, *arif*, *rais* or *sheikh*. This person managed the funds, monitored the quality of the goods and settled internal disputes on the *muhtasib*'s behalf. A president, known as the *shahbander* in Egypt, *kethuda* in Istanbul or *sheikh al-masheikh* in most other countries, was elected from the guild leaders. He acted as an intermediary between the citizens and the authorities on all important matters. His appointment was for life, but had to be ratified by the state authorities.

The Islamic associations differ from the medieval guilds in Europe in certain respects. Although they were a strong influence in the town and the bazaar, they did not have as much political independence and power as the Hanses in Northern Europe or the groups in Germany, France or England which, early on, secured the right to representation in the city governments. Their internal hierarchy was – and still is – less structured. The bazaar craftsmen do make a distinction between apprentices, journeymen and masters, but this simply implies different levels of competence and not a relationship of dependency. The people employed in a workshop are usually partners who negotiate their reciprocal rights and duties individually by contract.

Stoical old men, sometimes smoking water pipes, are a frequent sight in the Islamic world. Above: old men in the bazaar in Rissani, southern Morocco. Below: a Saidi from Upper Egypt indulging in his favourite pastime in the Khan el-Khalili in Cairo.

In the Iranian revolution in 1979 Ayatollah Khomeini was backed by the bazaar traders, concerned at the Shah's forced industrialization of the countryside. His stirring speeches also rallied the support of the impoverished peasants and slum dwellers and it was mainly from their ranks that he recruited the Pasdaran, the Revolutionary Guard. Although their influence is now much reduced, they are still a 'parallel police force' with special powers. The white turban is the mark of the mullahs, who number about 180,000 in Iran. Only the few hundred ayatollahs (the 'Seyyids' descended from Mohammed's family) are entitled to wear black turbans. Above: a brotherly kiss outside the Imam Mosque in Isfahan. Below: at the sheep and goat market, Rissani, southern Morocco.

In theory, the guilds are open to anyone. There are even joint Muslim-Jewish and Muslim-Christian guilds. In practice, a master's position is usually passed on to his son or nephew. Beginners have to serve for many years in a menial capacity, making tea, cleaning up and observing, before they are entrusted with a piece of work. When they are released to become journeymen, a solemn ritual takes place, with the master and guild leader symbolically untying a knotted belt worn by the aspirant.

In both Christianity and Islam, guilds have always been linked to religion. It was mainly the Sufis, the mystics, who helped spiritualize the world of work. They constantly reminded people that the glory of God is reflected in everything, no matter how ordinary and mundane, and any act of creation is a step closer to God. The endless patience which an artist shows in carving, writing, weaving or engraving brings more than just material gain.

The distinction between guilds, orders and brotherhoods was always fluid. What united them all was the ideal of *futuwwa*. In heathen times, this Arabic term – which literally means 'youth' – referred to a young man's praiseworthy qualities, notably selflessness, bravery and social justice. But in early Islam it also acquired religious connotations. In the Middle East in particular, men joined associations whose highest goal, like the Christian monastic orders, was to lead a morally pure life. Their customs and structure bore a slight resemblance to those of the freemasons. They too attached importance to formal initiation to distinguish themselves from the common herd. Initiates had to put on the '*futuwwa* breeches' and drain a cup of salt water. Even the tying of the belt described above was an esoteric act. There are still groups which practise spectacular rituals; for instance, some brotherhoods in the Maghreb send themselves into a trance by fire-eating or cutting open the tops of their skulls with a hatchet.

At their height, these groups were so influential that their members even included caliphs and sultans. But they were already beginning to decline by the end of the Abbasid period. *Futuwwa* was coming to be used as a camouflage for dubious revolutionary movements. Particularly when state authority collapsed, militant groups organized robberies in its name, extorted protection money and orchestrated revolts. Historians justifiably described the *fityan*, the group members, as rogues and vagabonds. Their kindness to women, children and old people was all that remained of the original ideals. Before long, they began to operate like the mafia. In many places, *fityan* had infiltrated the police over the centuries or formed a kind of semi-legal militia, a problem that the army and the state police have only recently managed to eradicate in many cities.

The final decline of the *futuwwa* ideal is just one of the radical changes that have been taking place in the bazaar community over a long period. As a result of westernization, much of the machinery that previously regulated social relationships is now controlled by the state. For instance, the role of the guilds has been taken over by trade unions, chambers of commerce and trade, the role of neighbours by anonymous insurance organizations. The traditional practice of almsgiving is being eclipsed by modern taxation systems. Foundations everywhere have long since been nationalized.

Even the fabric of the buildings is under threat. In many places, the bazaars have been adversely affected by urban redevelopment schemes. In some cases (but fortunately relatively few) they have been almost completely destroyed, for instance by the English in Kandahar and Kabul in the 1870s during the Afghan wars or by the Soviets in Turkestan fifty years later. The industrial products flooding the markets in ever greater numbers are also an obvious threat to the survival of traditional local crafts.

However, the biggest threat to the bazaars is the population explosion. In just one generation there has been a sharp rise in the populations of many cities. As people from the countryside flood into the cities, mainly into the old parts where accommodation is cheaper, the old-established elites and their businesses are moving to the 'European quarters' built in the colonial period, taking jobs and purchasing power with them.

Despite all these setbacks, the bazaar is still an essential part of Islamic society. A social experiment in Libya showed how important it is. In the 1980s Colonel Gaddafi and the General People's Committee had all the country's bazaars closed and replaced by a chain of people's supermarkets, on the grounds that private profits from trade were immoral. The old shopkeepers were compulsorily retired, the young detailed to clear shelves and work at the checkouts. In no time at all, the effects were felt and supplies dried up. The government was soon forced to reinstate the old system. Supermarkets and bazaars have coexisted peacefully in Libya since 1987. There are no prizes for guessing which has the biggest turnover!

The typical businessman in the bazaar combines the role of producer and salesman (the same word is often used in Arabic to denote the maker and the seller of particular goods). The traditional businessmen, however, are wholesalers and long-distance traders who often reinvest their profits in production. It is through them that Islam has spread peacefully as far afield as East Africa and South-East Asia. Above: scene from the souq in Hajjah, in the north of Yemen.

Mosques, shops and caravanserais

Few words conjure up more clichés in the western mind than the word harem. It evokes the whole opulent, magnificent and dangerous world of the Thousand and One Nights – exotic eunuchs, sensual odalisques, imperious sultanas. But few Arabic words are more misunderstood in the West. Harem, or *haram*, does not just mean the mysterious gilded cage; it is a general word for a sacred, protected or forbidden place. The holy areas around Mecca and Medina are *haram*. So too are the prayer halls in every mosque. The root *h-r-m* is in *ihram*, the state of devotion of pilgrims in Mecca, and in *muharram*, the Shiite month of mourning. The carefully screened-off part of every house where the women, children and servants live and visitors are not allowed is called *haramlik* or harem (the other area, in which the

The front door is the carefully guarded dividing line between the private living area and the semi-private life of the cul-de-sac. It is a typical feature of every Arab house (bait) *that the interior cannot be seen from the street. The outside walls are high and bare, the lobbies and corridors dark and winding.*

Discretion is extremely important, especially where women are concerned. Front doors often have Koranic verses on them, or amulets to ward off evil spirits. Visitors have to go through an entry ritual – they knock, announce themselves and wait to be taken inside. Male strangers especially cannot enter unless they are with a male member of the family. In many places there is a small niche with a candle in it next to the door. Its position indicates to the outside world when all is well inside the house, the head of the household is away or there is illness or death in the family. The mashrabiya, *a wooden bay window, used to be a popular way of preventing anyone looking into the house (left: in the old quarter of Jeddah, Saudi Arabia). Right: a secluded corner of old Cairo. Below: the town gate in Taroudannt, southern Morocco.*

master of the house receives friends and visitors, is known as the *salamlik*).

The harem and the bazaar are very closely connected. The distinction between the internal and external, private and public, female and male domains is the key to understanding the structure of an oriental city and, by analogy, the bazaar.

In his brilliant book *Architektur und Lebensformen in der islamischen Welt*, the Swiss town planner Stefano Bianca writes: 'The concealment of phenomena which are sacred or taboo is a theme that runs through the Semitic view of the world. Just as the inner sanctum of the Islamic cosmos, the cube-shaped Kaaba, is enveloped in a woven cover (a ritual that is repeated every year), people's auras also have to be protected and guarded against inappropriate contacts. This is particularly true of women and their female aura...'. Bianca goes on to say that this concealment is also a characteristic of Islamic architecture. He calls it 'man's third skin' (after clothing), 'the garment of the family'. If a stranger enters a house without permission, its occupants defend it as if they themselves were being attacked. It is significant that the Arabs use the same word for family and house, *bait*.

The subject of houses in the Middle East deserves a book to itself. The half-timbered buildings on the Bosporus, the monumental stone palaces in Lebanon, the Maghrebi and Arab clay fortresses and the multi-storey stone towers in the old parts of Jeddah and Sanaa ... the variety is endless. Regional features are similarly diverse: the wind towers (*badgir*) in the Gulf, the pillared entrance halls (*tarma*) in Iraq, the wooden bay windows (*mashrabiya*) in Cairo and the huge vaulted courtyard niches (*iwan*) in Iran – every region has its characteristic style. But what is most interesting is what they have in common.

In North Africa and the Middle East, a builder does not usually need an architect to show him how to build a house. The general aesthetic and social principles are so deeply ingrained in every individual that he will automatically try to incorporate them in his building. Most traditional town houses have an inner courtyard with cooling fountains. Their roofs are flat and closely dovetailed, often creating a spacious area which people can walk across. In the summer the whole family sleeps up there and all year round the women do many of their household tasks there and chat to their neighbours away from the men, as they would at the village well. The façade on the courtyard side is usually richly decorated with carving, moulding or coloured incrustations. The street side, by contrast, is forbiddingly plain. If the outside walls have any openings at all, they are small and barred and so high up that no one can see in. The entrance is closed off with a solid gate, usually reinforced with iron and firmly locked, and also a (symbolic) threshold. The passageway beyond is curved once or twice to ensure privacy.

There are two reasons why the exterior is so remarkably unadorned. Firstly, it is traditional for the appearance of the street to reflect the equality of all men before God. Secondly, the plain walls clearly demarcate the family's private domain.

An important feature of the city layout is the cul-de-sac (Arabic: *hara* or *darb*). Like a military glacis, it protects the privacy of the residents in the adjacent family 'strongholds'. Not so long ago, it was a physical defence – against rivals from other parts of town, for instance, or marauding Bedouin, mercenaries or gangs of youths. Up to fifty years ago, outsiders could not enter a *hara* without a local escort. Nowadays, the cul-de-sacs are merely psychological barriers. They are the common property of the neighbours, a kind of privatized public space. Each houseowner can use his half of the street more or less as he wishes – keep his animals on it, store goods and, provided he does not impede passers-by, even build bay windows over it. But, legally at least, he is only allowed to use the part from there to his front door.

The cul-de-sacs give each medina its characteristically eastern appearance. After dark, in particular, they are often used as an extension to the living room. People watch television, play, gossip and on hot summer nights even sleep in them. The maze of cul-de-sacs is in a sense the *haramlik* of the city. The main streets (Arabic: *shari*) are the *salamlik*, a public space essentially open to everyone. But the heart of the city is the bazaar.

Just as houses constitute the core of the residential districts, shops (Arabic: *hanut* or *dukkan*) are the core of the bazaar. They

The roofs are traditionally a female domain in the old cities. The women are much freer there than in the male preserves of market and mosque. Above: impressively renovated multi-storey houses in the medina in Jeddah. Below: most goods are still carried around the bazaar by donkey, as seen here in the alleyways of Fez.

are tiny booths, often measuring less than 2 square metres (about 20 square feet), open to the street. Behind them or – less frequently – on the upstairs landing are stores, offices or workshops. The owner's home and main store are usually in another part of town. In the traditional market, the shop is 0.5 to 1 metre (2 to 3 feet) above street level. In front of it is the *mastaba*, a bench for salesmen and customers. Shops can be closed like cupboards with several folding wooden flaps. The top flap is sometimes used during the day as protection from the sun, the bottom flap as a counter. This traditional type of bazaar shop has now become a rarity. Nearly everywhere – the Kapali Carsi in Istanbul is the most obvious example – the appearance of the old shops has already been marred by shutters and advertising boards, shop windows and doors.

The rows of thousands of shops lining the main thoroughfares are a typical feature of every bazaar. Until recently, the souqs (Arabic *suq*) could be closed off with gates, and even now they are guarded at night in many places. The way in which the various trades are divided up and grouped together has always been the subject of speculation.

In fact, different trade associations already had their own sections in the markets of the Roman and Byzantine Empires. However, the markets in North Africa and the Middle East are laid out in a way that makes them unmistakably Islamic. The great world traveller ibn-Battuta is often quoted on this subject. On his journeys through the Islamic world, he was struck by the similarities between the markets. Even the bazaar he found in the Muslim quarter of the Chinese town of al-Hansa was like the one in his home town in Morocco.

The ritual purity of the goods was probably a crucial factor right from the beginning. It is popularly believed that that is why the shops selling candles and books, spices, perfumes and incense have settled around the Friday mosque. Eugen Wirth writes that, in the Iranian places of pilgrimage, photographic studios, bus stations and cheap hotels, confectionery and souvenir sellers – i.e., trades which have no particular religious connotations – are located immediately beside the most important shrines. That suggests that the locations are also chosen for practical reasons, for instance (political) security. When Baghdad was founded, el-Mansur decreed that the butchers' market should be sited at the end of the bazaar. Obviously, it is usually desirable for dyers and tanners, potters and butchers, smiths and gunpowder sellers to be on the periphery, not just because of the smells and noise and dirt associated with their trades, but also because of the risk of fire and the amount of space they occupy. Moneychangers and moneylenders need to be in the centre of the bazaar, which is well guarded. But at the same time it was pointed out by travellers and historians, even in the Middle Ages, that the location depends on the target customers. For instance, as well as the markets for pilgrims there are also markets offering goods specifically for women (traditionally in the centre near the jewelry bazaar) or for visitors from the countryside (near the city gates).

The layout shows the close links between religion and trade in the bazaar (above: in the cloth bazaar in Aleppo). Until the invention of the refrigerator, blocks of ice were kept in the hermetically sealed Moayedi ice house in Kerman, Iran, all through the summer (below). Preserved from the Safavid period, it is unique in the Islamic world.

For some time now, however, the traditional layout has been changing. It has survived to some extent in ancient cities like Tunis or Fez, where there has been relatively little modernization, but those are exceptions. In most bazaars, the goods are now mixed up together. The main culprits are tourism and industry – cheap souvenirs and consumer goods. Also, shopping habits have altered since the development of 'European' quarters. The best customers, the elite, used to be found around the Friday mosque. Now the well-to-do mostly live well away from the medina, in the residential areas. Either they spend their money in the new part of town or they drive to the city gates and go to the nearest shop. These days, people are so anxious to save time that what used to be the less profitable locations are now the most lucrative.

Obviously, the markets in the ancient world prefigured many of the features of later bazaars, such as covered halls or inner

The Hossein-e-Bakhshi sarayi *in Kashan, Iran (above). The roofs look as if they were built haphazardly, a small dome here, a couple of tiers there, a few openings for light and air in between and the whole covered with a soft mixture of straw and clay the same colour as the nearby desert, hardened in the sun. Below: the three domes, with their glazed openings, of the Amin ad-Dole* timce *(market hall), also in Kashan, show the inventiveness of local builders.*

courtyards lined with arcades. Various excavations – from Palmyra to Ephesus, from Volubilis at the foot of the Atlas mountains to Apamea in what is now Syria – show that narrow streets with workshops and retail shops were already common in those days. Archaeologists in Dura-Europos on the banks of the Euphrates in Syria have unearthed the remains of the oldest 'bazaar' dating from at least the 4th century BC.

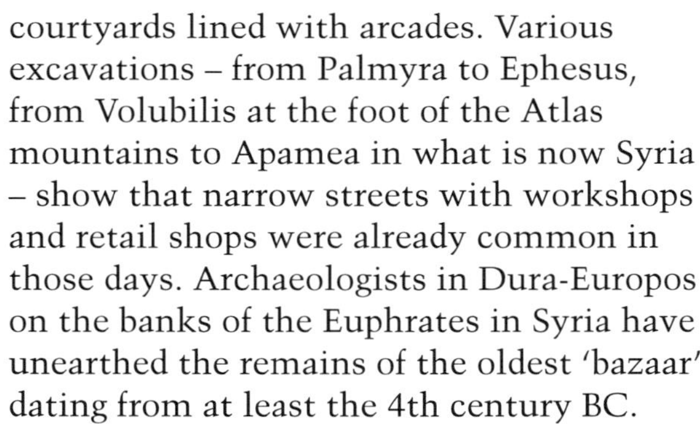

But the streets in which the Romans, Palmyrenes and Hellenes used to stroll and do their shopping were boulevards lined with colonnades, designed for heavy military and goods traffic. They bore little resemblance to the narrow bazaar streets of later periods, which were only intended for pack animals. In a famous, although not uncontroversial, study written in the 1930s, the French orientalist Jean Sauvaget, taking Aleppo and Damascus as his examples, showed how the change might have come about. According to him, after the Islamic conquest people began setting up stalls haphazardly along the broad main streets until the colonnaded walkways completely disappeared. These early souqs had nothing in common with today's complex network of buildings. If they were covered at all, it was only with makeshift mats or boards. It was not until the late Middle Ages that the barrel or groined vaults – many of which can still be seen today – were built as permanent protection against the weather or fires. That was probably when the bazaar acquired its characteristic appearance.

The warehouses and *khans* in the city centre only date from the Middle Ages. Until then, goods were always unloaded and stored on the edge of town, in large caravanserais similar to the lodgings along the overland routes. Around them were open spaces where the camels could be kept while they were being loaded and unloaded.

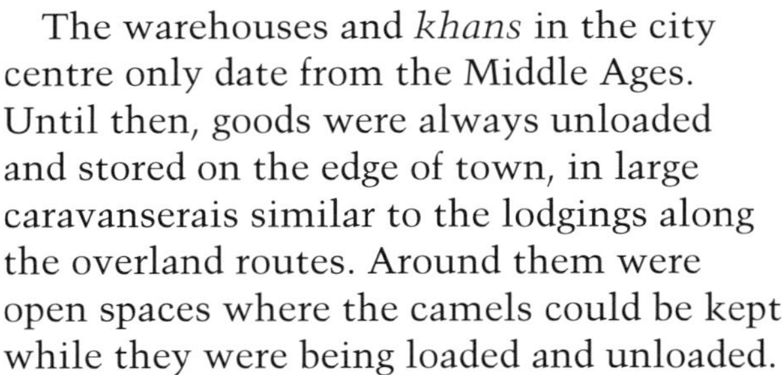

It is not clear why the traders gradually moved into the town centres from the 12th century onwards. Certainly security was a factor and probably also shortage of space – the retail trade could no longer accommodate the growing volume of goods in the souqs. But possibly the move was ordered by the authorities, because initially the new shops and warehouses in the bazaars are believed to have been mainly for non-local traders. No doubt they could be kept under tighter control inside the city walls and made to pay taxes and duties.

All over the Islamic world *khans* are more or less the same: buildings with several storeys around an inner courtyard, usually connected with the outside world by a single access route which can be closed off. The animals sleep on the ground floor, the people on the floor above. Access to the rooms is generally via open galleries. As with houses, the external walls are mostly unadorned, although the door is sometimes decorated. The façades on the courtyard are often very elaborate.

There do not seem to be any set rules for the location of the *khans* in the bazaar. The essential factor always seems to be proximity to the shopping streets and commercial districts. This is logical, considering how many different functions the *khan* has – of which more later.

Although there are basic similarities of design, certain regional variations have developed over the years. In Cairo, for instance, there are still several dozen *wakalats*, massive buildings with four or even five storeys. The top floor, with *mashrabiyas*, is often used for *raba*, rented accommodation. Appreciably more modest in size, but often with colonnades and elaborately carved timberwork on the courtyard side, are the *funduqs* in the Maghreb. Fine examples have been preserved in Tunis (from the 16th and 17th centuries) and Fez (from the 13th century). The *samsarahs* in Sanaa are also multi-storeyed. They are used mainly for accommodation and storage, but until recently they also housed religious scholars whose task it was to examine the religious credentials of incoming traders. That is obviously why *samsarahs*, which usually belong to the nearest mosque, are still in a sense religious sites.

The *khans* of Damascus have a unique architectural feature, in that most of their courtyards are roofed over with domes. Very similar to these halls in their layout are the *qaiseriyas*, 'imperial halls'. These (not to be confused with the much more modest inner courtyards of the same name in some bazaars in the Levant) are networks of narrow streets which can be shut off on all sides, found mainly in the old quarters of Moroccan cities. They originate from the Roman and Byzantine basilicas. The first is believed to have been built by Julius Caesar in Antioch – hence the name.

The typical *bedestens* in Istanbul and Western Anatolia and the Persian *timce* halls are closely related to the domed halls of Damascus, although they are actually much older. The *qaiseriyas*, *bedestens* and *timce* halls do not offer overnight accommodation. They are purely stores and, as such, represent the treasure houses of the bazaar in which particularly valuable goods such as gold, jewels, fine fabrics and sometimes carpets are sold. Moneylenders and moneychangers often have their offices there too. The *bedestens*, with their heavy gates and barred windows, were originally strongrooms in which citizens kept their money and documents.

The *khans* have as many different functions as they have regional variations. The large *khans* were generally used as accommodation and storage for wholesalers from outside the area and as offices and depots for locals. In most cases they are still in use, housing workshops and businesses. In some of them – Aleppo being a prime example – the European trading powers had their offices and consulates. When the *khans* were built, it could not have been foreseen that they would end up being used for car parks and bus stations, corrugated-iron stalls selling cheap imported goods or temporary camps for refugees from the countryside. As a result, the fabric of the buildings is rapidly deteriorating.

The names of the city caravanserais vary from one region to another. In the Maghreb they are called funduq, *in Egypt* wakalat, *in Yemen* samsarah, *in Turkey* han *and in Iran* sarayi. *Although architectural traditions vary, their basic structure and function are the same everywhere. Cells around an internal courtyard on the ground floor are used as stables and warehouses. On the upper floors are the dormitories for foreign traders and offices, and sometimes also living accommodation for locals. Above: the façade of the Vakil caravanserai in Kerman, decorated with coloured tiles. Below: one of the many* funduqs *in Marrakesh. Bottom: the five-storey inner courtyard of the el-Ghouri* wakalat *in Cairo with its* mashrabiyas.

There are many different types of minaret. The earliest, built in Syria, were similar to the ancient Christian watchtowers or church towers. In Spain and the Maghreb the minarets are square; in Turkey and Turkestan, Iran and Afghanistan they are polygonal or round. Cairo has a variety of shapes, reflecting its chequered history (above: the minaret of the mosque containing Mohammed el-Nasir's tomb; right: the skyline of the el-Azhar Mosque and University). A UNESCO study in Fez revealed that there are strict criteria for the positioning of mosques. The call of the muezzin *must be audible without a loudspeaker for up to about 60 metres (200 feet). Circles with that radius and the mosque at the centre drawn on the city map correspond almost exactly to the bazaar and residential district. Top: the weekly market in Boulmane, southern Morocco.*

The development of the city *khans* was encouraged by the Ottomans. The complexes built during their rule over the eastern Mediterranean (including the domed halls of Damascus) were more imposing than ever before. They contain several inner courtyards and market halls, including souqs, wells, baths and prayer houses. The most magnificent examples cover several hectares and were mostly owned by wealthy foundations. These were soon imitated in Persia; huge *sarayi* complexes were built in the Safavid period, notably in Isfahan.

Eugen Wirth compared the old bazaars with modern office blocks and shopping centres in the West. This might at first seem far-fetched; what could modern open-plan offices have in common with medieval *khans*? What connection could there possibly be between McDonald's or Pizza Hut and a food stall, a video centre and a teahouse, or a high-tech gym and a *hammam*?

In fact, their structures and functions are surprisingly similar. Both have offices and banks, food outlets, service and repair shops concentrated in a small area. In both pedestrians walk along covered, climatically controlled shopping streets – shopping malls or souqs. Both have not only local businesses and trades but also links with international trade and finance. No one lives in them; from early evening, both bazaars and business centres are deserted and often locked up.

But there are two important differences between the office block and the bazaar. Firstly, bazaars have existed in their present form for hundreds of years. Then there is the religious aspect. It is not by accident that the mosque is the centre of the bazaar. This was the place where court hearings were held and laws promulgated, it was a hospital and shelter for the homeless, a pastoral centre and a soup kitchen for the poor. Also – a mundane but none the less important factor – with its washrooms and public conveniences it provided sanitary facilities. Before the first *madrasas* (schools for traditional subjects such as medicine, mathematics and especially Koranic law) were built around the beginning of the second millennium, it was also an educational centre. But the *masjed* – the Arabic word means place for prostration – is, of course, chiefly a venue for communal prayers.

The history of the first purely Islamic settlements shows how closely the market

was linked to the mosque. Wherever the conquerors established a garrison town in the years after Mohammed's death, in Basra or Kufa, Fustat or Kairouan, the first thing they did was to designate a communal prayer and meeting place and build a wooden pulpit (*minbar*) and prayer niche (*mihrab*) modelled on the Prophet's house in Medina, indicating the direction of Mecca. Early historians agree, however, that the second step was always to set aside part of the area as a market place. Its use was governed by Bedouin custom, so that anyone occupying a particular site could keep it until he went home or had sold his wares.

It is clear from the first sight of a city where its inhabitants find spiritual fulfilment. In an 18th-century city in Europe the building that stands out above all the others is usually the political assembly building. In modern capitals the tallest edifices are the administrative buildings, the centres of economic life. In most medinas, on the other hand, the domes and minarets of the mosque are the highest, as were the cathedrals in medieval Christian cities. Below left: the holy city of Qom, a centre of the Iranian Shiite religion. Below right: the Dome of the Rock in Jerusalem, where Mohammed stopped on his ascent to Heaven. Above: tomb of a saint in Mocha, Yemen.

The importance and use of water

The story, like so many stories in this part of the world, begins with Abraham, the patriarch of the Jews and the Arabs. When Abraham was 85, he and his maid Hagar had a son, Ishmael. Abraham's wife Sarah then gave birth, at the age of 90, to her first son, Isaac, whereupon Hagar and Ishmael were banished into the desert – tradition has it to the waterless, burning-hot, rocky valley which is now the site of Mecca. There, after days of thirst and pleading, God sent them a spring, which soon turned into a well called Zemzem. Abraham went in search of Hagar and Ishmael and the two men built a small cube-shaped temple, the Kaaba, as he had been told to do in a dream. Ever since Mohammed's conquest of Mecca, every pilgrim has been anxious to drink the water from the holy well, which is said to come from one of the three rivers of paradise.

This legend shows the importance of water in Islam. It is venerated as a gift from God, essential to life and a sacred elixir which heals the soul.

'You can steal another man's wife, his horse, his honour, but not his water', according to the Koran. The writer of the Book of Books knew what is most essential to the peoples of the desert. The efforts made to collect and conserve water in all dry regions from the Atlantic to the Indian Ocean show how precious it is.

The water-drawing devices operated by oxen, camels or men and the networks of irrigation canals, dams, aqueducts and cisterns were not necessarily invented by Muslims, but Islamic engineers and builders played an important part in their development. One example is the highly complex system of canals in Fez, carrying fresh and waste water to and from every house, which is nearly a thousand years old. Other examples are the aqueducts designed by Sinan which once supplied some of Istanbul's ten thousand and more public wells, the huge Aghlabid basins on the outskirts of Kairouan and weirs like the two-storey Pol-e-Khajou in Isfahan, which is also a road bridge and a promenade.

The costly shaft-and-tunnel system still used in Marrakesh and in many Saharan oases and also in the Iranian highlands, for instance around Yazd and Kerman, is particularly impressive. It goes by various names, *khettara*, *foggara* and in Iran *qanat*, but it always works on more or less the same principle. Shafts lead into the earth about every 20 metres (65 feet). Where they meet impermeable layers of rock, they are connected by a slightly sloping canal which drains off the ground water, minimizing loss by evaporation in the desert climate. The tunnels can be anything up to 70 metres (230 feet) deep and 70 kilometres (more than 40 miles) long.

The Arab bath house is a place for relaxation and enjoyment as well as ritual purification. After the washing and massage, visitors are covered in towels in the maslakh, *the changing room, and offered coffee or tea. Occasionally even the supervisor indulges in a little nap (opposite: the supervisor of the Hammam an-Nahaseen in Aleppo). When it comes to supplying water to towns and fields in the deserts and steppes, no effort is spared. The famous old* norias, *creaking wooden wheels, raise the water of the Orontes to the level of the aqueducts in Hama, Syria (below).*

Although in some ways efforts are made to save water wherever possible, in other ways people are, or rather were, fairly extravagant with it. For instance, canals, fountains and pools have always been essential features of gardens. This is partly because they are cooling in the hot summers, but also because every garden is seen as an earthly reflection of paradise and in paradise the blessed are known to expect not only fruits, perfumes, heavenly peace and *houris* (pure maidens), but also streams flowing with milk, honey, wine – and a never-ending supply of pure spring water.

Spectacular fountains or cascades like those so popular in the European Renaissance and Baroque periods are never seen in the Islamic world. Muslims prefer their water to splash softly or trickle or drip, or even to be completely still. If the water is still, they feel that time itself is standing still. The borders between reality and imagination disappear in its smooth surface; heaven is reflected in both senses.

This cosmic dimension can still be experienced nowadays in a few of the major gardens, the Shalimar Bagh in Lahore for instance, the Taj Mahal in Agra, the Generalife in Granada or the Agdal gardens in the royal cities in Morocco. But it can also be found in any small house in an old part of town or in any mosque with a well in the centre.

A clean body and a pure soul. Both are very important in Islam and they can only be achieved with the aid of water. The Prophet is quoted in the Hadith as saying that the key to paradise is prayer and the key to prayer is washing. According to the Koran, he advised the faithful: 'When you go to pray, wash your face and your hands up to the elbows and rub your head and your feet as far as the ankles with your wet hand.' Only in an emergency is it permissible to rub oneself down with stones or fine dry sand – in the desert, for instance, when there is no clean water available, or when one is seriously ill.

The 'lesser ablution' before prayers is obligatory for every Muslim, whether at a magnificent well like this one at the Imam Reza Mosque in Mashhad (above) or in makeshift fashion by the roadside (below: in an Anatolian village near Erzurum). Although the ritual is only mentioned briefly in the Koran, all its details have been established by tradition.

This 'lesser' ablution (*al-wudu*), which has to be performed daily at the five prayer times, is not sufficient when a person is really unclean. After sexual intercourse, during illness and, if possible, before going to the Friday mosque, the whole body has to be washed 'from head to foot'. For this 'greater' ablution (*al-ghusl*) Muslims go to the baths (Arabic and Turkish: *hammam*). As well as complying with the religious prescriptions, it is also a social occasion.

Since the time of the Crusaders, nowhere else in the entire Orient has inspired the imaginations of Europeans like the *hammam*.

It was seen as a refuge where people could relax completely and give themselves up to unbridled pleasure. Like the harem, it was a symbol of oriental eroticism. The frescoes in the Ommayad baths at Qusayr Amra in the Jordanian desert with their scenes of naked frolics, the risqué verses in the *hammam* tracts and many other works of classical Arabic literature do seem to suggest that the steam baths were dens of iniquity. But it was nothing like the medieval bathrooms in the north, with men and women romping together. The sexes were, and still are, strictly segregated.

Some Islamic baths are reserved for men or women only; others have separate areas for each. In most, however, each sex takes it in turn to use the same rooms. Sometimes a veil is hung diagonally across the entrance when it is the women's turn. Fortunately, men who enter a 'closed' bath, even if by mistake, are no longer put to death. But any stranger, unaware of the significance of the veil, who comes into the lobby still receives murderous looks and is firmly ejected by the exclusively female staff.

The 'greater ablution' for men (above: in the et-Taba hammam *in Tunis) is a gruelling process. First comes the massage. Then their bodies are scrubbed down with a rough glove. After that their hair is washed and they might have a haircut or a shave. Finally they are soaped and rinsed down three times. Below: the cisterns in the Yerebatan Sarayi, Istanbul, the 'sunken palace'.*

Men usually go to the *hammam* in the morning or just before midnight, women between the midday and evening prayers. In the traditional society of a medina, an afternoon at the baths is often the only opportunity for women to meet female friends away from home. Here they can gossip to their heart's content and discreetly choose a bride for their sons from the other women's daughters. As the Koran requires, they can shave their underarm and pubic hair and afterwards gorge themselves with sweets to make themselves even more like their husband's ideal of beauty.

But it would be a mistake to think that the social barriers were broken down when people cast off their clothes. According to historians, women loved to flaunt their wealth and show off their clothes and jewelry. The *qabqabs*, wooden pattens which they

wore in the baths to avoid scorching their feet on the heated stone floors, were often decorated with strings of pearls, the ladling cups were made of gold or silver gilt and rooms where they relaxed after bathing had silk or brocade on the walls.

Nowadays women take a make-up bag to the *hammam*. Most of the cosmetics it contains are modern, but there are also all kinds of pastes, creams and perfumed essences made from ancient recipes – for instance, *kohl* for the eyes, *tfal* (aluminium oxide mixed with orange-flower water and rosewater), which is used on the hair, and henna for hair colouring.

Now that more and more people have their own bathrooms (and televisions), fewer people go to the baths. Gone are the days when Fez had more than 100 large public steam baths, Istanbul 155 and Aleppo as many as 195. But a few can still be found in most historic city centres. Some of them are 400 or 500 years old, in Damascus and Aleppo over 600 years, and they are open to anyone, whatever their religion.

Like the baths in the ancient world, they are basically divided into three sections: the *maslakh* (Turkish: *camegah*), the *frigidarium* of the ancient Romans, where people pay admission, change and relax afterwards; the moderately heated *bait al-auwal* (*sogukluk*, or *tepidarium*) for acclimatization; and the hot central area, the *bait al-harara* (*sicaklik*, or *caldarium*), consisting of several rooms. They have alcoves in which people wash and low marble platforms for relaxation and massage. The cold and hot water is collected in small bowls (bathtubs are believed to be breeding grounds for evil spirits and are only allowed as an exception in thermal baths). The water flows away through stone grooves at the side after use.

The baths are heated by a hypocaust system. Air heated by a huge wooden stove passes through hollow spaces under the floor and clay pipes in the walls. The steam comes from a tank and is brought into the bath through a thin, perforated internal wall. The central section usually has several domes, both for aesthetic reasons and to allow the steam to circulate and save water and fuel. They are set with convex tiles of opaque glass, protecting the modesty of the people inside and giving a dim light which encourages contemplation.

Even the staff are just as they were in the old days. As they come in, people are handed their personal sandals, towels and soap by the supervisor who, at the end, also wraps them in long loincloths, and attendants proffer tea, coffee or a water pipe. The *musaubin* (Turkish: *tellak*) scrubs and massages them three times, in accordance with the ritual. The boilerman sits in his underground room, feeding a glowing furnace with pieces of wood and wood shavings. Occasionally a barber still offers his services in the lobby.

The traditional baths, still owned by charitable foundations, have a central role in many ceremonies even today. Pregnant women go to them to prepare for the delivery and for the ritual purification forty days afterwards. Boys are brought there for circumcision. Brides come three times during the marriage festivities: seven days before the wedding, for purification; three days later, with their friends, to be decorated with henna; and the evening before the wedding night, with their future husband.

But the *hammam* still has its place, too, in the everyday lives of many people living in the old quarters. This is partly because of the religious prescriptions and also because it is useful in preventing and treating rheumatism and other ills. But mainly it is because anyone who has gone through this exquisite torture knows that nothing does you more good than to be soaped by expert hands, have your hair washed, your limbs pulled about and the skin loosened, and afterwards, completely rejuvenated and glowing all over, to sit wrapped in a sweet-smelling towel and suck on a water pipe.

The centre of every bath house is the steam room, the bait al-harara. *Instead of windows it has small opaque glass holes, set into the domes like stars. Its marble floor is usually heated. The niches round the edge are used to bathe in, with water scooped out of the washbasins. The hottest place in the room is the raised pedestal in the middle, where the* musaubin *gives massages which are both physically and mentally relaxing. (Opposite above: in the Cagaloglu* hammam *in Istanbul; below: in a bath house in Kerman, eastern Iran). Above: a believer at a purification ceremony in the Muayyid Mosque in Cairo.*

Overleaf: mirror and antique shop in the souq, Marrakesh.

CRAFTSMEN AND SHOPKEEPERS

THEIR WORK AND GOODS

Carpets
Clothing
Chechias
Jewelry
Perfume
Coffee, tobacco and sweetmeats
Medicine and magic
Calligraphy and painting
Wood
Glass
Metal
Ceramics
Leather

From loom to living room

The scene is repeated in every carpet bazaar countless times a day. A resourceful guide leads tourists into a shop 'just for a look!' The visitors sit down, beguiled by the shopkeeper's charm. Civilities are exchanged. Tea is offered and carpets unrolled one after the other. It is rare that somebody does not take a fancy to one and go home with it as excess baggage.

Luckily the bad old days of aniline dyes are over. Dyers are increasingly going back to natural substances such as indigo (blue), madder and cochineal (red), delphinium and dyer's weed (yellow). Opposite: wool dyeing in the bazaar in Kashan, Iran.

However, only a minority of Oriental carpets are brought to the West individually in this way. The vast majority are bought by wholesalers. The best example is Iran, where around ten million people are currently employed directly or indirectly in carpet-making. Carpets are the second largest export, coming after oil but before agricultural produce. Iran is the biggest

Carpet makers working at home usually invent their own patterns. Vagirehs *(Persian for patterns) are also used – these are particularly complex knotted designs with a variety of motifs. In the factories, however, the patterns are transferred to graph paper, then cut up, mounted on cardboard and hand-coloured. There are still a few* salims *left, men who read or sing out the pattern rhythmically for the carpet knotters to follow.*

Further stages in the life of a carpet: washing and then drying in the sun (right: in a khan *in Isfahan); trimming the rough pile (opposite above) and interim storage in the bazaar (opposite below: in the Farsh Forushha carpet bazaar in Isfahan).*

carpet exporter in the world. Although connoisseurs complain that standards are declining and that nowadays people in the villages are more interested in money than quality, carpets of excellent quality can still be found, at least in and around Isfahan and in Tabriz.

The *bakhtiari* can serve as an example of how carpets find their way from the loom to the end user via the bazaar. These carpets are woven to the west and north of Isfahan by Luris, Kurds and Tajiks and also by Arabs and Armenians. The background is usually ivory or cream, less commonly red, blue, green or brown. The style is rustic, almost crude. The warp and weft are made of cotton, the pile of sheep's wool. The most popular design is a garden with stylized flowerbeds and watercourses. Other common motifs are trees of life, bouquets of flowers, medallions and rococo roses. The manufacturing centre is the town of Shahr-e-Kord in the wild and inaccessible Zagros mountains.

As in other parts of the Middle East, most of the carpets and kilims are made without a needle. The factories in the towns often employ men, but in the villages the carpets are made by women at home, who, like other women in rural areas, have no employment rights.

The women collect the wool from their own herds and buy in the cotton. They spin by hand in the old-fashioned way, with a spindle or spinning wheel. First of all, the most valuable part of the wool is pulled from the fleece. It is beaten with wooden clubs, then washed and dried and pulled through the metal teeth of a card comb to make strands of even width.

Dying is mainly done synthetically, in the larger towns. The older, more natural dyes are coming back into fashion in Turkey, but less so in Iran. Workshops usually employ specially trained designers – artists who painstakingly transfer their designs on to cardboard covered with graph paper and use a numerical code to identify the colours. With village carpets like the *bakhtiari*, however, it is the weavers who choose the colours and patterns.

For the first few years, the *bakhtiari* is kept by its maker, unlike carpets from the cities, which are sold as soon as they are finished. It is only when it has acquired a certain patina that it is offered for sale in the nearest large town through a middleman. This arrangement suits both people in the East, who prefer the look of a new carpet, and westerners, who like the more muted colours after it has been used for a while.

It is unlikely that European buyers will have tracked down carpets themselves in

remote villages, as they sometimes claim. In fact, the wholesalers go to the bazaars in the large towns and retailers obtain their supplies from Hamburg, Zurich or London rather than from Iran.

The tales of valuable old carpets that someone has discovered tucked away in a corner of the bazaar are equally unlikely to be true. A few shops have two or three interesting specimens hanging on the wall, but these are not generally for sale. The truth is that stocks have run out. Iran has even been reimporting expensive Persian carpets from the West since the government began allowing this again in 1993.

In the meantime, the *bakhtiari*, still in its original dirty and dusty state, is awaiting a buyer with thousands of others in the carpet bazaar in Isfahan. The arrival of a wholesaler from Europe signals the beginning of a long and laborious process. The customer chooses the ones he likes from the enormous piles with an Iranian agent who has briefed him on current supplies and prices beforehand and is now acting as interpreter and middleman. Then the negotiations start. The margin is only 5 to 10 per cent, much lower than it is when bargaining with tourists who are not in the trade. The prices and numbers are noted and a *hammal* (a self-employed porter) takes the carpets in his four-wheeled cart, to a specially rented store watched over by a *sarayi* guard. Here the dealer inspects all the carpets again at the end of his buying trip and allocates them numbers. Two *adelbandi* (packers) wrap them up expertly. Then they are taken on open trucks to the Shah Abdol Aziz laundries on the southern outskirts of Tehran, where there is plenty of water to wash them and no shortage of sun to dry them.

The dust is finally removed from the *bakhtiari* and it is cleaned, usually with chlorine. New carpets which have not yet acquired a lustre are given a finishing wash, making them soft and springy. Sometimes they are also given an 'ageing wash' with strong chemical additives, in other words artificially aged, which is not officially allowed. An expert can spot this straight away because the pile is deep-coloured at the base but pale on top.

After being washed, the carpet is dried on rails in the open air. Then it is nailed on to boards with the lower side uppermost, trodden, wetted again and dried. The pile is roughened in the wash and has to be trimmed with electric clippers. It is checked for minor defects and any loose weft rows are picked up, threads cut off and individual knots dyed.

The last stage is the customs formalities. For tax reasons, the value of the carpet is usually declared to be a fraction of the real price. After that it goes to its final destination, nowadays often by air. The normal land route via Azerbaijan and Ukraine is not only long but has recently become very risky; more and more valuable carpets have been simply vanishing into thin air.

A loom in the souq in Aleppo (opposite). Weaving might have become more technically advanced, but the basic principle of warp and weft, the two threads crossing at right angles, has remained the same for 7,000 years. Until the Second World War, most oriental carpets were taken straight from the bazaars to Vienna, which became the main centre for the whole of Europe. Now the biggest import warehouses are in Hamburg and London. Above: a shop in Aleppo. Below: Isfahan.

Chadors, veils and kaftans

Arabs are very clothes-conscious. They give free rein to their imagination and are fond of contrasting bright colours, gold trimmings, silk braids and cords, buttons and tassels. Being inured to the heat, they wear two or three layers on top of each other, with furs and ties and sashes. The German traveller Fritz Max Hessemer, who was so impressed by the costumes he saw in the Orient in the early 18th century, would have been sorely disappointed nowadays. Especially in the cities, the colourful costumes are being replaced by drab-coloured grey and brown trousers, sports jackets, coats and skirts, even tracksuits and jeans. It is only amongst the peasants and nomads in the rural areas that the traditional costumes in light, bright colours have to some extent survived.

Although it is centuries since luxury fabrics were made for princes and dignitaries in state-run weaving mills, most Arabs have not lost their love of fine clothing. Old looms are still in use in most bazaars (below: the en-Nayar funduq *in Tunis). A wide selection of trimmings (opposite above) is always available.*

In most Islamic countries, the basic garment for both sexes has for centuries been the *sirval*, ankle-length baggy trousers in a light material, and the *qamiz*, a loose knee-length collarless shirt. Over that they wore (and still do in some regions) large, loose scarves. The only difference between men and women was the way the garment was wrapped, the colourfulness of the fabric and the accessories and ornamentation. At the same time, different regional styles developed – partly following pre-Islamic custom and partly because of the climate.

In the Maghreb, for example, the men wear a light-coloured hooded woollen robe to protect them against the extremes of temperature. The Arabs and Turks also have their own types of robe: the *aba* (a dark-coloured woollen garment) or the *kaftan* (long-sleeved, opening at the front, made of cotton or brocade). Palestinian women prefer a coloured embroidered cotton dress (*thawb*), North African women

Thirty years ago, Titus Burckhardt quoted an elderly Moroccan who took him into a warehouse full of machines: 'We lived without this for 1,300 years and didn't do badly. There were price rises, wars and sometimes epidemics, but never the worst epidemic of all, unemployment.' The old man might be reassured by the sight of these people sewing (below: Istanbul) or ironing (overleaf: Isfahan).

a sleeveless tunic, the *jubba* or *gandura*, with a shawl tied around the waist. Everyday wear for the Egyptian *fellahin* is the *galabiyya*, a simple cotton robe.

Headgear is equally varied. Traditionally, people in the Middle East did not like to go bareheaded. Muslims, like Jews, keep their heads covered as a sign of humility and respect, mainly, although not exclusively, while praying, and only uncover them if the circumstances are exceptional.

In most cases the basic headgear is the *taqiya*, the small embroidered cotton lace cap, usually white, nowadays affected by male fundamentalists as an anti-western gesture. Around the *taqiya* long cloths are wound into turbans, following the example of the Prophet. Iraqis, Syrians and Palestinians and the people of the Arabian peninsula wear headcloths tied with cords on top of theirs. The typical red felt hats – the flat *chechia* in Tunisia, the Egyptian *tarbush* and the Turkish *fez* – are closely related to the *taqiya*.

In the West there are many misconceptions about another common form of head covering, the veil. There are actually three different types: that worn mainly in Saudi Arabia and the Gulf States, which covers the nose, mouth and neck; the type with a transparent crochet slit for the eyes, common in North India, Afghanistan and Pakistan; and the Persian *chador* (meaning tent), often referred to in the West as a veil. This covers the head and shoulders, but not the face as is generally thought in the West.

It is widely believed that, throughout its history (it predates Islam by many years), the veil has been simply a means for men to restrict women's freedom, but again this is a misconception. Although it was (and is) true in many societies, the veil does have other functions. For instance, it protects against the sun, sand and dust and against the evil eye and molestation, it signifies membership of a tribe and it keeps away the spirits popularly believed to enter the upper bodily orifices. In any case, the veil was often worn by men as well as women and still is amongst the Tuareg.

The meanings of colours are difficult for Europeans to grasp. Although their significance varies, green and white are the colours of the Prophet, black was originally the colour of the Abbasids, red that of the Shiites, while in the Middle Ages yellow was reserved for Christians and Jews. The colour of mourning might be black, blue or white, depending on the region.

As far as women's clothing is concerned, the Koran merely requires that it should be restrained and modest. Women are exhorted not to expose their 'treasures'. When outside the home, they should cover their faces and breasts, not emphasize the curves of their body unnecessarily and not wear transparent materials or extravagant finery, to avoid arousing lust in the opposite sex. Mohammed also forbade men from wearing 'decadent' silk ('to prevent lice and skin diseases').

These rules were observed strictly by the Prophet's moralistic companions, but after only one generation they were being ignored by the rulers. The Omayyad caliphs set up state weaving mills, the *tiraz*, producing heavy gold- and silver-embroidered fabrics. At the same time they issued edicts requiring Christians and Jews to wear particular colours (for instance, yellow) and distinctive symbols (such as special belts).

Qalamkaris – *printed cloths – are a speciality of Isfahan. The traditional patterns are figures of ancient Iranian Zoroastrian deities and* termeh *(what Europeans call Paisley). The patterns are stamped on by hand; the cloths are then boiled on the river bank, washed and dried. The industry employs over a thousand men, but only one in a hundred is a master craftsman. Below: outside a* tarbush *shop in Cairo.*

Under the Abbasids, stockings and ankle-length, richly decorated ceremonial robes from Persia came into fashion. The Fatimids then began dressing their officials in magnificent costumes of silk and brocade. At the same time they set up workshops all over the kingdom, producing goods of superb quality which can still be seen in museums today. The famous coronation mantle of the Norman king Roger II in the Schatzkammer in Vienna is one example.

Right from the beginning, textile manufacturing was the most important industry in the Islamic world. Its products were used for furnishings – beds, divans, cushions, covers – as well as clothing. Especially valuable fabrics were status symbols and assets that could be passed down as family heirlooms and were often presented to important foreign guests. Silk (*harir*) came from Damascus and Aleppo and from around the Caspian Sea. Cotton (*qutn*) was grown mainly in Syria and the Nile valley, flax (*kattan*) in the Nile Delta, halfa grass, used to make mats and sandals, on the high plateaux of the Maghreb. Wool (*suf*) was found wherever there were sheep, goats or camels. Documents from the genizah in Cairo (the place where documents are kept in the synagogue) tell us that in the 11th and 12th centuries many, if not most, of the craftsmen and traders were engaged in the manufacture and sale of textiles.

In the 19th century the situation changed dramatically. Cartwright in England and Jacquard in France had invented and developed the mechanical loom, enabling the Europeans to flood the countries they had recently colonized with mass-produced textile goods. Although less durable and aesthetic, these were popular because they were cheaper. The traditional textile crafts continued to decline when industrial spinning and weaving factories were set up in many countries after independence. Today hand-weaving is done mainly in remote

villages and by the Bedouin. The few tailors still working in the bazaars are used only by a small well-to-do clientele hankering for the good old days. The children who once used to spin agave silk to be wound on hand bobbins, especially in the Maghreb, are becoming a rare sight nowadays.

European clothing was first copied in the Orient at the beginning of the 19th century, in the military uniforms. Influenced by the western envoys and businessmen and the mission schools, the local Christians and Jews followed suit. After the First World War, more and more Muslims from the urban upper classes had regular contacts with the West and dressed accordingly. Women acquired a new self-confidence and rebelled against wearing the veil. At the same time there were dramatic interventions by the state. In 1828 Sultan Mahmud II banned the

turban by law in Turkey and introduced the *fez*. Then in 1925 Kemal Atatürk ordered his subjects to wear hats or caps instead of the *fez*. In 1939 the Shah of Iran, Reza Pahlevi, took a similarly radical step, banning the *chador*. The unveiling was brutally enforced by the police.

As well as altering people's outward appearance, the disappearance of traditional dress also signals the decline of an attitude of mind and way of life. The Swiss Islamic scholar Titus Burckhardt has written that the loose oriental robes are much better suited to the extremes of climate in the East and that their combination of ascetic simplicity and male or patriarchal dignity reflects a particular way of thinking. What is more, the bowing and prostration and the ritual ablutions required in Islam are much more difficult to perform in European dress.

The plain high-necked, long-sleeved garment and the headcloth covering the neck and hair which modern fundamentalists try to impose on women as a reaction to the westernization of countries such as Algeria, Egypt or Turkey has very little to do with old Islamic customs. It is an attempt to adapt clothing which has long since been Europeanized to male ideas of female morality ordained by God.

The only occasion on which every Muslim, regardless of origin and status, abandons modern fashions is on the pilgrimage to Mecca. Whether rich or poor, men have to take off their everyday clothes and put on a special robe consisting of two seamless white wraparound cloths signifying a state of devotion (*ihram*). Women have to dress as simply as possible, with no perfume or make-up, and normally wear a headscarf rather than a veil.

The textile trade, especially silk, has always been extremely important to the economy of the Islamic world. The European powers had offices at the main transfer points from very early times. Raw bales and finished products were bought and sold according to strict rules under state supervision. In the 16th and 17th centuries war broke out between the Safavids and the Ottomans because the Persians were trying to gain a foothold on the European markets, by-passing Istanbul. Soon afterwards the growing competition from machine-made European products led to a decline in traditional textile manufacture in the Middle East, radically altering the structure of Islamic society. Left: a corner in the fabric and clothing bazaar in Fez. Above: a tailor in the Souq al-Juh in Aleppo.

The cap makers of Tunis

In the heart of the medina in Tunis, halfway between the Mosque of the Olive Tree and the government building, is a small souq with an atmosphere unique in the Islamic world. Its few short, vaulted alleyways are unusually straight, clean and quiet. It has barely two dozen shops, like oversized chocolate boxes with their pastel wainscoting. Their owners or tenants, mostly dignified elderly men, radiate the serenity that comes from an ancient tradition and long experience of life.

The red of the chechia *(opposite: a dyer) is obtained mostly from cochineal insects, bred in cactus plantations in the Canary Islands. The advantage of their pigments, also used for expensive lipsticks and aperitifs, is that, unlike the cheaper synthetic dyes, they do not fade or run. Below: staff of a traditional shop in the Rue de la Kasbah, Tunis.*

Not only does the Souk des Chéchias, home of the handmade felt cap of the same name worn by millions of Muslims from the Atlantic to the Gulf, have a magical atmosphere, it is also of great historical significance. Tunis is the only city in North Africa in which attempts are being made to revive, at least to some extent, the medieval

Stages in making a cap: the fulling mills of Tébourba, where soapy water is heated with gas, and the dye works on the outskirts of old Tunis.
Opposite: still life in the chechia *souq. A pile of felt caps, a leather shape on which the caps are smoothed, teasels and metal brushes for carding, a block for stretching and, of course, a picture of the boss.*

system of craft corporations. The cap makers' guild was always the most traditional and powerful corporation of all, and even today its honorary head, the *amin*, is the head of all the groups in the souq, a man of integrity and substance elected for life by representatives of the various trades.

The *chechia* makers have enjoyed the independence protected by the *amin*'s authority since their ancestors came to the north of Tunisia from Andalusia in the early 17th century, although their monopoly has on occasion been threatened. Just before the First World War, for instance, the East was flooded with factory-made caps from Austria and France. Shortly after the war the Tunisian government was going to allow Italian manufacturers to start mass-producing *chechias* in the medina. In the exodus from the city during the Second World War, many cap makers changed to other occupations. Some now make caps purely as a sideline and the number of workshops is declining all the time. But the ancient and complicated technique of cap-making has nevertheless survived all these pressures.

Like their great-great grandmothers before them, thousands of women still do piecework at home for starvation wages, knitting the *qabbus*, the white wool cap from which the famous headgear is made in a highly complex process. Even today the caps are brought to the souq by the sackful and then taken to the banks of the river Mejerda near the village of Tébourba (where the minerals apparently give the best quality) and immersed in wooden tubs of hot soapy water. They are tumbled in a huge noisy cast-iron machine for several hours. By the end they have shrunk by a third and turned into felt. Next the men in the souq workshops card the caps with dried teasels, clean them, smooth them with clippers and scissors and beat them with long wooden sticks. Finally the bosses' wives put the maker's mark on the inside edge (they are the only people allowed to do this). Then comes the dyeing process, in a vault wreathed in steam. First the caps are put in an alum solution for an hour and a half to impregnate them and then into the concentrated dye. How long they are left there depends mainly on the

شاشية

Intermediate and final storage: the newly dyed chechias *are wrung out, fitted over a clay block and dried in a wooden cabinet. Even in the 19th century the high-quality locally made caps on sale in the shops were kept separate from the mass-produced ones made in factories in Marseille and Bohemia.*

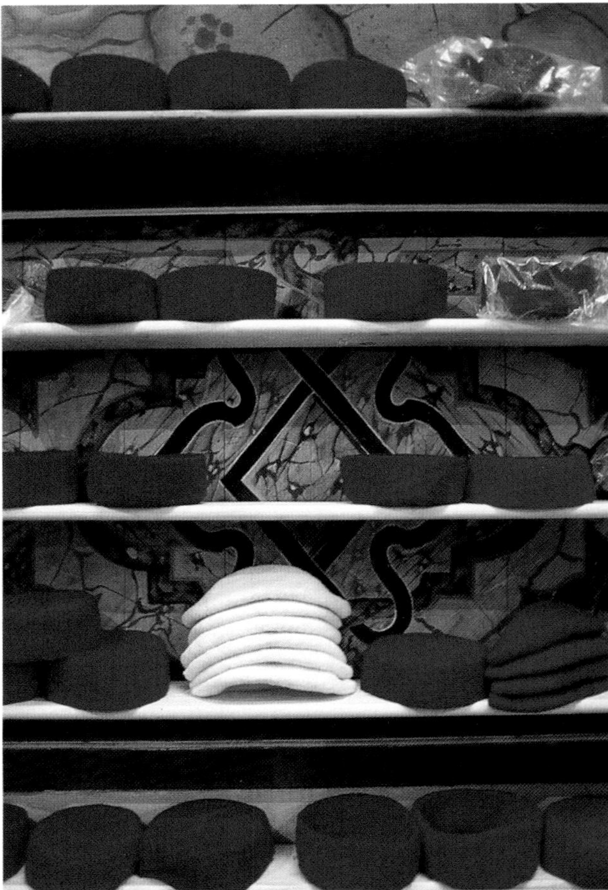

Opposite, below left: The chechias, *now almost finished, are combed, brushed and kneaded, mothproofed, folded and pressed. A few are sold by weight in the shops just around the corner (left and opposite, below right), but most are exported, priced individually. Below: the basic caps, made of white merino wool, are hand-knitted by women.*

materials; the old, precious natural dyes need longer than the cheaper new chemical powders. After rinsing, the caps are shaped. Each one is turned over a cylindrical clay block with a firm flick of the wrist and put into a furnace, still on the block, to dry. They are brushed and combed again, kneaded or chewed with fingers and teeth and then sprinkled with perfumed water and *burra*, the red felt powder. Finally they are folded, pressed between two wooden boards and flattened under the weight of a man whose sole job it is to sit on a pile of such boards. The finishing touch is reserved for the boss himself: sewing on the *qubbita*, the characteristic black tassel on the side.

The caps come in an atonishing variety of shapes and colours: the black ones worn in Tripolitania, the pale-red ones worn in the city of Tunis, the cylindrical *saqs* not covering the ears which other Tunisians wear, and the semicircular *qalabus* for export, which partly cover the ears. The tassel is significant, too – the longer the threads, the higher the wearer's social status.

However, the *chechia* has lost most of its old abstract connotations. The days of the Young Turks, when the *chechia stambuli* became the symbol of the modern Islamic nation in the early 20th century, are long gone, and so too are the days of the *destour*, the Tunisian independence movement, which in the 1920s chose the *chechia* as a visible symbol of resistance to the French occupiers. The future of the famous felt cap is uncertain. Will it degenerate into a tourist souvenir or a nostalgic memento of the past? Or will new export markets open up in the future, as Nigeria did in the eighties? There is no reason to be too pessimistic. In the early nineties, the workshops in Tunis were still producing over a million caps a year, almost as many as in previous decades.

Wealth and protection

The theories are more than a little bizarre by present-day standards. In the Middle Ages the Arabs believed that gold grew on trees or just under the earth like carrots and was picked at sunrise. Many people thought that it was grown by ants or by naked men living in caves. At the beginning of the 14th century the historian al-Umari asserted that the precious material started growing in August, 'when the sun is at its strongest and the Nile is rising'. When the water receded, bushes with roots made of gold could be found on the previously flooded land. The highly successful visit that the emperor of Mali, Kankan Musa, made to Cairo on his way to Mecca in 1324 created total confusion. Where on earth, people asked, could he possibly have got the fabulous quantities of raw gold which he was carrying with him on more than a

Amongst the wealthier people in the cities, gold has replaced silver for reasons of prestige. It is the done thing for a husband to give his wife a chain, a ring or a necklace. It does not seem to make any difference that many of the goods have been imported ready-made from Europe via Istanbul and Dubai.

hundred camels and distributing with such extraordinary generosity to his hosts?

The Arabs might be familiar with gold in processed form, as coins or jewelry, but they had no idea where it came from. What they did not know for a long time was that, unless it was from melted-down booty from looted Syrian churches, Egyptian tombs or Persian treasure houses, their gold came mostly from West Africa. Only Kankan Musa's men knew exactly where and the Saharan caravaneers who acted as middlemen did not disclose the routes by which the gold was taken north and east to the Arab traders.

On the other hand, the Arabs were well aware that their silver came from the traditional mining areas of Transoxiana and Khorassan, and also from Europe. From the 16th century onwards, and in the 18th century in particular, huge quantities of silver were exchanged for coffee from Saudi Arabia. The best-known means of payment was the Maria Theresa thaler, still used today by the Omanis and Yemenis and known as the *riyal fransi*. Around 200 million coins were estimated to be in circulation in Ethiopia and Yemen in 1900, about 6 million kilos (6,000 tons). They were the raw material for one of the most fascinating crafts in the Islamic world: the silver jewelry of southern Arabia.

Fine amber necklaces and amulet holders, rings, bracelets and belts can still be found in the Suq al-Fidda, the silver market in Sanaa, as well as curved silver daggers. Real Bedouin jewelry is rarely more than a generation old. It was customary in the rural areas for a woman's possessions to be melted down after her death and new ones bought for her successor.

Devout Muslims always believed that the manufacture and sale of precious metal articles corrupted the soul. As in many other cultures, gold- and silversmiths were believed to have connections with the occult, with magic, alchemy and healing. The trade – but not the wearing of their products – was usually restricted to members of the non-Muslim communities, the *jimmis*. In nearly every jewelry-making centre, whether it be Tunis or Isfahan, Istanbul or the south of Morocco, the trade was dominated by Jews. In Syria, it was Armenian Christians; in Cairo, it was mainly Copts.

Harqus *painting – the custom of decorating hands, feet and face and also other parts of the body with coloured patterns and motifs which fade after a few weeks – is common throughout the Islamic world. Like tattooing, it is both a decoration and a magic symbol to ward off evil spirits. All kinds of herbs, ash and charcoal are used, but the most common is henna, which gives a reddish-brown colour. It is made from the dried and powdered leaves of the henna bush, mixed with water and lemon, and applied with sharpened* kalame, *pieces of wood. In many places – Marrakesh for instance, where these pictures were taken – professional henna painters still come to people's houses. They work either freehand or from previously applied patterns.*

The most striking example of this religious specialization was the former Jewish community in Yemen. In every village in the highlands, in Hadhramaut or the coastal plains of Tihama, Jews made the distinctive solid or filigree belts, chains, rings and bracelets, coin pendants, hollow spheres and amulet containers. Several hundred Jewish jewellers worked in the Suq al-Fidda, the silver souq in Sanaa, the capital. The trade used to be passed on from father to son, but at the end of the 1940s this old tradition abruptly came to an end. The Jews emigrated to Israel, as they did from most other Arab countries.

The exodus was not the only reason for the decline of the silversmith's art. The radical social changes in the Arab world have been equally catastrophic. Oil wealth attracted many craftsmen to Saudi Arabia, where they are now simply traders. At the same time there has been a decline in the numbers of Bedouin, who traditionally wore silver. The gulf between rich and poor countries also means that most people can simply no longer afford as much jewelry as they used to. Elsewhere, on the other hand, people have suddenly amassed so much wealth that they are only interested in gold.

Even so, valuable traditional jewelry is still available. Whether amongst the Berbers in the south of Morocco or the Tuareg in Algeria, the Tunisian, Egyptian and Syrian Bedouin or in the courtyard workshops in the large urban souqs, everywhere there are a few master craftsmen, mostly elderly, who know the old techniques of engraving and embossing, chasing, casting and enamelling. Even in the Suq el-Sagha, the gold market in Cairo, high-quality individual pieces representing many hours of work by an expert can be found amongst the hundreds of mass-produced cartouches, Coptic crosses and Koranic verses engraved on medallions. Where there is a shortage of gold or silver, people improvise with brass or aluminium, inlaid with coloured glass or plastic instead of precious stones or the popular amber.

Often jewelry has retained its traditional function. Apart from its aesthetic effect (the primary purpose is obviously to please the opposite sex) it symbolizes a family's wealth (and sometimes their ethnic origins). It also reflects the wearer's social status. A striking example is the *jambiya*, the Yemeni curved dagger, still an indispensable mark of manliness and adulthood (even now, rhinos are being killed to make the finely carved horn handle). But, above all, jewelry is a form of financial security.

To protect married women's possessions against men, Islamic law provides for the separation of property. Nowadays a previously agreed sum of money is deposited when a couple marries. If they should divorce or the husband dies, this *mahriya* safeguards the wife's standard of living. In traditional societies, the dowry is still in the form of valuables. In Yemen, for example, there was an unwritten law up to a generation ago that a young man wishing to get married had to pay the bride price to his father-in-law in silver, half before the wedding and half if the couple divorced. Sometimes in rural areas the wife still acts as a 'walking bank' for the family and the better the harvest the more jewelry she wears. That is why the Bedouin in particular weigh bracelets and anklets and in many markets jewelry is still sold by weight rather than for its aesthetic quality.

In the Middle East jewelry is still believed to have a highly important protective function. Many Muslims wear talismans for luck and amulets to ward off danger. The main aim is always to guard against the evil eye (Arabic: *nazar*; Turkish: *göz boncugu*) and the *jinns*, invisible spirits which can cause serious harm, especially to children, pregnant women and brides. The objects come in a variety of different forms, for example keys (symbolizing virility or the life force), palms (affluence), coins (wealth and good luck on journeys) or animal signs such as snakes, doves and fish.

The material is also significant. Silver, the metal of the moon, is seen as particularly beneficial, copper as healing. Shells and corals encourage fertility. In many regions people wear dried and pressed fragrant herbs around their necks for their soothing effect. If the number of people wearing them is any indication of their effectiveness, flat blue beads with a white or yellow 'iris' seem to be especially protective. *Hijabs* – cylindrical or square receptacles containing pieces of paper with Koranic verses or blessings by a revered sheikh – are also common, either stitched to clothing or worked into belts or chains.

The five-fingered hand is the ultimate protective symbol. The Muslims call it the hand of Fatima, after the Prophet's favourite daughter, or *khamsa* (Arabic for the magic number five). Its *baraka*, healing energy, is regarded as so essential that it is hung in nearly every house and bazaar shop and often painted on the walls with henna. Even lorry drivers in the East, certainly not the most spiritual of people, trust their luck on the hazardous local roads to the hand, attaching it to the bonnets of their trucks as a talisman.

Above: the unofficial currency of Arabia is still the Maria Theresa thaler. Why these 28-gram (one-ounce) silver coins with a portrait of a foreign woman showing a great deal of hair and cleavage have found favour with Muslims will remain for ever a mystery. More than 250 million coins were struck in Vienna alone and another 50 million or so were minted in London and Paris after the Second World War. Below: a woman with fresh harqus *painting offering 'antique' bracelets for sale.*

بسم الله الرحمن الرحيم
سورة الفتح

Fragrances from the Thousand and One Nights

The love of sweet-smelling substances is as old as civilization in the Middle East. Even in Assyria, Babylonia and the Egypt of the Pharaohs, incense and anointing oils were part of every sacrificial ritual. In ancient times resins were brought to Greece and Rome in great quantities along the Incense Road. But their possession always symbolized the power to commune with the gods and was therefore reserved for the ruling families and high priests. It was only through Islam that perfumes became democratized.

According to tradition, Mohammed said that he loved women, children and sweet smells. On another occasion he said, 'Perfume is the food that refreshes my mind.' His followers were encouraged to collect and process anything sweet-smelling that grew in the desert. The aromatic roots and herbs (some of them hallucinogenic) not only delighted the faithful but also protected them against insects and diseases in the hot climate.

By the time the Crusaders eventually introduced the lore and use of perfumes into Central Europe, they had long been an established part of everyday life. The pleasure-loving Arabs had done a great deal to improve distillation methods. Instead of perishable oils or bundles of dried plants, barks and wood, they now only had to carry tiny phials. They also researched the therapeutic effects of perfumes on mind, soul and body. Sometimes the Sufis, the Islamic mystics, were almost addicted to subtle scents, which helped them purify their thoughts and made them more alert. Sweet-smelling essences were sometimes even mixed with the mortar used for building mosques.

Even with the ancestor smiling down so innocently from the wall, a perfume market is always a place of subtle eroticism. Every perfumer knows dozens of recipes containing such stimulants as amber, musk and civet, essence of roses, violets or camomile, which can rejuvenate old men and make women passionate. Some people, the Atlas Berbers for example, are so fond of perfumes that they wear flowers as 'organic jewelry', in decorative capsules or pressed and dried around their necks. Opposite: detail from a shop in the Souk el-Attarine in Tunis. Below: a bunch of roses in the bazaar in Bukhara.

The example of neroli oil, highly prized as a miracle remedy, shows how important perfume still is to many Muslims. In accordance with an age-old tradition, thousands of families in the Maghreb and Egypt distil it from the hand-picked flowers of the bitter-orange tree every year. Newborn babies are given milk mixed with it to drink and are washed with neroli water. Brides wear a wreath of neroli flowers at their weddings to allay their fears on their wedding night. The sick are given it as a medicine and the dying as 'food for the journey to Paradise'.

The vocabulary used by the cosmetic manufacturers to describe their 'Oriental' perfumes – scented with ambergris, honeyed, spicily sensual, full of impact and symbolism – leaves very little doubt as to the images they are trying to evoke: odalisques reclining in opulent rooms in the harem, perfuming their bodies to make them irresistible to men. The myth of oriental sensuality is conjured up and enhanced by fanciful product names like Cleopatra, Roxane and Scheherazade. When words are not evocative enough, the maker of the perfume adds an extra dash of civet (a secretion from the civet cat which is bred only in Ethiopia), ambergris (a mysterious substance from the intestines of the sperm whale), musk (a rutting secretion from a type of Himalayan deer) and castor (a sexual secretion from beavers). These smell terrible in their pure state, but, used in minute quantities, they give the perfume its characteristic 'sinful' quality and have the desired aphrodisiac effect (on either sex).

Even where there are still plenty of perfume shops – in Tunis, Damascus or Cairo, for instance – there is no hint

of this sinfulness nowadays. Few of the shopkeepers have the knowledge that was once an integral part of their trade. Few can still convey the subtle distinctions between top note, middle note and basic note. Few have any idea of the complex manufacturing process – the distillation, maceration or enfleurage (extraction of perfumes by means of steam, cold or hot animal fat), let alone the synthetic processes with all the benzols, phenols, terpenes and their hundreds of derivatives.

But these expert psychologists make up for their lack of knowledge with a surfeit of charm and rhetorical skill. Rubbing essences into the backs of their customers' hands and their forearms, they reveal their 'secrets'. They bring out a flask of 'genuine' ambergris or musk. They explain that they sometimes make amber into a paste to mix it into cigarettes or tea and ask if the customer would like to buy some of this forbidden, and therefore costly, aphrodisiac (of course, the customer is enjoined to secrecy). They boast of the purity of their rose oil ('from Bulgaria'), saffron ('from eastern Iran') and incense ('from the provinces of Dhofar and Hadhramaut in southern Arabia'). Some Cairo shopkeepers claim to own a flower farm in the Nile Delta or the Fayum oasis which supplies extracts to the European cosmetic groups.

For the amateur in particular, it is difficult to distinguish between fact and fiction in all this. Are a handful of flower growers really keeping the ancient tradition of perfume-making alive in Egypt? Does the Middle East really have hundreds of recipes unknown in the West – including cures for impotence? It is a fact that musk and ambergris have been banned for many years to protect the animals, and so are virtually priceless. In Asia and America, the trees from which the sweet-smelling but relatively cheap resin is obtained for the perfume industry are known as ambergris trees. Roses have mostly been replaced by synthetically produced rose oxide since the Bulgarians drastically reduced their rose-growing. And who can tell whether incense might not by a blend of different cheap resins or that saffron is, in fact, safflower?

Despite these misgivings, buying perfume can still be a pleasure. Some of the tricks are easy to spot (for instance, if an extract which is alleged to be pure leaves dye and oily stains when it evaporates, it has obviously been diluted with glycerine, turpentine or even olive oil). But origin and quality should not in any case be taken too seriously. It is, after all, no secret that most people in the bazaars (it is the exceptions that prove the rule) import their ingredients ready-made from Europe or mix them themselves with synthetic ingredients. The old theory that, if something was natural, it was automatically better than something synthetic no longer applies. Many artificial substances have the very same chemical composition and scent as the original; in fact some smell even more 'typical'. Others cannot be produced naturally at all at the moment.

If most buyers find their souvenir perfume a little overpowering later on in different surroundings, this might be because European suppliers do not give away all their secrets even to their best customers; but it might also be because the local clientele have different tastes.

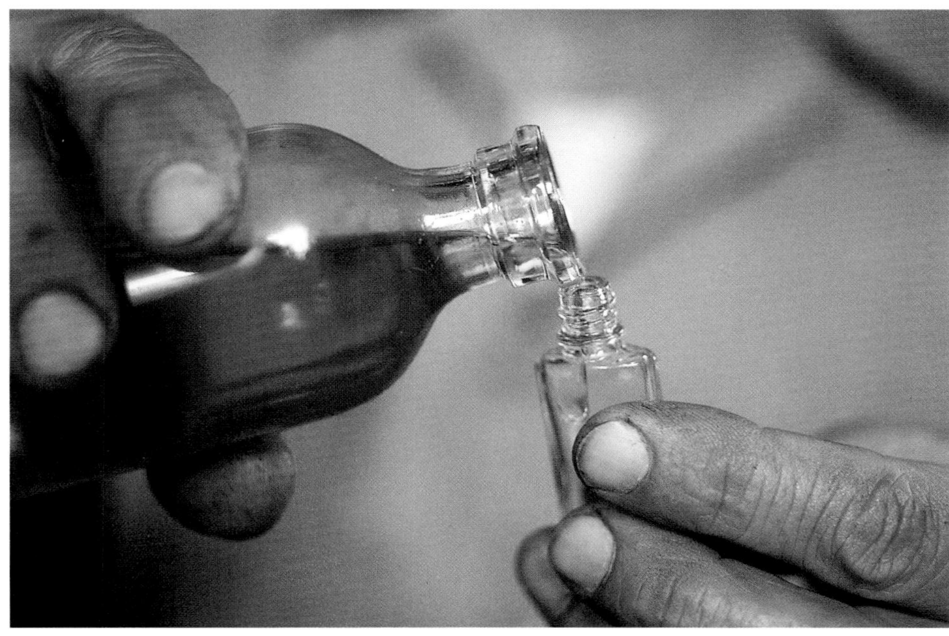

Some of the 'villains' of the perfume trade find astonishingly complicated and ingenious ways of maximizing their profits. A few years ago, for instance, people were selling what they claimed were bags of musk, but which were actually bags of clotted blood, scrap metal, coffee, earth and leaves, with forged seals. Most dealers, however, frown on such practices – and not only because they now obtain synthetic compounds from Europe or mix their elixirs themselves from artificial ingredients. Most are so honest that they sell their perfumes in opaque brown glass flacons instead of transparent ones, so that they keep longer.

Life's little pleasures

According to legend, in the early 16th century the sheikh of Mocha on the Red Sea, Ali ibn-Omar al-Shadili, offered traders from Portugal who put in at the port a strange black brew. He said he had made it from beans that had been roasted, ground and boiled up in water and he drank it every day. The foreigners liked the aroma and powerful effects of the *qahwa* and took several sacks with them on the ship straight away.

Historians are not convinced that coffee actually came to Europe via Lisbon. They believe that dervishes in southern Arabia first discovered its stimulant effects when it was imported from the Ethiopian province of Kaffa and used it to prolong their trances during their religious rituals. It is also said that at first orthodox theologians were vehemently opposed to it, believing it to be spiritually harmful. For a long time anyone found drinking coffee was severely punished or even put to death. This did not make it any less popular. It was not until the second half of the 17th century that the sultan admitted defeat and finally declared it legal. At the time, coffee was also popular in Europe and America and coffee houses were opening up everywhere. Most of the coffee came from the highlands in the north of Yemen and was exported mainly from Mocha, so there was at least an element of truth in the Sheikh al-Shadili story.

Coffee from southern Arabia has long since been superseded on the world market by other varieties. Nowadays it is imported from South America and the West Indies. *Coffea arabica* is only prized as a flavouring for chocolate and a rare luxury. But the social institution which it created still survives in the Islamic world.

Making coffee (or tea) is an essential daily ritual for every Arab. A Moroccan poet once said that it is a reflection of the universe. 'The sinai, the round tray, is the earth, the coffee pot the sky and the glasses the rain. The sky and the earth come together through the rain.' Opposite: a typical café in Damascus.

Whether it is a simple bench with three rickety chairs on the pavement or an elegant saloon, for men in the Middle East the coffee house is the centre of daily life, even since the advent of the telephone, radio and television. No one seems to mind if the seating is not very comfortable and the lighting comes from flickering neon tubes.

What is important is that it is a place to meet friends, exchange news, think up jokes and play backgammon, cards or dominoes. Even if you prefer not to take part in these daily rituals, that is no reason to stay away. You can just sit in the corner holding your beads (Arabic: *misbaha*; Turkish: *tespih*) and meditate on God and the world. Water pipes, which can be rented for a small sum, bubble away in the background. The only interruption comes from a shoeshine boy or beggar or – more rarely – a *hakawati*, a story teller.

Tobacco first came to the Middle East from America in about 1600 and became an essential part of any visit to the coffee house. Like coffee (and also hashish), it was initially used mainly by mystics and frowned on by the orthodox as being ritually impure. Like coffee, its consumption was for a time banned on pain of death, but this was eventually revoked after long argument. It was grown mainly in Macedonia, northern Greece and Anatolia under a state monopoly and smoked in long clay pipes.

The well-known water pipe (*narghile* or *shisha*, as it is called in Turkey and North

A real oriental coffee house (above: a street café in Damascus) offers a variety of sticky sweetmeats. Nearly every city has its own speciality: Damascus its sugared almonds, Kairouan its filled pastries and Mashhad (previous page, below) its nabat*, golden rock candy. Opposite top: a shop in the bazaar in Kashan.*

Africa respectively) was not introduced until the 18th century. The elaborate glass bowls came from Bohemia. The mouthpieces and the meerschaum 'curls' on which the balls of tobacco and glowing charcoal were placed were from the region of Eskisehir in western Anatolia. However, the long tubes and the artistically wrought brass tops were made in the local bazaar.

Sugar, too, is a relatively recent arrival in the Orient. It was already known to the great Arab doctors of the Middle Ages as a remedy and tonic and was imported from India and Khuzestan in south-western Iran in small quantities. But as a sweetener it was for a long time known only to a few rich people. It was not until sugar-cane began to be grown on huge plantations in

the New World that it was 'democratized'. Nowadays, walking through a sugar bazaar like the one in Isfahan with its white cubes and loaf sugar, its honeycombs and rock-candy crystals piled so high that they can give you tooth decay just looking at them, you wonder how this society ever survived without it. On the other hand, the Bedouin still manage very well without, at least in coffee. They add ground cardamoms to make the drink less bitter and insist that this is the only way it will help digest fatty foods, which for them is the real reason for consuming it. The custom of ordering a *qahwa siadeh* (with plenty of sugar), *masbut* (medium) or *arriha* (a little) or even, as is common in Iran, putting a cube on the tongue and washing it down only became popular in the 19th century, when tea was starting to rival coffee as the favourite drink in the East.

Nearly every city can boast its own (usually sticky) speciality. Istanbul has its *lokum* (Turkish delight), a glutinous mass made of cornstarch, sugar, water and nuts sprinkled with coconut; Damascus its *mlebbas*, sugared almonds; and Kairouan its *maqroudh*, pastry envelopes filled with dates. From Mashhad comes *nabat*, a yellow sugar with particularly large crystals, and from Isfahan *gaz*, a rare and expensive manna from a particular species of tamarisk. There are hundreds of other varieties as well: sweets, candied fruits, cakes dripping with oil. Even the holy city of Qom, spiritual home of the Ayatollah Khomeini, has its own sinfully sweet speciality – *sohun*, sprinkled with pistachios and made from oil, sugar, flour and a special kind of root.

But it is in classic Syrian-Palestinian cuisine that the greatest variety is to be found. *Baklava*, *karabij*, *ghoraybiyeh*, *muhallabiyeh* – there are countless recipes

Arabs were not always able to smoke their pipes in the relaxed manner of the camel dealer at Imbaba market in Cairo (above). When tobacco came to the Orient around 1600, orthodox scholars declared its use ritually impure. Anyone smoking it was severely punished – even put to death in the time of Sultan Murad IV (1623–1640). Above centre: tobacco sellers in the souq in Sanaa.

for these little pastries, desserts, biscuits and confectionery, flavoured with orange-flower water and rosewater and usually drenched in syrup. *Kunafeh,* made from a very thin multi-layered puff pastry fried in hot oil, filled with nuts and sprinkled with threads of pastry, is a particularly delicious example. The most famous is *kunafeh nabulsiyeh* from Nablus, filled with soft sweetish sheep's-milk cheese.

Even at normal times the Arabs love their delicacies, but in the fasting month of Ramadan it becomes a passion. As soon as a gun has been fired or the *muezzin* has given the official signal that the sun has gone down and people can eat again, the gas is turned on in thousands of kitchens. The evening meal begins modestly: to break their stomachs in gently, people eat a couple of raw dates or drink a sweet tea made of dried *mishmish,* apricots. But the obligatory visit to the mosque is followed by a convivial feast lasting for several hours. The most popular dish during Ramadan, particularly in the Middle East and the Gulf States, is *kataef,* a thick flour or semolina pancake filled with cheese, walnuts or *kishtah,* rich cream.

But the undoubted high point is the feast that marks the end of Ramadan, *id al-fitr* (Turkish: *seker bayrami*). Children are bought new clothes and given extra pocket money which they can spend as they want without any criticism from their parents. Most spend it on chocolates and sweets and *helu,* a kind of meringue in the shape of a small doll specially made for the occasion. The overdose of sugar is seen as fair reward for fasting with the grown-ups for a month without complaining.

Men while away many hours in the coffee and tea houses – opposite: a splendid example in what used to be the Hammam-e-Vakil in Kerman. The musicians, dancers and story tellers have all but disappeared, but card and dice games and water pipes are still available everywhere. Other popular entertainments, apart from the cafés, are belly dancing (bottom left) and, for Iranian men, physical training (top left: Kamal Zour Khaneh, a physical training centre in Isfahan). However, karagöz, *the shadow theatre which was once so popular, has long since died out. The best-preserved example can now be seen in the Kasr al-Azem (Azem Palace) museum in Damascus (centre left).*

يوجد
عسل غذاء ملكة النحل
غذاء - شفاء - قوة

Healing through faith

Opposite the entrance to the Azem Palace at the beginning of al-Bzouriyeh, the confectionery market in Damascus south of the Omayyad mosque, is a tiny shop. At first, it looks like something out of an old horror film. Lizard and snake skins, tortoise shells, dried hedgehogs and globefish, rabbit, fox and cat skins, roots, giant fungi and hundreds of other mysterious objects hang from the ceiling. On shelves on the wall are rows of glass containers and the counter is full of bags and boxes filled with strange substances.

In the olden days, fostering, maintaining or restoring reproductive capability was seen as the supreme public-health objective in all eastern cultures. That must be why so many traditional remedies are designed to arouse the libido. Opposite and below: Dr Aidi's shop in the bazaar in Damascus.

The shop's owner, Dr Mounif Osmane Aidi, is young, serious and busy. If the queue of customers lets up for a moment, which it seldom does, he is willing to reveal a few of his secrets. He opens the tin of powder made of ground-up salamanders,

which increases potency, and the tin of ox tongues, which reduce inflammation. He explains that hedgehog stops hair loss, Indian cucumbers prevent stomach-ache and benzoin and small crabs relieve all kinds of pain. Turtle shells should be put on children's chests to keep nightmares away.

In these days of government licences, medicines carrying strict directions for use and polyclinics, bazaar dispensaries like Dr Aidi's have become rare. Dentists' signs with a huge hand-painted set of teeth which even the illiterate can understand are much more common in the old parts of town. Often the dentist is just a *hadjam*, a barber, who traditionally also pulls out teeth. Some barbers have a curious way of attracting custom. They pile up all the teeth they have extracted in their shop window. The bigger the pile, the higher will be their reputation.

Sometimes these 'surgeries' have cupping glasses, cauterizing irons, needles and surgical scissors alongside the shaving brushes, knives, teeth and forceps. Traditionally, the *hadjam* also does blood-letting, tattooing, cauterizing and circumcision. This last is still common. Every *mulid* (saint's day), small boys or even teenagers, dressed in festive costume, undergo the painful operation. In Arabia and Egypt, girls are sometimes circumcised too.

Circumcision is not in fact specifically prescribed by the Koran; it is simply an old-established custom. But even now it is seen as a symbol of acceptance into the Muslim community and is not open to question. In most other respects medicine has developed along secular and scientific lines.

The 'medicine of the Prophet' handed down in the Hadith was based on the simple practices of the pre-Islamic Bedouin. But in the time of the Abbasid caliphs hundreds of ancient Greek medical texts were translated into Arabic. Many standard works were introduced into Muslim, and subsequently Christian-European, thought in this way.

In traditional medicine, the right word is often used as a remedy; for instance, a verse from the Koran may be recited over a sick person. A sura *written on a piece of paper and rolled up in an amulet protects against the evil eye. Below: a healer in the streets of Mashhad. Above: a* hadjam *in Ibb, Yemen, shaving a customer – only one of the numerous services he offers.*

Care of the sick was extremely advanced. Cairo and Baghdad already had hospitals in the 9th century. One famous example was the Bimaristan Nur ad-Din in Damascus, now the Museum of Arab Medicine and Science. As well as providing free treatment and medicines, it also kept records of the patients' names, diets and medicines – and this was in the middle of the 12th century! Ibn-Jubair reported that, when it was discovered that music speeded up recovery, singers and story tellers were brought in. Patients were given foot massages, perfume rations, free clothing and five gold coins when they were discharged, so that they did not have to worry about money while they were convalescing.

Many hospitals were also teaching hospitals. The teaching was much more wide-ranging than it is nowadays, embracing botany, pharmacy, chemistry, astronomy, theology, law and philosophy as well as medicine. Graduates were awarded the title *al-hakim*, which means wise, philosopher and doctor. Even famous doctors like ibn-Rushd (Averroes), his Jewish pupil Maimonides and ar-Razi were polymaths, renowned as natural scientists, alchemists and philosophers as well as doctors. Abu-Ali ibn-Sina (Avicenna) even went into politics and became vizier.

The range of goods includes miswak *(fibrous stalks for tooth cleaning), wooden containers for* kohl, *ground malachite eye make-up and even dried chameleons, which are crushed to powder as a treatment for warts (and, of course, as an aphrodisiac). Below: Spanish fly.*

Obviously some doctors specialized in particular branches of medicine, but the most noteworthy achievements of the Islamic doctors were in medicinal lore. A shop like Khedr el-Attar's in the spice bazaar in old Cairo, for instance, gives an idea of the huge range of medicines – most of them herbal – that are still used: myrobalan for high blood pressure, betel for jaundice, cardamom for circulatory problems, camphor, turpeth and tamarind ... there is a herb for every disease. Khedr says that nigella, black cumin, is currently being tested as a cure for AIDS in American laboratories.

The Nuredin hospital (Bimaristan Nur ad-Din) in Damascus was a centre for Islamic medicine. Even in the 12th century, surgery, orthopaedics, fevers and mental illness were regarded as separate branches of medicine. Nowadays the building where abu-Ali ibn-Sina (Avicenna) once worked (below: a memorial bust) is the museum of science and medicine. The holistic approach of Islamic medicine is reflected in the language: attar *still means both a perfumer and a person who sells herbs and medicines. Opposite: Khedr el-Attar, the famous dispensary in the bazaar district of Ghouriya in Cairo. Above: scene at the spice market in Taizz (Yemen).*

The practices of the alchemists, who tried for hundreds of years to turn base metals into gold or silver, have long since disappeared from these traditional dispensaries. *Theriak*, the legendary universal elixir, is no longer available, nor is *benj*, a once popular antidote made of black and white poppy seed, hemp and an extract of henbane. Not even hashish and opium are available any more – at least, not officially. However, small magical objects and pieces of paper with mysterious symbols and figures can still be found amongst the pots and jars. These are talismans which protect their wearers against invisible evil forces and apparently they are still very popular.

At sites like the famous Djamaa el-Fna in Marrakesh, respected healers practise alongside the travelling quacks and charlatans. In Morocco they are known as *fkih*. A *fkih* says the prayers at funerals, teaches children about the life of the saints at the Koranic schools and, above all, keeps the traditional medicine alive. Now modern science is rediscovering its secrets.

During his long training, a *fkih* has to work with occult forces. He has his own personal spirit, who helps him choose the right Koranic verses and numerical symbols to exorcise a person who is possessed. Unlike many more modern doctors, he still has plenty of time to listen and advise. A *fkih* knows about the meaning of dreams and sympathetic magic, the relationship between the movements of the stars and the incidence of diseases, how to cure animals by magic before they are sacrificed and how to use owls' blood and hyena brains for healing. He knows the right incantations and aphrodisiacs for people who have been unable to have children. The most gifted *fkihs* still emit healing energy after their deaths and thousands of people seeking help go on pilgrimages to their *marabouts* or graves.

العطار
Khedr

Letters and pictures

La ilah illa allah; Muhammad rasul allah; 'There is no God but God and Mohammed is his Prophet.' This profession of faith is whispered into the ears of Muslim children as soon as they are born. They are the first words everyone learns to say and the last they will utter when they die.

The beauty, rhythm and guttural sound of the Arabic language developed among the heathen Bedouin as they passed the long desert nights around the campfire and when poets met together in the towns. However, it was not until the Koran was revealed and disseminated that the language was perfected and acquired its universal significance. Orthodox Muslims believe that the holy book had existed in heaven since time immemorial and the Prophet's messengers took it all over the world as an invisible bond uniting the Muslim community.

Of the four processes involved in the making of a book – calligraphy, illustration, illumination and binding – calligraphy has always been the most highly regarded. Even princes saw fine handwriting as a way of enhancing their reputations. The name of the sultan is still sometimes covered with fine gold leaf.

The Koran has been the key element of Islamic religion, culture and politics since the 7th century. It reintroduced an archaic idea which was to prove crucial in the development of Islamic art. It is based on the belief that all pictures, even figurative decorations, are essentially already in existence and waiting to be brought to life. But since only Allah can bestow life, it is an inadmissible presumption for man to try and imitate natural phenomena. Moreover, the formal recording of a work of creation destroys the immediacy of the divine act and detracts from its deeper, real nature. Even today many people in the East are reluctant to have their photos taken.

In the Koran the prohibition of images is only explained in very vague terms. But according to the Hadith, the collected sayings and deeds of the Prophet, 'no angel ever enters a house in which there is a picture or a dog'. People who make pictures are warned that, at the Last Judgment, they

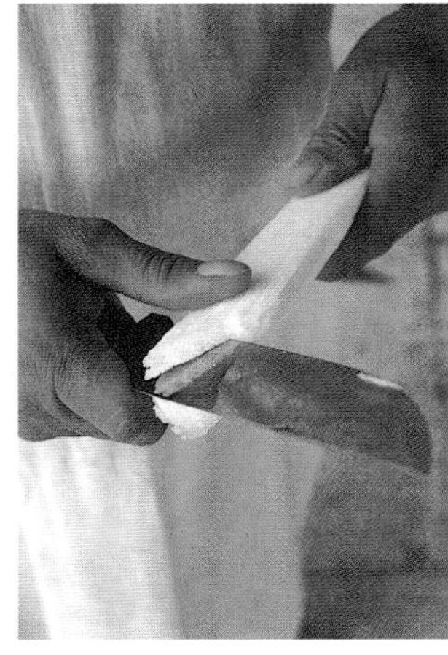

Thousands of years ago, parts of the Nile delta were overgrown with papyrus, but in Egypt it had long since been eradicated until Dr Hassan Ragab began cultivating it again at his institute in Cairo in the mid-sixties. Now papyrus painted with pharaonic motifs and hieroglyphs can be bought in the tourist bazaars.

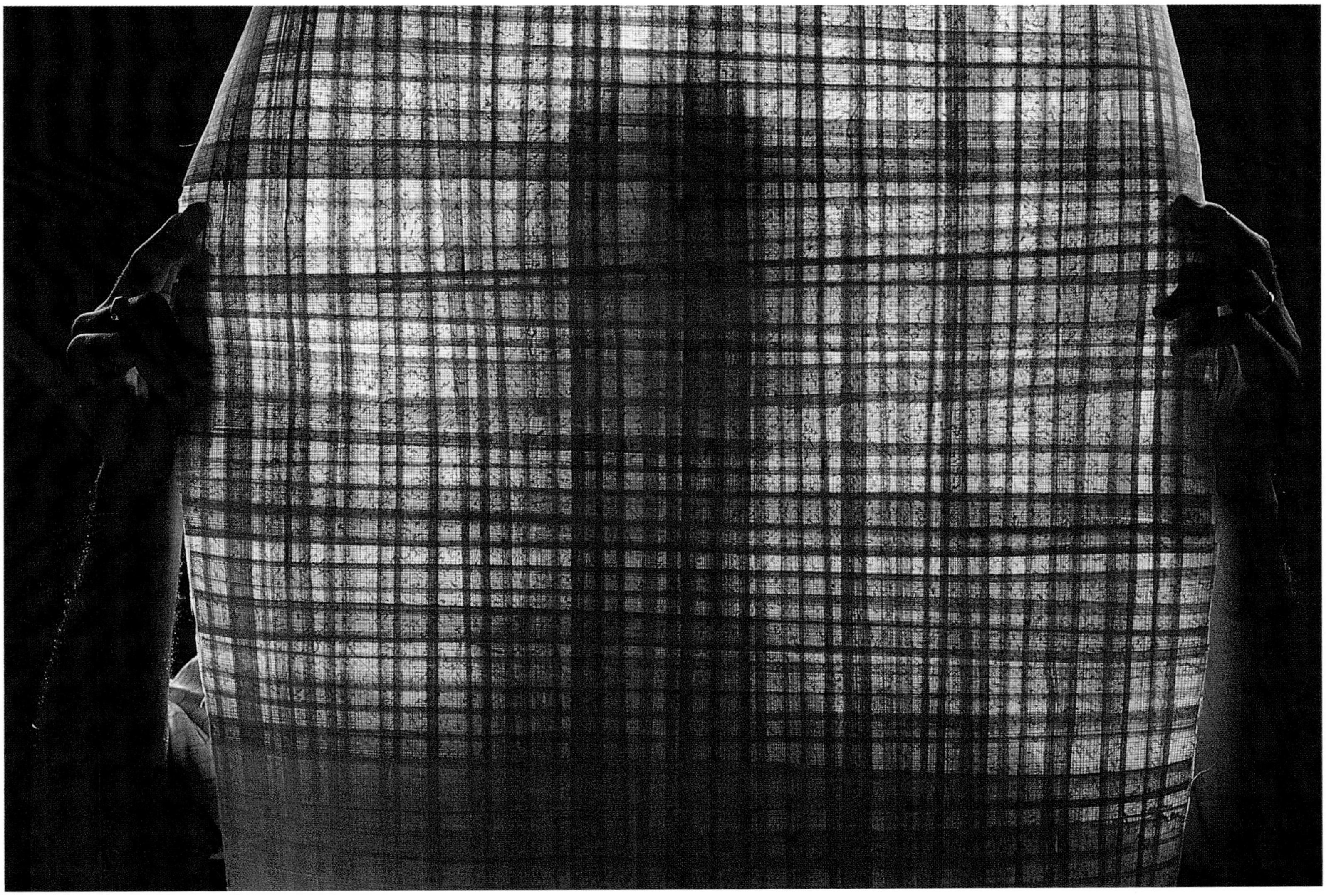

will be forced to try in vain for eternity to breathe life into their creations. According to the canonical laws of the four major law schools, tattooing, usury and the pictorial arts are all considered equally reprehensible.

These beliefs were based on well-founded social and political considerations. At the beginning, Islam had to establish a foothold in a society in which painting and sculpture were often religious symbols and many of the beings depicted were prayed to as idols (one of Mohammed's first acts after conquering Mecca was to remove the statues of the local guardian deities). Islam therefore had to make a clear distinction between the belief in the One God and polytheism and at the same time show a willingness to compromise. Its interpreters would not allow the portrayal of 'viable' beings, but allowed those with their heads removed, their necks severed or their bodies pierced – like the figures in the popular shadow theatre. The argument was that these were no longer 'theoretically viable'.

The prohibition was not, in fact, strictly observed. The Omayyads decorated the walls of their desert fortresses with elaborate frescoes. Fatimid viziers in Egypt became patrons of artists. Later on, Ottoman sultans even employed portrait painters from the West. Scientists, especially anatomists and technicians, were soon illustrating their theories with pictures. The iconography developed in the 13th century in the eastern provinces of Iran illustrated themes from the Prophet's life and the sufferings of the martyrs Ali and Hussein, although Mohammed's face was always covered by a white disc or a veil.

Also in Iran, a new artistic genre, miniature painting, was introduced by the invading Mongols. At first this was seen in Arab countries as being extremely offensive. It depicted landscapes, animals and human beings, initially in the soft pastel shades of the Far East, but later in strong, bright colours. The favourite themes were scenes from the great national epics and illustrations to verses by the love poets Hafiz, Saadi or Omar Khayyam. The artists were not concerned with shade or depth or central perspective. Their figures had no individual personality; they were clone-like, all of them radiating the same supernatural serenity. Even so, the realism of masterpieces such as those from the art schools in Tabriz, Shiraz and Herat was unrivalled in Islamic art until the 16th and 17th centuries, when Ottoman artists were commissioned by the sultans to paint their portraits and to illustrate their military campaigns and life in the seraglio.

But, despite its refinement, miniature painting always took second place to another art form, calligraphy. After the Koran was revealed, the Arabs looked for a way of writing it down which did justice to its beauty. Between the 7th and 8th centuries, they created their own characteristic style for the 28 consonants and 3 vowels, their abbreviations and the special symbols of their script. Called *kufi*, it was similar to the old ornamental script of the Nabataeans. At first it was archaic, angular and stiff, but it soon became more decorative. At the beginning of the 9th century, paper began to replace papyrus; writing was revolutionized and *naskhi* script was developed. This was a relatively flexible cursive script which, being easier to learn and write, appealed equally to the millions of converts and to the hundreds of scribes at the Abassid courts who had to transcribe the old works from the conquered regions into Arabic. The new script imposed strict rules on the calligraphers, defining the proportions of the up and down strokes and the body of the character and the relationship between height and width. *Naskhi* became widespread. It formed the basis for printer's type and for modern written Arabic.

But this was not enough to satisfy the creativity of the calligraphers. Since some letters could not be joined, they made a virtue out of necessity and put whole sections of text in the spaces between letters of different heights, embellished with loops and knots and entwined with floral patterns. Thereafter various ornamental scripts were developed, such as *thuluth*, used mainly in architectural decoration, the Persian-Indian forms *nastaliq* and *shikaste*, all kinds of Maghrebi-Andalusian styles and the *diwani*, the Ottoman court chancery script often found on old documents in which the name of the sultan, the *tughra*, was intertwined. In the most ornate style, the letters were artistically arranged to form human, animal and plant shapes or complicated geometrical patterns – a neat way of circumventing the ban on images.

The Koran contains 114 *suras*. It takes a proficient scribe about twelve months to

With illiteracy rates of up to 50 per cent, public scribes are still a necessity in many Islamic countries. They sit offering their services outside courts or police stations with their pen and paper or typewriter (opposite above: in the bazaar in Hajjah, Yemen). They have preserved the old traditions of miniature painting (above: a battle scene painted in the bazaar in Isfahan) and ebru, *paper marbling (opposite below: a master craftsman at work in Istanbul). The brocade embroiderers have developed a special process for transferring the pattern to the fabric (below). They perforate a piece of silk paper and sprinkle powdered chalk through the holes on to the dark fabric underneath.*

copy, although ibn-al-Bawwab, head of the calligraphy school in Baghdad, is said to have made 500 copies in his lifetime. At that time (the 11th century), a craftsman known as a *warraq* copied books and also made and ornamented their covers and decorated the inside of the book with illuminations and calligraphic borders. The workshop often had a bookshop attached to it.

Whole armies of copyists were employed in libraries, known at the time as 'houses of learning'. Their enormous stocks of books were nearly all lost in the late Middle Ages. The legendary collection in Tripoli, with its three million volumes, was sacked by the Crusaders, the one in Baghdad by the Mongols. The treasures of the Fatimid library in Cairo, said to have filled forty rooms of the palace, were piled up by zealots and burned (a strategy later to be imitated in Europe).

Now, at the end of the 20th century, writing is a neglected art. Schools require no more than an approximation of typewritten letters. Simple new scripts are even being invented to speed up illiteracy campaigns. But the elitist art of calligraphy is still popular. Its students still have hours of breathing lessons (to enable them to hold the pen steady), have to practise the correct posture when sitting cross-legged (to perfect the countermovements of the supporting and the writing hand) and exercise their mental powers daily.

Arabic, the holy script of the Koran, is used on every conceivable material for the greater glory of God (opposite). The Assil brothers, sura *embroiderers in the Khan el-Khalili in Cairo (opposite bottom), inherited a special legacy. Their ancestors embroidered the* kiswa, *the brocade cloth covering the Kaaba in Mecca, with verses from the Koran. The* warraq, *a person who creates documents and copies, binds and sells books, has long since become obsolete. Now the Koran sellers' goods come from printers (above: a street in Abu Dhabi). They also sell prayer beads.*

Pens have changed very little over the years. The calligrapher still dips a reed pen trimmed at the end (Arabic: *kalam*; Turkish: *divit*) into the traditional ink-well. The ink and writing medium, however, have changed. The mixture of soot from oil lamps and other substances has mostly been replaced by synthetic ingredients (although children in the Koranic schools in the Maghreb still write with *suif*, black wool fat from sheep). At a very early stage, paper replaced camel bones, scraps of leather, palm bark, papyrus and parchment. Paper was invented by the Chinese and its first appearance in the Islamic world was in Samarkand. Harun ar-Rashid set up the first large paper mill in Baghdad in 795. The first paper book was produced in 870. Calligraphers soon began to improve the paper, colouring it with lime blossom, tea, saffron, straw, tobacco or onion skins, and smoothing it by rubbing raw egg on it with marble or ivory polishing discs. The Islamic countries had a paper monopoly until the 14th century, when it was broken by the Europeans.

Where printing was concerned, the East was not so advanced. The mechanical reproduction of texts was for a long time forbidden because the rulers feared blasphemy and religious conflicts, and it was also out of the question, for instance, for a printing plate reproducing the name of Allah to be contaminated with a cleaning brush made of pig's bristles. The Hungarian Ibrahim Müteferrika had to fight for many years before the sultan finally allowed him to operate the first press in the Islamic world in Istanbul in 1727. In Egypt it was the reformer Mehemet Ali who set up the first printing works in 1833. The first official printed version of the Koran did not appear until 1925, nearly 400 years after it had been published in Arabic in Venice.

Turners and carvers

Little boys and men can still be seen crouched on low stools in dark corners turning pieces of wood day after day, although nowadays it is a rare sight. Their simple wooden lathes, *makhrata baladi*, are relics of the Middle Ages. These are worked with their hands and feet, a knife, a wooden bar and a piece of string. The wood is wedged in the vice, the string wrapped round it and pulled tight on the bar. The resulting arc is moved backwards and forwards with the right hand. They hold the knife on the rotating wood with the left hand and guide it with their toes.

Of course, this work is now done by machine in many places. But some hand turners have managed to survive, protected by the internal economy of the bazaar with its minimal transport and material costs and rents. *Ustas*, old master craftsmen, still

A carver proudly exhibits his shebeke *– a kind of jigsaw puzzle made of hundreds of artistically patterned pieces of wood – at a private carpenter's shop on the outskirts of Samarkand. It took him about two years to make and will be used as a door panel. Opposite: a flat roof resting on tall slender pillars, a common feature in Uzbek mosques.*

Wood has a multitude of uses. Above: a lute maker in Damascus. Below: two fine examples of mashrabiya *work in Cairo (inside and outside). Opposite: a specialist turner's in the bazaar in Isfahan. It is here that they make the* mils*, the elmwood clubs weighing up to 40 kilos (88 pounds) swung by Iranian men in the* zour khaneh.

conscientiously initiate new apprentices into their secrets. It is as if the community feels it owes a debt to this great tradition. After all, the *minbar* (pulpit) from which the Prophet spoke to the faithful in his house in Medina, the very first work of art created in the name of Islam, was made of turned wood.

It is often said that the shortage of wood in most Islamic countries hampered the development of carving and architecture, but that is not generally true. Certainly in some desert regions, the Arabian Peninsula in particular, wood was for a long time reserved for the rich. It was used mainly as a costly decoration for relatively small areas, such as panelling for recesses or frames for mirrors, or at most a wooden door. Especially fine varieties were almost as prized as ivory for carving.

However, many of the regions that are now bare were once wooded. In Fatimid and Ayyubid Egypt (11th and 12th centuries) large areas were actively reafforested. Plenty of wood was available. Even the smaller and poorer mosques, for instance, had pulpits, lecterns and book chests. In secular buildings, too, wood was widely used. Nearly all the big old town houses in Damascus, Tunis, Cairo or Fez have – or at least had – wooden walls and balustrades, coffered ceilings and wall panelling. The fact that there was no wooden furniture was not because of a shortage of the material. People ate, sat and slept on the floor, on cushions, mattresses and carpets. Only the highest dignitaries sat on chairs. Food was served on metal trays and household goods and books were kept in wall niches. Often the only wooden items were the chests in which clothes, bedclothes and possibly jewelry were kept. It was only with Europeanization in the late 18th and early 19th centuries that western furniture such as armchairs, tables, shelves and cupboards came into fashion.

In wooded areas – the Balkans, Anatolia and parts of Persia, the north of Tunisia and Morocco – the situation was quite different. There, wood had always been an integral component of architecture. The traditional Ottoman house was often built entirely of wood. It had outside steps and open balconies, decorated façades and sometimes also half-timbering. The *yalis* – summer residences of the Istanbul elite on the banks of the Bosporus – are a particularly impressive example of the Ottomans' skilful use of wood. Some of these two- or three-hundred-year-old buildings have recently been renovated. In Central Asia, too, characteristic styles were developed. Long and massive trunks were used as pillars to support porches or *iwans*, vaulted door niches. Outstanding examples are the Ali Qapu and Chehel Sotoun Palaces in Isfahan, the Bolo-hauz Mosque in Bukhara and the Friday Mosque in Khiva (Uzbekistan) with its 213 richly carved pillars, some of them over a thousand years old.

The tradition of painted wood also comes from Central Asia, from the Uigurs. It was brought to Cairo in the 9th century via Samarra and spread to the whole of the Middle East and North Africa. Despite the Islamic prohibition on images, it was some time before the Buddhist- and Chinese-influenced naturalistic paintings of animals and human beings were replaced by abstract calligraphic and floral patterns. The best examples of traditional wood painting are in Morocco. In Tétouan, Chechaouèn and Rabat, and particularly in the carpenters' market in Fez, the Souk en-Nejjarine, hand-decorated Atlas-cedar furniture and wall panelling are still made on a large scale.

Cairo has for many centuries been the undisputed centre for woodwork. The

Fatimids, following the highly distinctive tradition of the Copts and influenced also by the Abbasid artists, produced decorated panelling of a rare quality. Its main feature was its elegant leaf decorations, but it also had figures and *kufi* letters, often combined with the finest ivory decoration. By the Mameluke period, the Egyptians had already exported their art all over the Mediterranean and they then developed *rumi*, complicated designs of hexagons, stars and arabesques, based on Seljuk patterns. At the same time, the ancient decorative technique of intarsia was revived.

The ancient Egyptians, like the Babylonians, Phoenicians and Byzantines before them, decorated their religious furniture with multicoloured woods, bone, ivory and mother-of-pearl. The Copts and Fatimids continued this tradition. In the 14th and 15th centuries, enormous quantities of mother-of-pearl were brought

The pillars in the harem courtyard of Tosh-Khovli palace in Khiva are a fine example of wood-carving (below). The fashion for painting wooden architectural features in bright colours originated in Central Asia and was soon taken up in the Middle East. Above: the arcaded vault in the Omayyad Mosque in Damascus.

into the country on the newly-opened trade routes and inlay work became very popular. The fashion soon spread to other countries, Syria and Persia in particular.

Mother-of-pearl has remained popular. Mosaic is used on every imaginable object in the bazaars in Cairo, Damascus, Isfahan and Shiraz. There are two ways of making it and neither has changed very much over the centuries. In the traditional method, the individual pieces are laboriously put on with tweezers according to a pre-drawn pattern and the edges and surfaces smoothed off with sandpaper when the final piece has been inserted. Fine putty mixed with sawdust is applied to fill the tiny cracks, then scraped off and the finished article painted with varnish.

In the second method, which is less complicated, a few thin coloured rods, about 60 to 80 centimetres (24 to 32 inches) long, are stuck together, sawn into wafer-thin disks and the cross-sections glued on. The rest of the process is the same as in the other method.

Mashrabiya was also developed on the Nile in the Mameluke period. This is lattice-work made of turned pieces of wood on pegs which can be inserted into each other in geometrical patterns. These three-dimensional 'jigsaw puzzles' remain popular today as partitions and decorations in mosques, churches and private houses and some are still made by craftsmen using their hands and toes. Until the beginning of the 20th century they were mostly used for the huge bay windows which were once found all over Cairo and can still be seen in many of the older parts. Similar to venetian blinds, they had various functions. They kept out the harsh sunlight and heat and helped the air circulate, and they allowed the inhabitants, especially women, to look out on to the street without being seen themselves. Clay jugs filled with water were placed in small overhangs (the literal translation of *mashrabiya* is drinking place). The liquid seeped out through the porous material and was evaporated by the slight breeze. The wooden 'refrigerator' kept the jug and its contents – and the air in the room – pleasantly cool.

Sawyers, carpenters, turners, carvers of wall decorations or locks: woodwork was already used in a variety of ways even under the Fatimids. Later exponents were the makers of mother-of-pearl inlay and painted wedding chests, still found in many bazaars. Above: in the joiners' souq in Marrakesh. Below: in the Wakalat el-Ghouri in Cairo.

The last glass-blowers

The system is so successful that it must be the envy of recycling experts in the West. Thousands of teenagers with wooden donkey carts go around Cairo collecting rubbish. From the heaps that accumulate daily, they pick out broken pieces of glass and bottles and take them to a tiny workshop in the old part of town. There the materials are sorted into different colours and melted down to be made into vases, carafes, cups or beakers to be sold in the tourist bazaar as the famous hand-blown Muski glass.

The green glass is made mainly from Seven Up bottles, the clear glass from Pepsi or Coke bottles, the amber-coloured glass from medicine or Stella beer bottles. Chemical colouring – magnesium powder or cobalt or copper oxide – is only needed for the purple and blue glass. One person

Long before the technique of glass-blowing began in Syria around the time of Christ, vessels were made in Egypt and Mesopotamia by melting glass around a sand core. In the 13th century, the Venetians imported the technique from the East and established a virtual monopoly in Murano. Below: vases made of Cairo Muski glass.

processes about 30 kilos (66 lbs) of broken glass a day, making between a hundred and two hundred objects. The *zabbalin*, the refuse collectors, are paid 10 piastres (about £1.80 or US $3.00) for a kilo of plain glass, half as much again for coloured glass.

This simple but efficient method of recycling is used only in Cairo and the biggest user is the 'Glass Factory' owned by the brothers Hassan and Reda Raouf. The business – immediately behind the Bab el-Futuh – is also unique in another respect. In the whole of the Middle East, there are only about a dozen traditional glass-blowing works left, three of them in Cairo. But only the Raoufs use the original techniques.

This all happens in a bare, dark room with roughly whitewashed walls covered in soot and a trodden clay floor. Canvas sacks filled with tons of glass fragments are heaped up in an outhouse. The brothers built the rough stone furnace themselves and they work by it six days a week. Their tools are spread out next to the rickety wooden stools – iron bars, pliers and enormous pincers like medieval torture instruments. The melting point of glass is about 1,000°C (1,800°F) and the men's foreheads are permanently bathed in sweat.

The Raouf brothers' workshop is one of only three remaining glass-blowing works in Cairo (see also overleaf). There is a certain irony to one of the reasons for the dramatic decline of the trade: apparently the Egyptian government refuses to issue new licences on the grounds that the work endangers the glass-blowers' health.

They make the glass in more or less the same way as the Mesopotamian immigrants who came to Cairo in the 10th century. The glass-blower dips his blunt-ended hollow metal tube into the molten mass and fishes out a small lump, which he puts on the mouthpiece and blows up into a ball. Then he swings the tube through the air with an artistic flourish to shape the glass and finally uses his 'torture instruments' for the details such as stems, handles or decoration. He flattens the base by pressing it against a stone and hands the piece to his assistant to be put aside to cool. The only concession to modernity is the new kerosene heating system. Now it no longer takes the Raoufs two hours to heat the furnace every morning and they only have to work eleven hours a day.

القزاز

Although people no longer put human embryos into the furnace as a tribute to the fire gods before lighting it for the first time, there is still something esoteric about the glass maker's art. Who can say that changing common substances like quartz sand, chalk and soda or potash into something so ethereal just with fire and then breathing shapes into them is not magic?

Nowadays glass-blowing is often low-grade piece work. The influence of the middlemen and the power of industry have put the remaining glass-blowers under severe pressure. But there is still much to admire in the almost erotic way in which the artist breathes shape into the lumps of glass, the variety of shapes (a master craftsman can make more than a hundred different types of vessel) and the instinctive sureness and speed of the well-practised movements.

Apart from Cairo, it is only in Damascus that real craftsmanship can be found, not surprisingly because Syria – along with Mesopotamia and Egypt – is one of the birthplaces of glass making. According to ancient writers, there was already a fully developed industry round Tyre and Sidon on the coast at the start of the Christian era. The purity of the sand and the plentiful supply of resinous pinewood from Lebanon, which was especially suited to this purpose, made it an ideal location. The technique of glass-blowing is also believed to have originated in Syria around the time of Christ's birth. It was there that the rock-crystal vessels and amulets so sought after in Europe were made. The famous enamelled or gilded hanging mosque lamps which the Mameluke princes ordered in vast numbers also came from Syria. The technique was brought to Venice in the 13th century by the Crusaders and 200 years later Tamerlane took expert glass-blowers to Samarkand.

Nowadays, however, Damascus typifies the pressures facing this traditional craft. In 1975 there were only thirteen workshops left. By the early nineties, this had fallen to just two.

Smiths and sword makers

When you first go into a copper and brass souq, you feel as if you have walked into a madhouse. Men are frenetically beating metal plates and objects with heavy hammers. Others are sitting there like automatons making patterns on plates and trays with their gouges and punches. Between them they are making such an unholy row that you would think it would drive them crazy. But if you just listen to the cacophony for a while, you realize that it does have a hidden cadence. The men are careful to fit in with the changing rhythms of their neighbours and you can tell from their faces that they are happy in their work.

The deafening sound of the *nahassin*, the coppersmith, can still be heard in most bazaars. Although in the last few years the need for hand-made nails and horseshoes,

The coppersmiths' concert – below: a 'drummer' from Isfahan – is the acoustic high point of any visit to a bazaar. Muhammad Asad wrote that this musical and social harmony reveals the hidden beauty of the oriental soul. Opposite: an Isfahani surrounded by his scrap metal.

provides work for a whole host of engravers and chasers.

Islamic metalwork originated far to the east, in Fars and Khorassan in Persia and in Sogdiana, in what is now Uzbekistan. As long ago as the 9th and 10th centuries, magnificent incense containers, pots, jugs, bowls and aquamaniles (large water containers) were made in Bukhara and Samarkand, Ghazni and Herat. The favourite material was bronze. In the ancient Orient and East Asia it was considered the ideal medium for occult and astrological ideas. Its figurative shapes showed Sassanian and Far Eastern influences (the best known are the animal figures, like the birds of prey still copied in Isfahan today), but the *kufi* calligraphy made it unmistakably Islamic.

The main streets in the bazaar are also processional routes. They are often draped with black cloth in Moharram, the month of mourning, when the Shiites commemorate their revered martyr Hussein. The most important requirements for these religious processions are supplied by the smiths' bazaar: the tree of life decorated with bells and iron peacock feathers, the scourges with which the faithful whip their backs until they bleed at the Ashura festival and the khamsa, *or hand of Fatima, that guards against the evil eye (above and below: in the Mesgaran bazaar in Isfahan). Opposite above: nickel-silver and silver trays in the bazaar in Fez. Opposite below: a varied selection of metal goods in the old quarter in Cairo (in the right foreground, a copper pinnacle for a minaret).*

hinges, locks and knockers has declined rapidly and many specialist smiths have already gone out of business, traditional copper tableware has withstood the competition from the cheaper plastic and aluminium goods, especially in the rural areas. In the cities, the huge pots for weddings, hospitals and barracks are still made by hand in the old way, and the insatiable demand for tourist souvenirs

Mohammed banned the use of gold and silver eating and drinking vessels on the grounds of extravagance, and Muslim craftsmen soon developed ways of treating the surfaces so that they looked like base metal. They were particularly fond of damascening, a decorative technique in which softer metals like copper (and later also silver) were applied to a hard brass, bronze or steel surface in which filigree patterns were engraved. This art, which was already practised in antiquity, was perfected in the Seljuk period and reached its acme in Mesopotamia, especially the city of Mosul, in the 13th and 14th centuries. The craftsmen had mastered both methods of damascening to perfection: the inlay technique (in which the patterns were cut deeply into the metal bodies and thin wires or plates hammered into the grooves) and the technique later known in India and the Ottoman Empire as *koftgari*, used mainly for steel, in which the base was scored with minute furrows and the intarsia applied with a round hammer. The Mosul school's decorative patterns – battle and festival scenes, rosettes, animal friezes, borders of script and medallions with figures – soon spread to the West after the Mongol invasion. The new centres of production were Damascus, Aleppo and Cairo. Even in Venice, a whole guild of Saracen craftsmen worked on magnificent vessels, candelabra, candlesticks, Koran stands and also globes,

astrolabes and quadrants in both Persian and Damascene styles in the late 14th century.

Compared with the glories of the past, what is being produced by the workshops nowadays seems of poor quality. Now and then, Syrian, Egyptian or Moroccan artists do still receive commissions from rich clients for individual pieces on which they work for months and have an opportunity to demonstrate their craftsmanship. Many of the consumer goods for local people still have an authentic old-fashioned simplicity. But much of the original creativity has been stifled by mass production for the souvenir trade. Increasingly nowadays brassware is prefabricated industrially and just given the finishing touches in the bazaar so that it can be passed off as handmade.

Gone are the days when even the pots in the charity kitchens, such as those in some Anatolian monasteries, were richly decorated works of art. Gone too the days when Istanbul still had a weapons bazaar and the Italian travel writer Edmondo de Amicis wrote (in 1883) about the 'elegant helmets and blades, breastplates, gleaming swords and daggers'. The 500-year-old tradition of the legendary Damascene swords has all but died out, but with one exception.

In the heart of Damascus, in the maze of tiny streets south of the Street called Straight, if you look carefully you will find an unobtrusive but unique workshop. Its owner, Daud Kahale, is one of only three men who revived the art of sword making in the sixties and seventies, two generations after it had apparently died out. In the front room of his family business he turns out magnificent-looking, but usually inexpensive, dress swords, mainly for customers from the Gulf States. Their blades are made of chrome steel, their 'gold' coating is actually paint and they usually cost only a couple of thousand Syrian pounds (about £30 sterling or US $50). In a tiny back room, however, he keeps the objects which are his real love: a few dozen old swords wrapped in canvas which even a non-expert can see straight away are something special.

Daud Kahale is a world expert on historic weapons from the Middle East. Many of the major collectors in London, Los Angeles and Qatar send damaged pieces to him for repair. When the British Museum, for instance, is planning a special exhibition, it consults him. The treasures entrusted to him are worth millions of dollars.

If he sees that a visitor is genuinely interested, he will happily reveal a few secrets. He will explain what gives a sword its quality: the delicate balance between rigidity and flexibility which prevents the sword from breaking when a hefty blow is struck. Or the fact that the hollow near the handle and the grooves in the blade are there to cushion the force of the blow or to introduce bacteria into the enemy's wound. He also explains the differences between the basic shapes: the elegant curved *shamshir* of the Safavids, the older curved Damascene sword whose name, *kalij*, translates from the Turkish as hair-splitting, and the rare double-edged swords always reserved for kings. Finally he tells you – not without a touch of *schadenfreude* – of the unsuccessful attempts by American scientists to solve the mystery of the damascened blade. As an expert, he is fascinated that no one (himself included) now knows how the solid steel alloys for the multi-layered swords were made and how, when they were welded in the forge, they produced the curious wavy coloured grain known as 'diamond'.

The Arabs are believed to have learned the technique of encrusting swords from Uigur prisoners in Samarkand in the 8th century, but the art of the armourer reached its height many generations later in Damascus. The unchallenged master sword maker was Asad-Allah, who was born in Damascus, taken to Isfahan and worked for the Safavid court around 1600. His stamp, a guarantee of the highest quality, still appeared many generations later on hundreds of Persian swords (above left), a typical example of early product plagiarism. Opposite: bargaining in the brass and copper souq in Aleppo. Below: a smith in Fez (not a chicken shop, as it might appear!).

Potters and tile makers

If it were not for the tower blocks in the new part of Cairo visible on the horizon through the drifting smoke, you could think you were back in the time of the Fatimids. The brick ovens here in Fustat cannot have looked so very different a thousand years ago. Even the way in which the raw material is obtained must have changed only very little: holes are dug with spades, their clayey base soaked with water and trodden until a compact but pliable mass of clay is produced. Even the *dulahs*, the potters' wheels on which hundreds of men, protected from the sun by makeshift walls of reeds and palm leaves, turn out pot after pot at breakneck speed, work on the age-old principle of footpower.

Thousands of clay bowls for water pipes drying in the ruins at Fustat (opposite). After being stacked into huge piles they are fired in ancient brick and clay kilns (below). More than 1,500 potters work in the north-west of Old Cairo in conditions that would horrify European health and safety inspectors.

But looking at the end-products, there is obviously no comparison with the far-off period when Cairo was known as the city

Mosaic tiles are one of the finest examples of Islamic craftsmanship. The process is a complicated one. First, motifs and patterns are drawn on a large sheet of paper, then the individual colours are carefully numbered and cut out. The patterns are then laid on tiles of the same colour and these are cut out with special tools and their edges rubbed smooth. Next, the patterns are laid out on a soft plaster surface, the outlines retraced with the point of a knife and the original tiles inserted. The block is covered with wooden boards and worked into the structure after it is dry. Opposite: a master craftsman from Fez showing the central star motif in 'God's spider's web', a popular pattern in the Maghreb. It consists of a number of strips radiating out from the centre in a rigid geometric pattern, intersecting and unfolding into a huge rose. Above: only holy places have green glazed roof tiles in the Maghreb. Below: a faïence maker in the bazaar in Isfahan.

of the potters. The thousands of pots drying here today in the Fustat ruins are just for everyday use: earth-coloured jugs, pots, plates, vases, mouthpieces for water pipes, or at best, a couple of the clay dolls which are sold in the bazaars before the feast of the Prophet's birthday. What was made here between the 1st and 2nd centuries AD was real art, unequalled in the known world.

Despite the various influences from older civilizations, Islamic pottery developed its own distinctive style at a very early stage. Its main characteristics were an unusual diversity of colours and patterns and new processing techniques. In the 9th century, it centred around the caliphs' courts in Samarra and Baghdad, where the new culture from Arabia first came into contact with Chinese porcelain. In an attempt to copy this fascinating material, the greyish-brown clay was covered with white pewter glazes, creating the first genuine faïence in the history of ceramics.

The lustre technique was also developed in Abbasid Iraq. After being fired the vessel was painted with a mixture of silver, sulphur, copper oxides and colour pigments. A second special firing process then gave it a gleaming metallic surface. Two hundred years afterwards artists perfected this technique in Fustat (it was revived many years later in the Italian Renaissance).

After the fall of the Fatimids they emigrated to Persia and Anatolia at the end of the 12th century, ushering in the golden age of Islamic ceramics. In Rayy, for instance, near present-day Tehran, they were instrumental in the development of *minai* ware – faïence on which colour was applied to the glaze in the style of court miniature painting. Aghkant, near Tabriz, became famous for its *sgraffito* ware, Nishapur for its special transparent glaze, Kashan for the particularly skilful use of polychrome effects, and Konya and Raqqa for the invention of *fritte*, a glass-like substance made from ground quartz and clay which made it possible for the pots to be fired harder.

The most popular background colour was cobalt blue, which for a long time could only be obtained from Persia. In the Chinese porcelain industry it became known as Mohammedan blue and was much prized. The inhabitants of distant Fez even chose it as their city's 'symbolic' colour. The faïence technique was also brought from the Middle East to the far west. Malaga, Valencia and later also Seville were centres of the Spanish-Moorish pottery which, via Majorca (hence the name majolica), was a major influence on the ceramic tradition in Italy, and later the rest of Europe, and still survives in the Iberian peninsula in the traditional blue-and-white wall tiles known as *azulejos*.

The architectural use of Islamic ceramics also began at a very early stage, originated by the Seljuks. In their capital, Konya, Koranic schools were decorated with faïence mosaics inside and out as long ago as the mid-13th century. Impressive examples can still be seen in the local museum, the Karatay Medrese. Soon afterwards, tile-making was developed in the Maghreb and in the east the Timurids perfected the art on their monumental buildings in Samarkand and Herat. But the heyday was under the Ottomans. At their factories in Iznik they constantly developed new forms and production processes (the faïence collection in the Topkapi Sarayi shows the astonishing diversity and quality). Large masterpieces were produced in their earlier seats in Edirne and Bursa, and especially in Istanbul – virtual carpets of ceramic with luxuriant ochre, turquoise and emerald-green tulips, flowering trees and arabesques on a mostly white or blue background.

The finest examples of tile decoration are found in Iran and Central Asia. Façades and interiors like those of the Medressa Tilla-Kari in Samarkand (opposite and below) and domes like this one on the Sheykh Lotfollah Mosque in Isfahan (above) are unrivalled, except possibly in Istanbul.

It was only in the reign of Shah Abbas I in Persia that this workmanship was surpassed. The combinations of colours and patterns in, for instance, the domes of the Shah or Lotfollah mosques in Isfahan were unrivalled anywhere. By the time the factories in Kütahya and Canakkale began making 'Turkish Rococo' work, the original inspiration and creativity had already been lost. The work produced in the 19th century was schematized and meticulously precise.

Despite its artistic decline, pottery has nevertheless retained a certain mystical aura. In the ceramics towns of North Africa such as Nebeul, Fez, Safi and Sale, for instance, every workplace is still seen as a holy place. If a potter establishes himself on the site of a competitor, it is said that his goods will crack the night after they are made. In Fustat there is an unwritten law that unfired vessels should not be sold, because of the belief that it is possible to do someone serious harm by scratching names or magic formulae into soft clay and throwing the pot in the Nile.

The tanners and dyers of Fez

One of the most truly breathtaking experiences in the bazaars is a visit to the tanners' quarter of Fez, in the Quartier Chouara to the west, where the polluted river flows out of the old town. It is a relic of the Middle Ages – like a scene from Dante's *Inferno*. At its centre is a large courtyard full of stone vats lined with tiles containing dyeing solutions in various colours, with half-naked men wading in them.

The daily grind of the pack animals (opposite). Day in, day out, they carry up to 6,000 uncured cow hides and at least half as many goatskins from the warehouses and collect them again a week or two later for the middleman (below), cleaned, tanned, dyed and dried.

There is a terrible stench of putrefaction, urine and sweat. On the peeling walls the hides of cows, calves, goats and sheep are hung up to dry and all the while heavily laden donkeys are bringing in new hides, still with blood on them. Some come from the city's slaughterhouses, the rest are brought from all over the country. The hides are auctioned at midday in four nearby *funduqs* which have specialized in the leather trade for centuries

– 3,000 goatskins and up to 6,000 cow hides every day.

In Chouara and a few smaller tanneries in other areas the hides undergo an ancient and lengthy process. First they are immersed in lime baths to remove the rest of the flesh and hair. Then they are put in a water bath with sulphuric acid and sea salt to pickle them. In the tanning process proper, the skins, now pliable and soft, are soaked in a mixture of oil and tanning materials. Synthetically produced chrome alum is now used instead of the old vegetable substances (usually oak or chestnut bark).

The next stage is the chamois tanning. The leather is softened again with a greasy solution, planed on the flesh side and smoothed on the outside, giving it its characteristic shine. It is then immersed in a dyeing vat with fixatives and lastly put out in the sun to dry in the fields outside the medina. In Fez they use only natural pigments for dyeing – indigo for blue, madder or cochineal for red, safflower for yellow and antimony or iron oxide for black. The white and pale-gold colours for the famous slippers, *babouches*, are obtained from tamarisk skins and camel milk or pomegranate skins and alum.

Leather was used in the Islamic world from the earliest days. The Arabs, originally a nomadic people who lived mainly in the saddle and in tents, ate, slept and prayed on it, drank out of it, dressed in it and bound their holy book in it. Leather was even used in their houses: for mats (in Yemen), as a wall hanging (in Cairo and Damascus) or, as in the famous Sala de los Reyes in the Alhambra, as a gilded ceiling covering. It was processed in various important centres, on the banks of the Euphrates, Nile or Bosporus, in Yemen, Persia and Tunisia.

But the country most famous for its leather was, and still is, Morocco. It is no accident that in Europe high-quality leather from sheep- and goatskins is called morocco. Complete libraries used to be shipped there for the books to be bound by Moroccan leather-workers and embellished with gold blocking or with lattice-work decoration. Every bazaar from Tangier to Agadir is full of bags and purses, cases, belts and pouffes. But the most popular items are the *babouches*, hanging from the ceilings of the shops like bunches of grapes or laid out in pairs in cases on the walls.

Thirty per cent of all Moroccan leather-workers live in Fez. More than 1,500 people make slippers there, mostly the standard white and yellow kind made from sheep or cattle hides, but there are also special grey slippers made from horses' hides, available only in Fez and considered an enviable status symbol.

All the pieces are cut and sewn by the men in the workshops. Young apprentices stick on the manufactured imported insoles, often (surprisingly) made from pigskin. Women working at home embroider the toecaps. The patterns they use are strikingly similar to the tattoos on the faces of the Berbers. The shoemakers slave away from seven in the morning to nine at night, six days a week, with no social security. For a pair of elegant *babouches* they are paid 150 dirhams (less than £10 sterling or US $16) – the price of five beers in a tourist hotel.

Chouara, the tanners' and dyers' district of Fez, as a passing tourist would see it (above and opposite). If you actually descend into this area, at first you can hardly breathe. The men working here have to live with the noxious smells all the time. They fill the vats with fresh water from the Wadi Fez (Oued Fès) and later channel the toxic coloured liquid, mixed with acids, lyes and oils, back through an intricate system of canals. Below: one of the countless leather shops in the medina in Fez.

Overleaf: scene in the bazaar, Rissani, southern Morocco.

THE HEART OF THE CITY

PORTRAITS OF THE FINEST BAZAARS

Cairo
Damascus
Aleppo
Istanbul
Sanaa
Dubai
Kairouan
Tunis
Marrakesh
Fez
Shiraz
Isfahan
Samarkand, Bukhara and Khiva

N
Danube
Edirne
Canakkale
Izmir
Córdoba
Granada
Algiers
TUNIS
Nebeul
KAIROUAN
Tétouan
Chechaouèn
Rabat
Sale
FEZ
Meknes
Djerba
Tripoli
Casablanca
ATLAS
Ghadaia
MARRAKESH
Sijilmassa
Ghadames
Agadir
S A H A R A
HOGGAR
Ghat
Taghaza
Bilma/Kawar
Agadez
Timbuktu
Gao
Niger
Kano

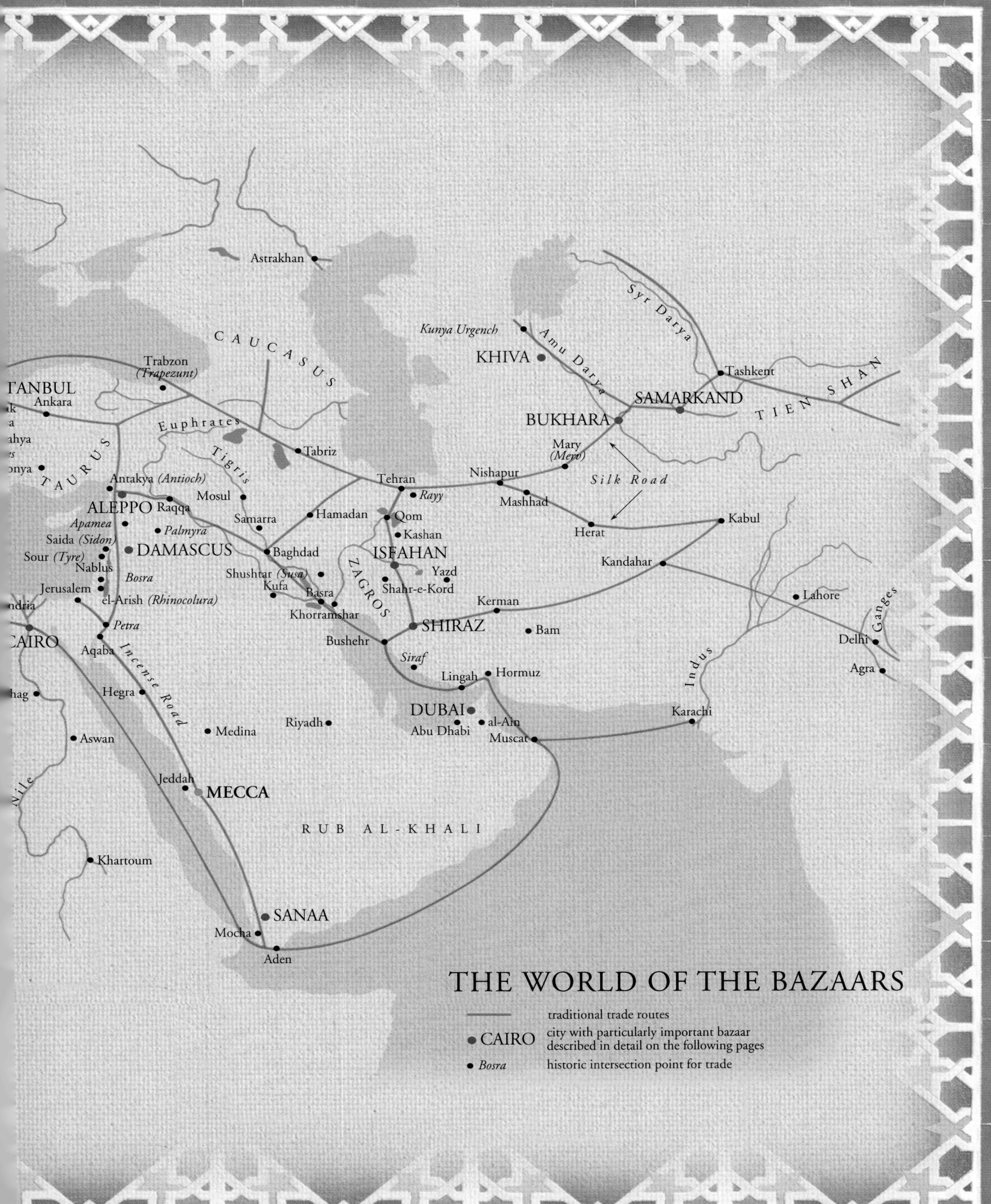

THE WORLD OF THE BAZAARS

traditional trade routes

CAIRO — city with particularly important bazaar described in detail on the following pages

Bosra — historic intersection point for trade

Astrakhan
CAUCASUS
Kunya Urgench
Syr Darya
Amu Darya
KHIVA
Trabzon
(Trapezunt)
TANBUL
Ankara
Tashkent
TIEN SHAN
SAMARKAND
BUKHARA
Euphrates
Tigris
TAURUS
Tabriz
Mary
(Merv)
onya
Antakya *(Antioch)*
Tehran
Nishapur
Silk Road
Mosul
Rayy
Mashhad
ALEPPO
Raqqa
Apamea
Hamadan
Qom
Samarra
Kabul
Palmyra
Kashan
Herat
Saida *(Sidon)*
DAMASCUS
Baghdad
ISFAHAN
Sour *(Tyre)*
Nablus
Bosra
Shushtar *(Susa)*
ZAGROS
Yazd
Kandahar
Jerusalem
Kufa
Shahr-e-Kord
el-Arish *(Rhinocolura)*
Basra
Lahore
ndria
Khorramshar
Kerman
Ganges
Petra
SHIRAZ
Bam
CAIRO
Aqaba
Incense Road
Bushehr
Delhi
Siraf
Indus
Hormuz
Lingah
Agra
hag
Hegra
DUBAI
Karachi
Riyadh
al-Ain
Abu Dhabi
Medina
Muscat
Aswan
Nile
Jeddah
MECCA
RUB AL-KHALI
Khartoum
SANAA
Mocha
Aden

القاهرة

Cairo

If you have never seen Cairo, you have not seen the world. A character in one of the tales from *A Thousand and One Nights* enthuses that its earth is gold, its Nile a wonder, every house a palace and its air is soft like the sweet-smelling wood of the aloe. Since its heyday about 600 years ago, the city has seen drastic changes. The gold has become tarnished, the Nile is polluted and the fragrance of the aloe has been replaced by the pungent smell of exhaust fumes.

Even so, Cairo – the biggest metropolis in Africa – is the quintessential fairy-tale Oriental city. This is partly because of its exceptionally large number of historic monuments; UNESCO has singled out 600 of the Islamic monuments alone for conservation. But, above all, it is because of its people's friendliness and zest for life

The most venerable of the countless mosques in Cairo and the second oldest university in the world is el-Azhar, built in 970–972 (below: the prayer hall). Its scholars are still regarded by orthodox Muslims as the highest authority on all fundamental questions of religious law. Opposite: the door of the Rifai Mosque.

القاهرة

Cairo – general view
A Old Cairo (formerly Babylon), B Fustat ruins, C Geziret el-Roda, D City of the Dead, E el-Qahira, F el-Gamaliya, G Ghouriya, H Citadel, I Moqattam Hills, J Azbakiya, K Abdin Palace, L Bulaq, M Garden City, N Zamalek, O Gezira, P Dokki, Q Imbaba, R Heliopolis/airport, S Giza/pyramids, T Nile.

El-Qahira – the old city
*BAZAARS AND MARKETS: **1** Khan el-Khalili, **2** Suq el-Attarin (spice market), **3** Suq el-Nahassin (coppersmiths), **4** Suq el-Lamoon (lemon, garlic and onion market), **5** Suq el-Muski (clothing, food, leather), **6** Suq Khiyamiya (tent makers' market), **7** Suq el-Hamam (dove market on Sayyida Ayisha Square). SPECIALIST WORKSHOPS AND SHOPS: **8** el-Daour (glass-blowing), **9** Ghouriya (clothing market), **10** Tarbush (felt hats), **11** Fawani (tin lanterns). MOSQUES, KORANIC SCHOOLS AND MAUSOLEUMS: **12** el-Hakim Mosque, **13** Madrasa Qarasunqur, **14** Suleiman Aga Mosque, **15** el-Aqmar Mosque, **16** Gamal el-Din Mosque, **17** Barquq mausoleum, **18** Madrasa Mohammed el-Nasir, **19** Qalaun complex, **20** el-Salih Ayyub mausoleum, **21** el-Azhar Mosque (university), **22** Madrasa el-Ghouri, **23** el-Ghouri mausoleum, **24** Fakahami Mosque, **25** Muayyid Mosque, **26** Salih Talai Mosque. CARAVANSERAIS: **27** Wakalat el-Ghouri (arts and crafts centre), **28** Qaitbey, **29** Qusun. WELLS AND BATHS: **30** Sabil-kuttab Oda Pasha, **31** Sabil-kuttab Abdul Rahman Katkhuda, **32** Hammam el-Sultan, **33** Sabil Mohamed Ali, **34** Sabil Nafisa el-Bayda. OTHER: **35** Fatimid city wall, **36** Beit el-Suhaymi, **37** Baibars el-Gashankir monastery, **38** Beit Gamal el-Din el-Dhahabi. CITY GATES: **39** Bab el-Futuh, **40** Bab Zuwayla, **41** Bab el-Nasr. STREETS: **42** Shari el-Muizz, **43** Shari el-Azhar, **44** Shari el-Muski, **45** Shari Mohamed Ali, **46** Shari Ahmed Maher.*

Khan el-Khalili and surrounding area
*BAZAARS AND MARKETS: **A** Suq el-Sagha (gold and silver market), **B** Suq el-Kuttab (books and writing materials). SPECIALIST WORKSHOPS AND SHOPS: **C** Narghile (water pipes), **D** Assil (sura embroiderers), **E** Khedr el-Attar (medicines and herbs), **F** Mahmoud Hamdy (foot ironer), **G** el-Khady (amber prayer beads), **H** Mashrabiya turners. MOSQUES AND MAUSOLEUMS: **I** el-Mutahar complex, **J** el-Hussein Mosque, **K** el-Azhar Mosque, **L** Barsbay Mosque. CARAVANSERAIS: **M** Wakalat el-Gallaba (former slave market), **N** el-Qutn. RESTAURANTS, TEA AND COFFEE HOUSES: **O** Café el-Fishawy, **P** Cafeteria Sinusi, el-Harram el-Husseini, Orabi, etc. **Q** Restaurant Khan el-Khalili, **R** el-Hussein hotel and roof café. WELLS AND BATHS: **S** Sabil-kuttab Ahmad Pasha. OTHER: **T** Public toilets, **U** Tourist police. STREETS: **V** el-Seke el-Gedida, **W** Shari el-Muizz, **X** Shari el-Azhar, **Y** Midaq.*

BORDER: Metal decoration from a door at the Muayyid Mosque. ILLUSTRATION: Bab Zuwayla.

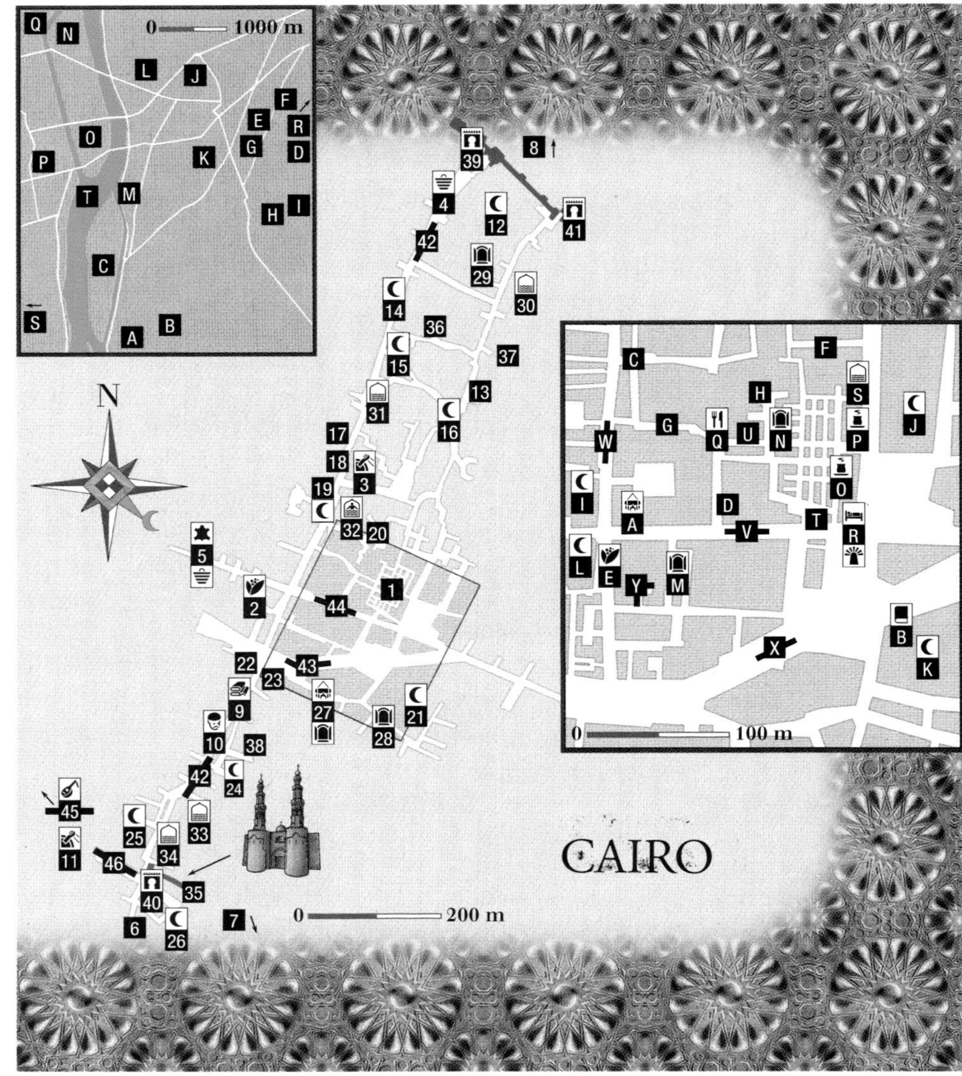

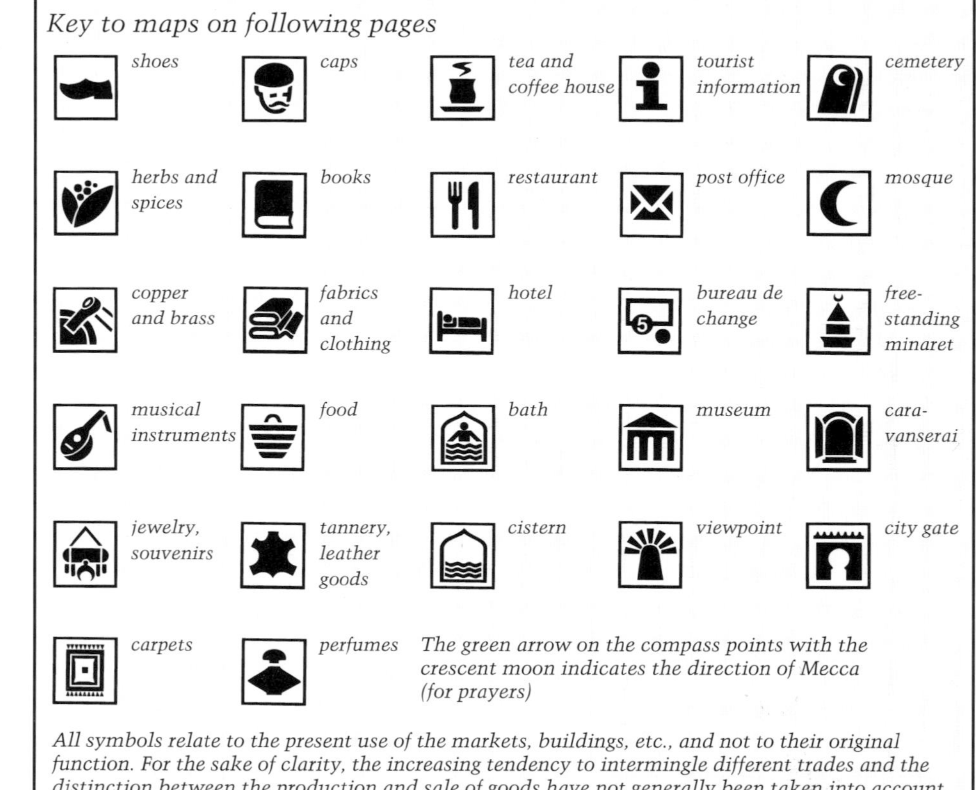

and especially their love of story-telling and bargaining.

The roots of this vitality go back 5,000 years, to the time of the first Pharaohs. 'The Residence of the White Walls', later Memphis, sacred to the worship of Ptah, was founded mainly for economic reasons. Its position, only 25 kilometres (15 miles) south of present-day Cairo, made it eminently suited to become a trading centre. Upper Egypt and the fertile Delta were both equally accessible and it was the easiest place to cross the Nile.

The Arab settlement at Fustat was even more important. Built outside the northern walls of the Roman city of Babylon by the conqueror Amr ibn-al-As in 641, this garrison town soon became the economic centre of the Islamic Empire, a powerful free-trade area. Governors of the Abbasid caliphs of Baghdad subsequently built other residences, but Fustat remained the transfer point for all goods from India, Arabia and the Mediterranean for over 500 years.

This only changed under the legendary ruler Salah ad-Din (Saladin). In 969 his predecessors, the Shiite Fatimids, had founded el-Qahira ('the victorious') nearby, a strongly fortified town whose name Italian traders later distorted to Cairo. El-Qahira was a palace district and access was forbidden to the common people. However, Salah ad-Din, who founded the Ayyubid dynasty, opened the royal enclaves to the lower orders. Thousands of craftsmen and traders from Fustat moved into the new metropolis. The present large souq grew up along the main street, the Qasabah, and in the adjoining streets, with the residential quarter, the *harat*, to the left and right. At the same time a second market district developed below the citadel which Salah ad-Din had built as a fortress against the Crusaders. This stocked weapons, horses and tents for the soldiers stationed nearby.

Cairo was at the height of its splendour in the time of the Mamelukes (1250–1517). Although these former Turkish and Circassian slave mercenaries had their barbaric side (most of the sultans were stabbed or poisoned by their successors), their military skill saved Cairo from being invaded by the Mongols and conquered by European armies. They also had a talent for building. The most able, like Baibars and Qalaun, an-Nasir, Qaitbey and al-Ghouri, left a legacy of magnificent palaces, mosques and mausoleums and also countless caravanserais (*wakalats*) still named after them. At the end of the 14th century the Egyptian historian Ahmad al-Maqrizi noted that in the 1.5 kilometres (1 mile) between the northern city gate, the Bab el-Futuh, and the Bab Zuwayla to the south there were no fewer than 58 *wakalats* and 87 markets, with more than 12,000 stalls selling every imaginable luxury: Indian silks, Italian velvet, painted glass from Damascus, muslin from Mosul, parrots and gold dust from Ethiopia. The spice trade was particularly important. Despite the Pope's threats to excommunicate them, city-states like Genoa, Pisa and Venice had settlements in Cairo (which was Muslim and therefore hostile territory) and imported up to 1,500 tons of spices a year.

The Khan el-Khalili, precursor of the commercial complex which now forms

The area around the el-Azhar Mosque is still the heart of old el-Qahira. Every day Shari el-Muizz, leading from el-Muski street to the Bab Zuwayla, becomes an enormous open-air market for inexpensive goods (above). Wakalat el-Ghouri, the huge caravanserai built in the Mameluke period (centre) has for many years been a centre for contemporary arts and crafts. The Khan el-Khalili (below) is a treasure trove for souvenir and antique hunters.

the tourist centrepiece of the bazaar, was built in the area around a Fatimid castle in about 1400. Named after its builder, Sultan Barquq's chief equerry, it was used as a hotel and store by generations of foreign traders. Many of them were Persians, which explains the proximity of the Hussein mosque – the Prophet's grandson Hussein is venerated as a martyr by the Shiite Persians and his head is said to be buried on the site. Hussein was for a long time patron of the craftsmen and guilds in the Khan el-Khalili.

Under Ottoman rule, Cairo's economic importance developed, although Vasco da Gama had in the meantime discovered the maritime route to the Far East. Indian spices were replaced by Yemeni coffee as the main trading commodity. The economy was given a major boost by the *hajj*, the pilgrimage to Mecca, on which a caravan of up to 40,000 people set out every year from Cairo. In its heyday in the mid-17th century there were 145 souqs and 360 *wakalats*. For the first time minorities like the Jews (mainly moneylenders and gold- and silversmiths), the financially astute Copts and the Armenian locksmiths and jewellers had their own quarters in the cosmopolitan city. Rich traders bought luxurious residences along the old canal, the Khalig, and on the banks of the lakes. Architecturally, however, the Ottomans contributed little of note to the markets. Their outstanding legacy is the *sabil*, the faïence-decorated public well.

The most radical changes in Cairo's commercial centre came about at the time of Mehemet Ali, the father of modern Egypt (1805–1849). He Europeanized the city, making Bulaq, the old Nile port in the west, the centre of his industrialization scheme. Modern shipyards and the first state printing works in the Arab world were built there. In the medieval city centre he had lanes built to provide better means of access for the new coaches. After Napoleon's troops had removed the gates between the individual souqs and stripped the guards of their office, he ordered the removal of the traditional stone benches

Although sometimes obscured by haze and exhaust fumes, the view across the roofs and domes of Fatimid Cairo to the towers of the Bab Zuwayla is unforgettable. Cairo has more major monuments than almost any other city in the world.

The necropolises at the foot of the Moqattam Hills. It is often thought that the reason why more than half a million Cairenes live here permanently (some even have running water and electricity) is the chronic housing shortage. In fact, mystics and pilgrims were already living in the two cemeteries soon after they were built (from the 7th century). Living side by side with the dead has been a tradition in Egypt since the time of the Pharaohs.

Mahmoud Hamdy is one of the last survivors of the exotic guild of foot ironers. He irons for eight hours a day in his tiny shop behind the el-Hussein Mosque, guiding the 15-kilo (33-pound) iron with his right hand and pressing down with his foot.

(*mastabas*) outside the shops and decreed that *mashrabiyas* – turned-wood balcony and bay-window grilles – should not be used in new buildings. In short, the bazaar underwent cosmetic surgery, with questionable results.

Further modernization took place under Ali's successors Said Pasha and Ismail Pasha. Cairo became the flourishing supply base for the building of the railway and the Suez Canal. Factories, dams and bridges were built, as well as parks and smart hotels. The Khedive rulers, the viceroys of the Ottoman emperor, now lived in the newly built Abdin Palace instead of the citadel. European-style residential and commercial districts developed around it. The old markets in the Fatimid city centre became what they essentially remain today, a place where the poorer sections of the population live and shop, a place for craftsmen, Bedouin and Saidis (immigrants from Upper Egypt). Progress brought debts and with them dependence on the western powers. In 1882 Egypt became a British protectorate. The decades before and after that were marked by foreign intervention and national revolts, culminating in 1922 in formal independence. But it was not until the thirties and forties that men like Talaat Harb and Ahmed Aboud managed to develop independent Egyptian industries on the outskirts of the city. These benefited particularly from the brief but spectacular boom during the Second World War. Finally, president Gamal Abdel Nasser brought

about a historic change when industry and agriculture were nationalized after the 1952 revolution and large private assets confiscated by the state. Most foreigners left the country. Thousands of shops in the city centre and the bazaar were taken over by Egyptians.

Since then conditions in Cairo have deteriorated dramatically. In 1952 it still

had a manageable two million inhabitants. Now the population is fifteen million, half of them minors. By the new millennium, there are expected to be twenty million. The government froze the charges for leases on the seized property and the rents for private houses in the 1950s and ownership rights have often not been settled. As a result, Cairo's housing stock is now in a state of advanced decay. The earthquake in the autumn of 1992 speeded up the decline.

But this urban disaster (which will at least be slightly alleviated in the near future by a new canal system) only affects the city's exterior. Behind it is another, much more attractive, picture: the amazing energy which keeps this huge city going against all logic, makes its inhabitants so wonderfully

Not many food markets have such a historic setting as the one in the Ghouriya bazaar district. On one side is el-Azhar Mosque and university, on the others the el-Ghouri and Qaitbey caravanserais. Above: a woman selling vegetables in front of an artistically carved mashrabiya.

cheerful and optimistic, and proves the truth of the chaos theory.

There are not many places where you can feel yourself transported back to the Middle Ages as you can in Cairo. You only have to look at the view from the minaret of the Muayyid mosque, which has captivated generations of travellers, or stroll north along the Shari el-Muizz, the former kasbah. The people you see in the souq in old el-Qahirah could have lived fifteen or twenty generations ago.

In the Suq Khiyamiya south of the Bab Zuwayla, the old place of execution, the tent makers are still sewing as they have done for centuries. In the Shari Ahmed Maher, people are making *faranis*, brass lanterns for the long nights of Ramadan. Behind the al-Ghouri mausoleum, shored up with scaffolding since the last earthquake, two magnificent brass steamers decorated with the royal emblem are still used to shape *tarbushes*. Tailors still sit cross-legged in their niches, working away on their antiquated but functional cast-iron Singer sewing machines.

It is true that many trades and products have disappeared, probably for good. The jewel and diamond markets on Shari el-Muski have gone since the downfall of King Farouk in 1952, as have the professional scribes since cheap printing methods were introduced. The slave market closed in 1870 and the guild of gunpowder sellers was banished from the bazaar in the 18th century after a series of disastrous accidents. No silk is brought from Sohag now and no raw gold from Nubia and Sinai. High-quality antiques, such as Coptic fabrics, Fatimid ceramics and Persian miniatures, are more likely to be found today in a museum than in the bazaar. Camel wool and gum arabic are virtually impossible to obtain from Sudan because of the situation there. *Shahi*, the famous cotton-silk mixture, is not available even from Ouf's, the leading fabric shop. There is only one old man left who still weaves silk by hand, right next to the Beit el-Suhaymi.

With its many magnificent mosques Cairo is recognized as the centre of Sunni Islam. In the courtyard of el-Azhar (above) the professors still sit in wooden chairs to teach as they have done for centuries. The Sultan Hassan Mosque (below) is one of the showpieces of the Mameluke period. The picture shows its central courtyard and the well for washing.

It is still possible to track down two or three old-fashioned perfume shops, where the essences are sold pure and not mixed with alcohol or olive oil, as they are elsewhere, and their owners grow their products on their own flower farms in Fayum on the Delta. Around el-Azhar, university bookbinders, engravers and calligraphers offer their work for sale. In a narrow street behind the Bab el-Futuh, just next to the cemetery where ibn-Khaldun is said to be buried, three glass-blowers still make the famous opaque Muski glass. In the Suq el-Nahassin, the smiths are hammering out the tops of minarets and the huge copper pots used to cook *ful*, the national dish. The spice souq has not lost its bewitching aroma and the painstaking *mashrabiya* work is now being revived. In the Khan el-Khalili, most of the 'antique' cast bronzes, coins and scarabs are forgeries, delivered newly made from the factory, and old papyrus drawings turn out on closer inspection to be painted banana leaves. But it is still possible to come across 'characters'. Mahmoud Hamdy, for instance, one of the last foot ironers, pressing suits and dresses eight hours a day with a glowing 15-kilogram (33-pound) iron. There are also the makers of prayer chains, who model the beads individually from amber, using their feet. Or the Assil brothers who, following in the footsteps of their great-grandfather, embroidered Koranic verses on the brocade cloth covering the Kaaba in Mecca.

The el-Hakim Mosque at the northern edge of the old city (above) was completely renovated with private funds in the early 1990s. It was built by the Fatimid el-Hakim who, although revered by the Druzes of Lebanon as the highest incarnation of God, was reputed to be cruel and eccentric. Below: the reception room of the Beit el-Kritiliya, also known as the Gayer Anderson Museum.

Even the areas outside the Fatimid city centre are hives of industry where the old traditions are kept alive. Anyone who has seen the lute makers' workshops in Shari Mohamed Ali or the potters' kilns in Fustat, the Sunday pigeon market below the citadel, the curious auto-spares market in Bulaq or the camel market out in Imbaba will agree: not only does Cairo have an enormous bazaar, the whole city is an enormous bazaar.

دمشق

Damascus

At first sight Damascus, capital of the Arab Republic of Syria, has a great deal in common with Aleppo in the north. Both are about 100 kilometres (60 miles) from the Mediterranean coast, where agricultural land meets nomad territory. Both have always been equally important trading stations in international caravan traffic. In their thousands of years of history both have frequently been shaken by earthquakes and depopulated by epidemics, occupied, plundered or burned down, but they have risen again like a phoenix from the ashes and remain the embodiment of urban culture. Both have outlasted many powerful competitors – Aleppo, for instance, the ancient settlements of Antioch, Seleucia, Apamea and Qinnesrin; Damascus, in turn, Petra, Bosra and Palmyra.

But in spite of – or perhaps because of – these similarities, the relationship between the inhabitants of the two cities has never been an easy one. The Syrians have a saying that the people of Aleppo speak like men, the people of Damascus like women. The Damascenes take this to mean that their northern neighbours are slow and uncultured. In Aleppo they retaliate by saying that people in Damascus are lazy. There are reasons for this perennial jealousy: for centuries Aleppo

Scenes from one of the most ancient cities in the world. In the picturesque streets of the Qaimarriyeh district (right) time has virtually stood still. The centuries-old clay and poplar-wood balconies still survive. Even the view of the Souq al-Bzouriyeh (left) could – at first sight at least – date from a much earlier period. However, the main street in the bazaar district which used to be the Street called Straight (opposite) has been radically altered. The tin roof was built around 1870. The holes were made by stones and bullets.

Construction of the Omayyad Mosque on the site of an ancient temple district began in 705. It replaced a Christian basilica, a relic of which was preserved in the old lookout towers converted to the first minarets for the new religion. The head of John the Baptist was buried in a shrine in the middle of the prayer hall (above).

was economically more successful, but politically, intellectually and artistically (at least until after the Islamic conquest) it was nearly always overshadowed by its rival.

As the seat of government of the Omayyad caliphs, Damascus (in Arabic Dimashq ash-Sham) was already the centre of a world empire in the 7th century. Nur ad-Din (Nuredin) and Salah ad-Din (Saladin) used it as a residence and base for their fight against the Crusaders and 800 years later it was a local capital for the Arab nationalists, from which they organized their resistance against the Ottoman, British and French occupiers. Damascus was – and to some extent still is – a centre for exquisite craftsmanship and luxury goods. The old quarter of the city, under UNESCO protection, has largely escaped the destructive effects of progress. In the narrow streets of the Qaimarriyeh district many of the traditional half-timbered clay and poplar-wood houses have survived.

The city also has religious significance. According to Sunni tradition, ash-Sham

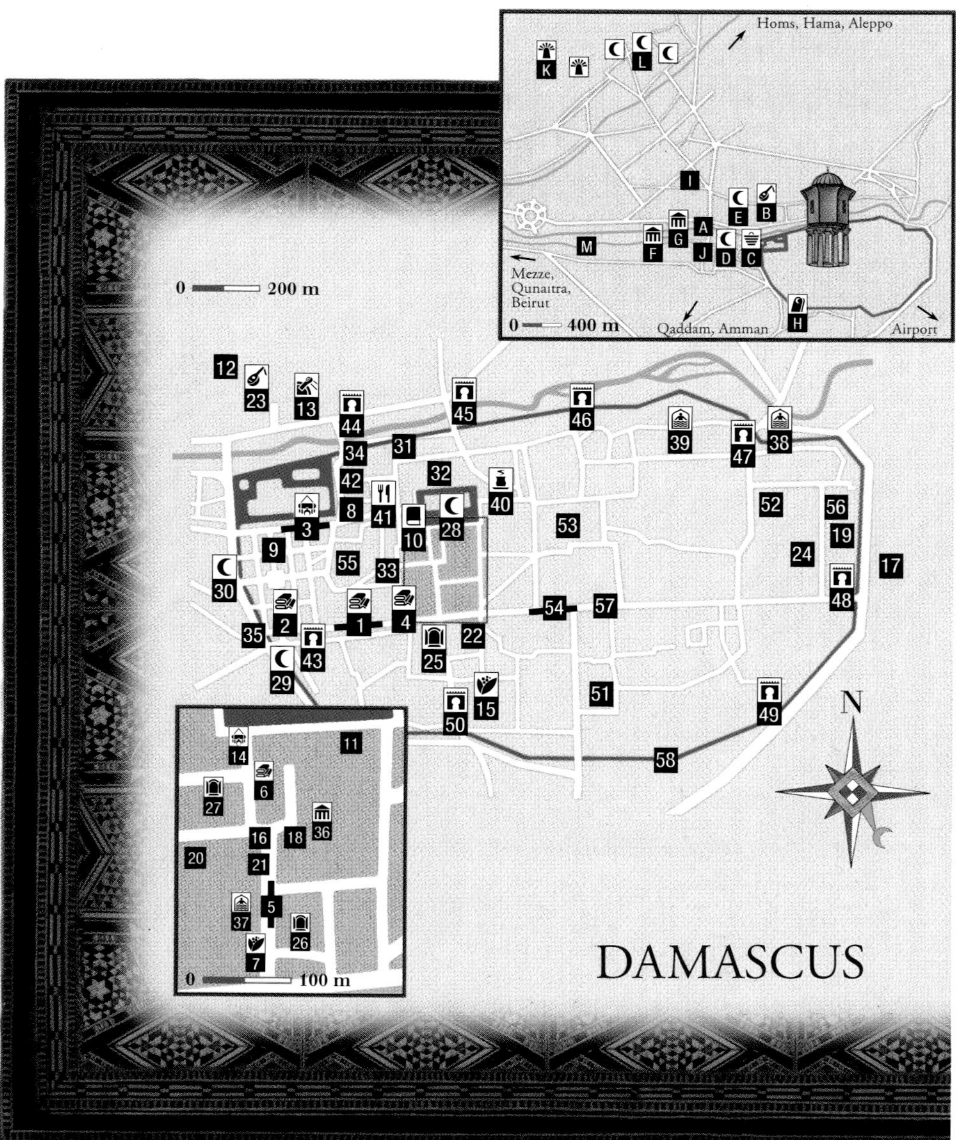

Damascus – general view
*MARKETS: **A** Craft souq (including glass-blowing) in the former al-Selimiyeh caravanserai, **B** Souq Suruiyeh (general goods, lute makers), **C** Food market. MOSQUES: **D** Tinkiz, **E** Yelbogha. MUSEUMS: **F** National Museum, **G** Military Museum. OTHER: **H** Bab as-Saghir cemetery (with Fatima's tomb), **I** Parliament, **J** Hejaz railway station, **K** Jebel Qasyun, **L** Salhiyeh, **M** River Barada.*

Old city
*SEPARATE MARKETS: **1** Souq Madhat Pasha (textiles, wool), **2** al-Kumeileh (secondhand textiles), **3** al-Hamidiyeh (textiles, jewelry), **4** al-Hayyatin (textiles, tailors), **5** al-Bzouriyeh (confectionery), **6** an-Niswan (women's jewelry, fabrics and clothing market), **7** al-Attarin (perfumes, spices), **8** al-Asrounieh (household goods), **9** al-Arrawan (furniture, flea market) **10** al-Miskiyeh (books), **11** al-Abbabiyeh (wooden articles), **12** al-Khunya (formerly the pilgrim market outside the citadel; general goods, leather accessories), **13** an-Nahassin (copper, leather), **14** as-Sagha (gold jewelry, **15** Shagour district (wholesale grains and spices). SPECIALIST WORKSHOPS AND SHOPS: **16** Dr Mounif O. Aidi (folk remedies), **17** Abu Ahmed (glass-blowing), **18** Dahdoub (antiques), **19** Khalil Daye (antiques), **20** Azem School (antiques), **21** Ghraoui (cakes), **22** Daud Kahale (swords), **23** Oud (lute) makers, **24** Various wood inlay shops (Hanania Street). CARAVANSERAIS: **25** Khan Suleiman Pasha, **26** Khan Asad Pasha, **27** Khan al-Harir. MOSQUES: **28** Omayyad Mosque, **29** Sinan Pasha, **30** Darwish Pasha. KORANIC SCHOOLS AND MAUSOLEUMS: **31** az-Zahiriya (Baibars' tomb), **32** Saladin's tomb, **33** an-Nuriya, **34** al-Adiliyeh, **35** Sibalya. MUSEUMS: **36** Arts and Popular Traditions (Azem Palace). BATHS: **37** Nur ad-Din, **38** as-Saher, **39** Bakri. RESTAURANTS, TEA AND COFFEE HOUSES: **40** Noufara, **41** Abul Ez, **42** Old Damascus. CITY GATES: **43** al-Jabiyeh, **44** al-Faraj, **45** al-Faradis, **46** as-Salaam, **47** Touma, **48** Sharqi, **49** Kaysan, **50** as-Saghir. OTHER: **50** Haret el-Yahoud (Jewish quarter), **52** Bab Touma (Christian quarter), **53** Qaimarriyeh district, **54** Madhat Pasha/Bab Sharqi street (formerly the Street called Straight/Via Recta), **55** Bimaristan Nur ad-Din (old hospital), **56** Ananias chapel, **57** Roman archway, **58** City wall.*

BORDER: Damascene wood mosaic on a jewelry casket. ILLUSTRATION: Treasure house in the courtyard of the Omayyad Mosque.

For general key see page 146.

(together with Kairouan) is the fourth most holy city in Islam after Mecca, Medina and Jerusalem. Abraham is said to have born there and it is where Moses was buried. It is the place where Saul became Paul. The Archangel Gabriel is said to have appeared in a cave on the neighbouring mountain, Jebel Qasyun; the Virgin Mary took refuge in another. The mausoleums of several of the Prophet Mohammed's close companions are in the suburb of Salhiyeh. The head of John the Baptist rests in the Omayyad mosque and it is prophesied that at the end of time Jesus will come down to its oldest minaret, the 'white' minaret, to slay ad-Dadjal, the antichrist.

One reason why the city is regarded as holy is its unusually favourable location. It is situated at the edge of a huge, cool and shady oasis, the Ghuta, and supplied with fresh water from the River Barada all year round. Damascus was extolled by poets as *al-Fayha*, the fragrant, diamond of the desert, bride of the earth, mother of all cities. It was always compared in old works to the Garden of Eden. Even Mohammed himself, reaching what is now the suburb of Qaddam on one of his journeys, refused to go on when he saw the orchards and canals, not wanting to enter an earthly paradise before reaching the heavenly one.

The recently restored Khan Asad Pasha (below) is one of the most splendid commercial buildings in the Islamic world. Four pillars divide its square courtyard into nine domed areas. Above: a state-room in the Azem Palace (see overleaf).

The many layers of the past can still be seen in the modern structure of the city and its souq. The Romans had their temple of Jupiter (of which the well-maintained west tower and the monumental surrounding wall in the south-west corner are relics) where the Omayyad mosque now stands. The remains of the early Islamic ring of fortresses and the present eight gates correspond to the ancient city layout. The route of the central shopping street, the *Via Recta* or the Street called Straight, has not changed since Roman times. It has been widened by 26 metres (85 feet) and is now lined with shops and businesses instead of pillared arcades, an amphitheatre and the governor's palace. Today it is known as Madhat Pasha or Bab Sharqi Street and the western part is divided into two parallel streets, a textile and a wool market. But it still divides the whole of the old quarter from west to east for over a kilometre (1,100 yards) and the streets are laid out at right angles in the old way.

In fact, the real centre of the market shifted to the area around the citadel in the Middle Ages. First of all the horse dealers moved. Under the Mamelukes they were joined by gunsmiths, cloth and clothing makers – trades which drew their customers from the army stationed nearby.

In the second half of the 19th century the western part of the bazaar was extensively modernized. Rows of shops with display windows and metal doors and a continuous upper storey for workshops and offices were built on either side of its main street, the Souq al-Hamidiyeh, and later (in 1873) the corrugated-iron roof with steel cross-beams which Syrians like to compare with the Galleria built in the same year by King Victor Emmanuel II in Milan. Since then the architecture has reflected the type of goods on sale: the bazaars at the foot of the citadel cater mainly for tourists and the rural population with tasteless souvenirs and ready-made clothes, cheap jewelry and plastic. The only exception is the Souq al-Miskiyeh, the book bazaar, at the eastern end of the street, where academics, students and imams browse through the political works, novels and Korans, especially on Friday afternoons.

The traditional trades and most of the magnificent old caravanserais are found in the narrow intersecting streets between al-Hamidiyeh and Madhat Pasha. In the Souq al-Bzouriyeh, for instance, there is a dispensary where aged healers buy the most obscure ingredients for their mysterious mixtures. In the old-established Confiserie Ghraoui next door, sinfully sweet home-made chocolates, sweets and candied fruits are still displayed in dusty mirrored windows and *mlebbas* (sugared almonds) are handed out to passers-by from sacks outside on the street. In the neighbouring perfume shops bottles of real rosewater from the suburb of Mezze can still be seen amongst the metal containers for synthetic fragrances. Three families have remained loyal to Damascus's most famous craft, sword making (although only one now knows how to repair the really valuable old swords). Sitting at a wooden loom in what used to be the Azem Koranic school, one last elderly man still occasionally weaves the legendary silk brocade.

Outside the central market area, some craftsmen have managed to hold their own against the avalanche of mass-produced industrial goods. A few of the couple of hundred people who still live in the Jewish quarter (Haret al-Yahoud), despite being given official permission to emigrate in 1992, continue to produce the typical copper vessels with silver and brass damascening. Wooden caskets with coloured veneer mosaics, cabinets, chairs, coffee tables and Koran stands with wafer-thin layers of mother-of-pearl are still made in the Christian quarter, Bab Touma. Two traditional glass-blowers are

Muslims regard the Omayyad Mosque as the fourth holiest site in the world after Mecca, Medina and the Dome of the Rock in Jerusalem. The main façades in the inner courtyard – above: an arcade – and the octagonal treasure house (below) are covered with magnificent mosaics. The Azem Palace (Kasr al-Azem), built in the mid-18th century (opposite), is the finest example of Damascene domestic architecture.

still working not far from the Bab Sharqi and near the Tekkiyeh, the mosque and resthouse for pilgrims designed by the great architect Sinan. Some 3 kilometres (2 miles) outside the city, on the road to Homs, stonemasons still carve the jigsaw pieces for the traditional stone intarsia work from different-coloured blocks of marble.

But anyone wanting to get an idea of the quality of products from the golden age of Damascene arts and crafts, the time when local artists helped decorate the Taj Mahal, the palaces and mosques of Constantinople, Isfahan and Samarkand, should visit the palace of the former Ottoman governor Asad al-Azem, which since 1952 has housed the Museum of the Arts and Popular Traditions of Syria.

Sunset over the Anti-Lebanon Mountains (the Jebel Qasyun). At this time the bazaar offers particularly good bargains because there is an unwritten law that the last customer of the day has to be given a special discount. Above: the clothes market at the western end of the Souq Madhat Pasha.

Aleppo

Many cities, especially in the Middle East, claim to be the oldest and most continuously inhabited in the world, but few have such a well-founded claim as Aleppo. Archaeologists believe there to have been a permanent settlement in, or even before, the 4th millennium BC on the same steep rocks on which the citadel stands today. Documents show that Aleppo had already become the seat of an independent kingdom around 1800 BC, about a thousand years before the founding of Rome and Byzantium. It was called Halab, which is still its Arabic name today. Its exposed position on a strategically important fortress hill, on the borders of several large empires, meant that the city's early years were very turbulent; it was conquered in turn by the Hurrites and Hittites and later by the Assyrians, Persians

The impregnable citadel of Aleppo, built in the early 13th century by Saladin's son Sultan Ghazi. Only the Mongols ever managed to storm it. The ruins on the 55-metre (180-foot) hill date from various periods and include the Ayyubid gateway (opposite) with the contrasting colours that are so typical of Syrian stonemasonry.

Both the outside and the inside of the Omayyad Mosque in Aleppo (above: the inner courtyard) are modelled on its namesake in Damascus, but after the massive destruction in the 12th and 13th centuries its original design was radically altered in the Mameluke period.

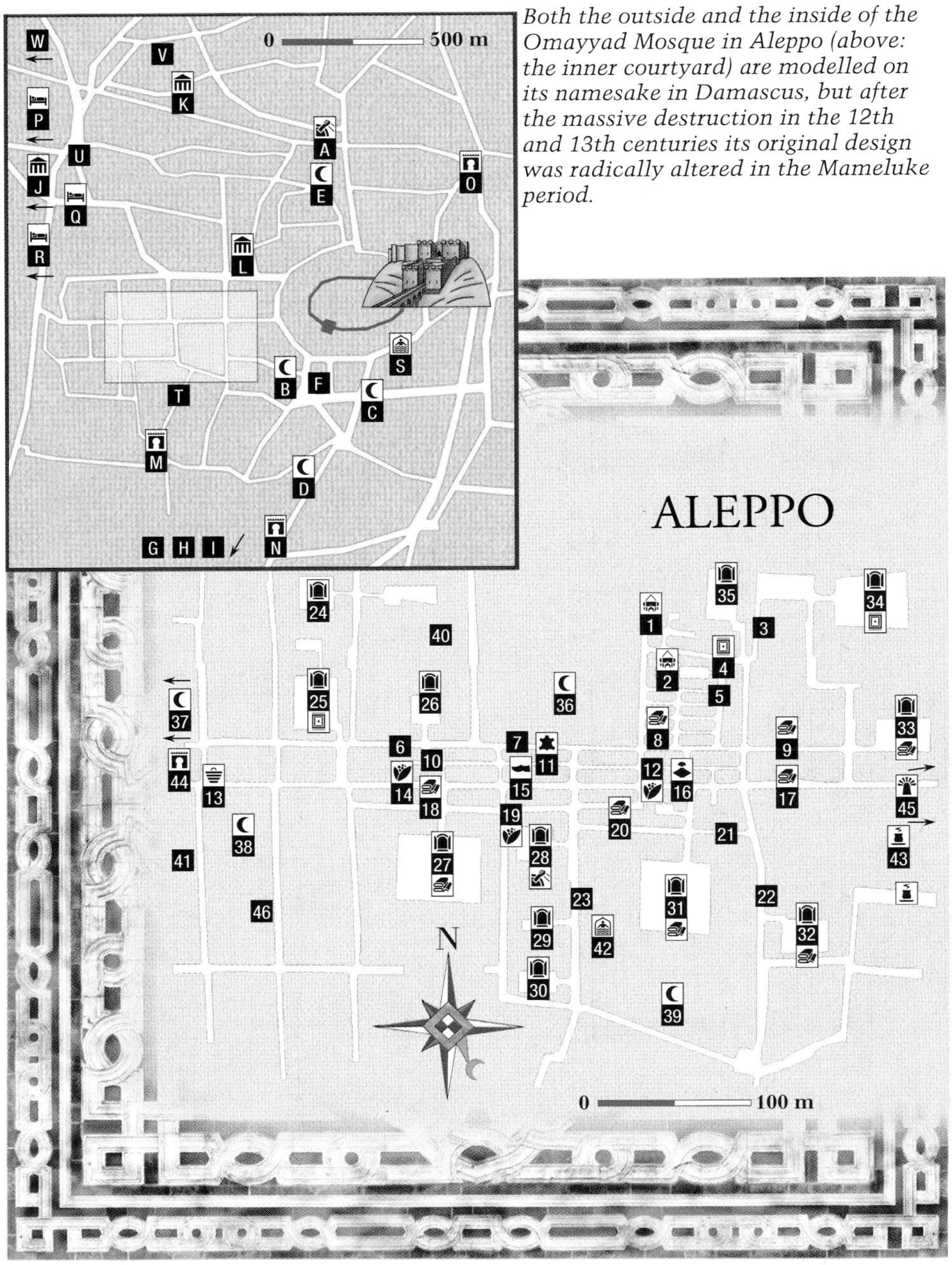

and Seleucids, partly destroyed and then rebuilt. It was only under the Romans that peace was restored. It is to them that the city owes the right-angled layout which can still be seen today, and also a phase of prosperity and the building of the first large market with colonnaded streets and an *agora*.

After the Arab conquest the Omayyads built their Great Mosque on the *agora* and immediately beside it the covered markets (*qaiseriyas*) which ibn-Battuta described six centuries later as the finest and biggest he had ever seen. The early years under Islam were not entirely without incident. The city was destroyed several times (by the Byzantine Nicephorus Phocas in 962 among others) but there were brief periods in which culture flourished. On the whole, however, it remained deeply provincial. It was only under Nuredin and Saladin, the legendary opponents of the Crusaders, and Saladin's son, the Ayyubid Sultan Ghazi, that it began to develop. They turned the citadels into a unique fortification with moats, glacis and a magnificent residence, set up Koranic schools and Sufi convents and boosted trade

ALEPPO

Aleppo – general view

*MARKET: **A** Souq an-Nahaseen (copper and brass). MOSQUES: **B** Khosrofieh, **C** Otrosh, **D** Tawashi, **E** Osman Pasha. KORANIC SCHOOLS: **F** Sultaniyeh, **G** Firdausi, **H** Zahiriyeh, **I** Kamiliyeh. MUSEUMS: **J** National Museum, **K** Folklore Museum (Beit Ajiqbash), **L** Arts and Popular Traditions. CITY GATES: **M** Qinnesrin, **N** al-Maqam, **O** al-Hadid. HOTELS: **P** Baron, **Q** Amir Palace, **R** Khahba Kham Palace. BATHS: **S** Hammam an-Nasri (formerly Lababidiyeh). OTHER: **T** Bimaristan Argon (old hospital), **U** Clock tower, **V** al-Jdaideh (Christian quarter), **W** Park.*

Central souqs

*SEPARATE MARKETS: **1** Souq al-Jedid ('the new'/gold and silver), **2** Stambul (gold and silver), **3** as-Sabun (soap), **4** al-Haraj (carpets), **5** al-Wazir (tablecloths), **6** al-Junfas (camel-hair bags), **7** al-Hibal (ropes), **8** at-Tabush (ladies' clothing), **9** al-Ibi (fabrics, winter clothes), **10** al-Haur (firewood), **11** al-Itaqiya (leather), **12** ad-Dra (corn), **13** al-Bahramiya (food), **14** as-Saqatiya, **15** al-Batiya (shoes), **16** al-Attarin (perfumes), **17** az-Zarb (fabrics, hats, cotton), **18** al-Gumruk (raw silk, cotton), **19** al-Han (henna), **20** al-Juh (cloth), **21** al-Hammam (bathing utensils), **22** al-Qutn (cotton), **23** al-Mahmas (seeds, pistachios). CARAVANSERAIS: **24** al-Harir (silk), **25** al-Qasabia (carpets, kilims), **26** al-Hibal (ropes), **27** al-Gumruk (cotton and silk), **28** an-Nahaseen (copper), **29** al-Burghul (wheatmeal), **30** al-Abasi (pistachios), **31** al-Alabiya (winter clothing), **32** al-Farrayin (wool), **33** Hair Bak (headscarves), **34** al-Wazir (craft work, carpets), **35** as-Sabun (soap). MOSQUES: **36** Omayyad, **37** Mulberry Tree, **38** al-Bahramiah, **39** al-Adliah. KORANIC SCHOOLS: **40** Halawiah, **41** Mokadammiya. BATHS: **42** Hammam an-Nahaseen. TEA AND COFFEE HOUSES: **43** al-Ahram and al-Attar. OTHER: **44** Bab Antakya (city gate), **45** Citadel, **46** Bimaristan Nur ad-Din (old hospital).*

BORDER: Stone decoration on the door of the Omayyad Mosque. ILLUSTRATION: Citadel.

or general key see page 146.

and business by enlarging the markets and signing a treaty with the Venetians giving them the right to settle in Aleppo (the Italianized form of Halab).

Twice between 1260 and 1400 the Mongols invaded northern Syria and laid waste to Aleppo. It also suffered devastating earthquakes, epidemics and internal unrest. But in the 15th century it experienced an economic upturn under the new Mameluke rulers. Antioch, which had overshadowed Aleppo since ancient times, was razed to the ground by Baibars' troops. By then Cilicia in Lesser Armenia and the Genoese trading stations on the Black Sea – which had both until recently been important staging posts between Europe and Persia – had ceased to exist. The starting point for caravans from east and west was now Aleppo. Within a few generations its population grew to nearly 300,000. New suburbs, new markets and the first large *khans* grew up. A large parade ground was built below the citadel for the garrisons strengthened to protect the trade routes.

The old part of esh-Sheba, the grey city, in the evening light (below). For 700 years, from the time of the Crusaders to the end of the Ottoman Empire, it was at the intersection of several transcontinental trade routes. Its 12 kilometres (7½ miles) of covered souqs make up the largest bazaar in the world. The textile trade (above) is still the most important branch of the economy.

After the battle of Dabiq (1516) the whole of Syria fell under Ottoman rule. Aleppo became the capital of a *wilayat*, an imperial province, and soon, despite massive tax levies, the most important trading centre in the Levant. The political stability of the new empire and the improvements in goods traffic (eventually many borders disappeared and currency was simplified) soon attracted the European trading powers. Once again the Venetians were the leaders, this time in the diplomatic field, setting up a mission in 1548.

The boom also made its mark on the old souqs. Some time in the 15th or early 16th century their wooden roofs were replaced by the stone domes, barrel and groined vaults still seen today. But the finest monuments to this new prosperity were the huge complexes that sprang up south of the market's main street. Mostly financed by state officials from religious foundations (evidently the cost was beyond the guilds and even the richest individual traders), these complexes usually housed several wells, *khans*, markets and mosques.

Obviously Aleppo was not without its problems. The discovery of the sea route to India, the rise of the rival city of Izmir (Smyrna), and later on the building of the Suez Canal all had an impact on trade, as did domestic political crises such as the Turkish-Russian war. Aleppo was so closely bound up with world economic trends that it could not escape the repercussions of the closure of vital sea routes through the Mediterranean during the Napoleonic wars, a poor coffee harvest in Yemen, a gold rush in California or the failure of the monsoon in India. But despite these setbacks, it still managed to maintain its position as one of the main centres of world trade during the 400 years of Ottoman rule.

There are various reasons why Aleppo was so successful. One is undoubtedly its geographical location. The border between the settled agricultural land and the grazing grounds of the nomads has always run past the city's gates, where the fertile hilly coastal area merges into the barren flat steppes. It was the obvious place for the farmers to exchange their crops for the nomads' trade goods and a natural stopping point between the Mediterranean and the Middle East for transcontinental caravans.

Like Nablus, Aleppo is famous for its olive soap. The biggest factory is in what was once the French governor's residence (below). Huge vats of water, soda and olive oil are brought to the boil in the cellar. The resulting paste is pumped into large flat basins and after it has cooled and hardened it is cut into pieces with a kind of harrow, to which two children lend their weight. The finished bars of soap are stamped with the firm's emblem and stacked up to dry for several months. Six tons (25,000 bars) are produced daily. Opposite: the Hammam an-Nahaseen, one of the finest public baths in the city, is over 700 years old.

Another reason was the fertility of the surrounding land. The rainy north-west in particular is covered with vineyards, wheat and melon fields, almond, fig and pistachio plantations. Since the Middle Ages the acres of olive groves have supplied a flourishing local soap industry. The large-scale production of cotton, wool and silks soon made the place what it is today, the centre of the Syrian textile industry. Then there is the mentality of its inhabitants. In recent times the people of Aleppo have been far too cosmopolitan and entrepreneurial to take much interest in politics. On the whole they are not known for their religious or nationalistic fanaticism or even hostility to strangers. Quite the opposite, in fact: all the trading nations –

Greeks, Arabs, Armenians, Iraqis, Iranians and Indians – had colonies there. The Christians, and to a lesser extent the Jews, were particularly respected and prosperous. Both minorities proved themselves very useful as intermediaries between the Europeans, the locals and the Turkish authorities.

Probably because they are so hard-working, the people of Aleppo are often accused of not being interested in the finer and more spiritual aspects of life. At first sight this prejudice seems to be confirmed. *Esh-Sheba*, the grey, as Aleppo is called because of the pale limestone from which it is built, certainly does not look like a romantic city. Its monotonous sea of buildings nestles in bare, ochre-coloured hills, often covered with dust, and in the long summers the heat is pitiless. On its outskirts are huge factories and barracks. Since the Second World War, its historic centre has been drastically redeveloped and new streets built. Apart from the citadel, it seems to have few sights of interest to tourists and few really high-quality goods are made in its workshops, at least compared with Damascus.

Whirling dervishes in the courtyard of the old hospital, the Bimaristan Nur ad-Din, attract both locals and tourists. Opposite: the Souq al-Juh (cloth market).

But if this city is really as dull as it is reputed to be, how does it come to have so many idyllic little corners tucked away? Such places as the shady café al-Attar outside the entrance to the citadel or the an-Nasri and an-Nahaseen baths, which are hundreds of years old. How did such splendid palaces come to be built, like the one in al-Jdaideh, the Christian quarter? Why do Sufis still dance for a selected audience in the courtyard of the medieval Argon hospital in the evenings? And what about the wonderfully dilapidated colonial hotels like the Baron?

Above all, why do most wholesalers still market their goods through the old Ottoman *khans* and not through modern terminals? Probably because they know exactly what they would be losing if they left the bazaar.

اسطنبول

Istanbul

Whether under Persian or Roman rulers, Macedonians, Greeks, Crusaders or Ottomans, whether as Byzantium, Constantinople or Istanbul, since the beginning of its chequered history the 2,500-year-old city on the Golden Horn has always been one of the most important trade centres in the world.

We know from historians such as ibn-Battuta that Istanbul had covered markets used by various guilds as workshops and stores from very early times, but their exact location is still not clear. Were they, as some have claimed, down at the harbour opposite the Galata, the Genoese quarter? Were they along the old colonnaded main street, the precursor of the Divan Yolu Caddesi? Or were they, as the Byzantine stone relief of an eagle above the eastern gate of the old market seemed to suggest, where the Kapali Carsi stands today?

What is certain is that the conquest of the city by the Ottomans in 1453 ushered in a new economic era. Suddenly it became the centre of a world empire which would soon stretch from the slopes of the Alps to the Arabian desert, from the Atlas to the Sea of Azov. To keep pace with this economic expansion, Sultan Mohammed II ordered the construction of a *bedesten* in 1461. The Internal (Ic) or Jewelry (Cevahir) Bedesten, modelled on the large markets in the former Ottoman capitals of Edirne and Bursa, is still one of the most important parts of the bazaar. It covers an area of 1,300 square metres (14,000 square feet) and is topped with fifteen large and eight small domes. It originally contained 44 shops selling especially costly goods such as velvet, silk, weapons and precious stones and members of the public could keep their savings and valuables there. Its walls are over 1.5 metres (5 feet) thick, with massive iron gates on all four sides. Towards the end of his rule the Sultan had a second *bedesten* built, the Sandal Bedesten, named after a particularly fine silk satin made in Bursa. Its roof consists of twenty brick-red domes supported on massive pillars. It is almost as big as its older counterpart and was mainly used by textile traders. A network of right-angled side streets soon grew up around these two original buildings and around them was a ring of about thirty caravanserais. The Kapali Carsi, the covered market, was soon regarded throughout the world as the perfect example of a well-organized bazaar.

The Misir Carsisi, the Egyptian bazaar on the Golden Horn (opposite) sells mainly herbs, spices and dried fruit. It was built in 1660 by Hatice Sultan, mother of Mohammed IV, on the site of the old Venetian markets and for a long time imported most of its goods from Egypt – hence the name. After a disastrous fire in 1954, Istanbul's central bazaar, the Kapali Carsi, was drastically 'modernized'. The last wooden benches and shop windows were removed, walls and arches covered with cheap whitewashed stucco and glass and aluminium doors fitted. At least the worst excesses like neon and plexiglas signs were removed again in the eighties and the colourful plaster on the arches was restored (below).

For more than 400 years the market remained a fabulous microcosm of the immensely wealthy and cosmopolitan state. Time seemed to pass more slowly than in the outside world and it was extraordinarily tranquil. The shopkeepers sat in their niches, *dolaps*, reading the Koran or sucking on a water pipe. There were no guards. No one shouted out prices or bargained. Customers could taste and buy unmolested. The only noise was the warning cry of a *hammal* (porter) or a caravan leader driving his heavily laden horses or camels through the crowds. The buildings were similarly discreet and tasteful. There were no displays or shop windows, no signs or advertisements. The only decorations were mural paintings. The thick walls kept the place cool in summer and warm in winter. The adjoining streets were lined with shady trees and entwined with passion flowers and wild vines.

Curiously enough, the structure of the bazaar remained untouched by the

The Kapali Carsi (great covered bazaar) as seen by the muezzin *of the Nuruosmaniye Mosque. The market covers about 40 hectares (100 acres) and contains banks and baths, workshops and tombs, prayer, coffee and tea houses and more than 4,000 shops. About half a million people pass through its 18 gates every day. The Sandal and Ic* bedestens *stand out in the centre and foreground of the picture.*
Opposite: one of the innumerable cloth and leather traders.

vicissitudes of politics for many generations. There are no records of malicious damage or serious theft. The tranquillity was only disturbed by natural disasters. Fires were particularly frequent, hardly surprisingly since, until the beginning of the 18th century, most of the buildings were made of wood, partly for fear of earthquakes and partly because, in the old Turkish nomad tradition, housing was not expected to be permanent. The worst fire, in 1589, destroyed virtually the whole city. No fewer than 28 mosques, 22,000 houses and 15,000 shops were razed to the ground. The only major robbery was by the Janissaries in 1750. With hindsight it was a warning to the government, because soon afterwards the splendour of the Ottoman Empire (and with it the bazaar) began to fade. Military power waned, important provinces were lost. The flow of raw materials, young craftsmen and taxes began to dry up. At the same time the first wave of European manufactured goods poured into the country and with it the spirit of mercantilism. In its wake came the first profiteers and tourist touts.

ISTANBUL

Istanbul – general view of the old city
BAZAARS AND MARKETS: ***A*** *Great Covered Bazaar (Kapali Carsi),* ***B*** *Egyptian (spice) Bazaar (Misir Carsisi),* ***C*** *Artists' market (Cedid Mehmet Efendi Medresesi),* ***D*** *Art and craft bazaar (Soguk Cesme Medresesi),* ***E*** *Junk market (Külliye Beyazit). MOSQUES:* ***F*** *Suleyman Mosque (Süleymaniye Camii),* ***G*** *Hagia Sophia (Ayasofya Camii, a museum since 1934),* ***H*** *Blue Mosque (Sultanahmet Camii),* ***I*** *Beyazit Camii. WELLS, BATHS, CISTERNS:* ***J*** *'Sunken Palace' (Yerabatan Sarayi),* ***K*** *Cistern of the 1001 Columns (Binbirdirek),* ***L*** *Cagaloglu Hamami. MUSEUMS:* ***M*** *Topkapi Sarayi (+ harem),* ***N*** *Museum of Turkish and Islamic Art (Ibrahim Pasa Sarayi),* ***O*** *Carpet Museum (Hali Müzesi and Kilim ve Düz Dokuma Yaygilar Müzesi),* ***P*** *Calligraphy Museum (Hat Sanatlar Müzesi). RESTAURANT:* ***Q*** *Pandeli. STREET:* ***R*** *Divan Yolu Caddesi. OTHER:* ***S*** *University,* ***T*** *Galata,* ***U*** *Eminönü,* ***V*** *Laleli,* ***W*** *Golden Horn,* ***X*** *Bosporus.*

Kapali Carsi – Great Covered Bazaar
BAZAARS AND MARKETS: ***1*** *Sahaflar Carsisi (book bazaar),* ***2*** *Flea market (Bit Pazari). MOSQUES:* ***3*** *Nuruosmaniye Camii,* ***4*** *Mercan Aga Mescidi,* ***5*** *Ic Bedesten Mescidi. CARAVANSERAIS:* ***6*** *Valide Hani,* ***7*** *Büyük Yeni Hani,* ***8*** *Imameli Hani,* ***9*** *Astarci Hani,* ***10*** *Kalci Hani,* ***11*** *Zincirli Hani,* ***12*** *Cuhaci Hani. WELLS, BATHS, CISTERNS:* ***13*** *Örücüler Hamami,* ***14*** *Kürkcüler Hamami. RESTAURANTS, TEA AND COFFEE HOUSES:* ***15*** *Havuzlu Lokanta,* ***16*** *Cay Bahcesi,* ***17*** *Savk Kahvehanesi. STREETS:* ***18*** *Kalpakcilar Basi Caddesi,* ***19*** *Cadircilar Caddesi,* ***20*** *Mahmut Pasa Caddesi,* ***21*** *Yaglikcilar Caddesi. OTHER:* ***22*** *Sandal Bedesten,* ***23*** *Ic Bedesten.*

BORDER: Detail from the portico of the Rüstem Pasha Mosque.
ILLUSTRATION: Suleyman Mosque.

For general key see page 146.

Like most empires just before their final collapse, the Ottoman Empire then entered a final 'golden age'. Craftsmen and traders, demonstrating all their skills and aesthetic sensibility, turned the Kapali Carsi into a virtual museum with exhibits for sale. For Western Europeans the 500 weapon shops and 1,000 or so fabric shops were a wonderland. The Frenchman Albert Millaud said in 1873 that a single shopping tour was 'enough to bankrupt several Rothschild families'. Another French visitor, overwhelmed by the range of goods on offer, found it even more impressive than the Burlington Arcade in London and the Palais Royal in Paris, at the time considered the best shopping centres in the western world.

Eventually, however, the *fin de siècle* lived up to its name. The famous bazaar degenerated. The prosperous traders, with their deep roots in tradition, moved in increasing numbers to Eminönü or Beyoglu to open up near the new businesses and banks. The people who replaced them were only interested in money; frauds and extortion became widespread. Then in 1894 there was a devastating earthquake which left huge gaps among the buildings. The two Balkan Wars (1912/1913) were the *coup de grâce* for the economy. The guild system collapsed and with it the whole social order. The Sandal Bedesten, which had long since become an ordinary store, was sold to the local council and since then has been used for carpet auctions.

During the First World War the Kapali Carsi was a depressing sight, with its deserted, crumbling streets lit by makeshift bare oil lamps and its impoverished shopkeepers. All its past elegance had disappeared. Of the 1,001 guilds that had existed in the 17th century only a handful remained. All the turban makers, bow and arrow makers, faith healers, hashish and opium dealers had gone. So too had the slave traders who had auctioned their live goods in the Ic Bedesten until this was banned by Sultan Abdülmecid in 1847.

It was not until the 1950s that the bazaar began to undergo a renaissance. Turkey, now a republic, was enjoying an economic boom and people were flocking to the city from the rural areas. Between 1920 and 1992 Istanbul's population rose from half a million to twelve million or more. For the Kapali Carsi the effects were catastrophic. The last old wooden benches and chests were replaced by formica or aluminium. The already tiny shops were divided into shoebox-sized units with glass windows, the finely decorated street arches whitewashed over and covered with hundreds of garish plexiglas advertising signs – although these were removed again in the eighties. The old bazaar was flooded with mass-produced goods and crowds of people. These days it has about half a million visitors a day, twice as many on public holidays, and the number is growing all the time. Since the collapse of the Soviet Union, black marketeers from Kazakhstan, Uzbekistan and other former Soviet republics with ethnic Turkic populations have picked on Istanbul as the best place to buy goods. Huge cheap markets have sprung up around the bazaar, extending as far as Laleli and Eminönü.

The Sultanahmet Camii or Blue Mosque was built opposite Hagia Sophia (which is over a thousand years older) between 1609 and 1616. The mosque is one of the masterpieces of Ottoman religious architecture. Its exterior (opposite), crowned by six minarets, is a perfect combination of half-domes, domes and flying buttresses. The prayer hall (above: chandeliers and minbar*) is of an impressive size. The dome, for instance, is 23.5 metres (77 feet) in diameter and 43 metres (141 feet) high. The tomb of Sultan Selim II was designed by Sinan, the most gifted of the Ottoman architects (below: the entrance door).*

But in this sea of kitchen utensils, imitation-leather bags and jeans a few islands of good taste still stand out. The Zincirli Hani, for instance, in the north-east corner of the bazaar, still has exquisite carpet and antique shops and many shop windows in the Sandal Bedesten display artistically carved meerschaum pipes. The Misir Carsisi, the Egyptian bazaar below the Golden Horn, is still full of the captivating scents of herbs and exotic spices, as it always has been. Hand-marbled paper and the cymbals well known amongst

اسطنبول

percussionists are now being made again in a few workshops. Even now some shops in the Sahaflar Carsisi, the picturesque book bazaar, are used as an unofficial meeting place by Sufi mystics. In the shadow of the adjoining Beyazit mosque old men and students from the nearby university drink their apple tea in a leisurely fashion from tulip-shaped glasses.

But it is almost entirely due to gold that, towards the end of the 20th century, the Kapali Carsi has again become the true commercial heart of the city. A survey in the late eighties revealed that nearly 100 tons of gold were sold in the bazaar every year and that much of it is smuggled across the Turkish border in exchange for oil, sheep or opium. More than half the 4,000 shop-owners earn their living directly or indirectly from gold: the jewellers on the Kalpakcilar Basi Caddesi, the main street of the jewelry bazaar, the goldsmiths in their workshops and the modern-day alchemists tucked away in back yards who check the pure gold content with silver, tin and nitric acid. The fact that the most successful trade is carried on behind the most discreet façades in order not to arouse the suspicions of the tax authorities has nothing to do with declining business ethics since the two world wars. It is a tradition whose roots go back to the Byzantine era.

Meerschaum pipes (below) are a speciality of the Istanbul bazaar. The soft, white, porous raw mineral is mined around the town of Eskisehir in western Anatolia. Being easy to carve, it is often made into jewelry, cigarette holders and pipe bowls. Opposite: evening on the Golden Horn, with the Atatürk bridge in the background. Above: a shop in the Misir Carsisi, part sweet shop and part chemist's shop.

صنعاء

Sanaa

Even as the plane comes in to land, you can see how extraordinary the 'Pearl of Arabia' is. Spread out beneath you are more than 6,000 tall 'gingerbread' houses and more than 100 minarets and domes, nestling in a high-lying rocky but fertile valley and framed by the deeply fissured mountains, Jabal Nuqqum (2,900 m/9,500 ft) and Jabal Ayban (3,200 m/10,500 ft). Looking down, you can see the old citadel, the al-Qasr; the central square, Maydan at-Tahrir; and next to it al-Mutawakkil, where the palace used to be. You can see the *maqshamah*, the vegetable gardens, the square of the Great Friday Mosque and, not far away, the dried-up bed of the Wadi as-Saila, which only turns into a river in the spring and summer rainy periods. You might even be able to see the two parts of the original town centre, to the west the suburbs with

The capital of Yemen, 'the beautifully built', lives up to its name. The houses, up to nine storeys (about 50 metres or 165 feet) high, are of natural stone and brick. On closer examination, pre-Islamic motifs can be found in many of the elaborate plaster and stucco decorations.

*Opposite top: the silver (or tin) curved dagger (*jambiya*) is to a Yemeni what a necktie is to a European, although outside the big towns the machine gun has for some time now rivalled it as a symbol of manhood.*
Opposite centre: blind, arthritic camels can still be seen turning ancient sesame mills in dim vaults near the Bab al-Yaman.
Opposite bottom: night market behind the Bab al-Yaman.

what used to be the Turkish and Jewish quarters, to the east the old town with the ruins of the walls which enclosed the whole city until thirty years ago, the Bab al-Yaman, the last of the four city gates, and immediately behind it the low buildings of the market.

Sanaa, a fortified town which, according to legend, was founded by Noah's son Shem, has always been vitally important to the Yemenis. With its favourable geographical position and its strong protective walls, it was predestined from early on to be a *mahram*, a hallowed and neutral place in which the farmers and warriors from the mountain tribes, often engaged in bloody feuds, could meet unarmed. Even today it is forbidden to carry weapons in the city and the government has posted soldiers on the approach roads to take pistols and rifles into safekeeping. At the same time Sanaa was a particularly coveted strategic target, lying as it did at the point where the territory of the Zaidites, a Shiite sect whose imams ruled the mountain villages of the north, bordered on the territory of the Ottoman and later Egyptian occupiers further to the south.

Because of the frequent fighting and pillaging, few of the buildings that remain are more than two or three hundred years old, but the atmosphere in the labyrinth of small streets is still medieval. Immediately behind the Bab al-Yaman, to which even nowadays the police nail the hands cut off thieves as a deterrent, deaf and

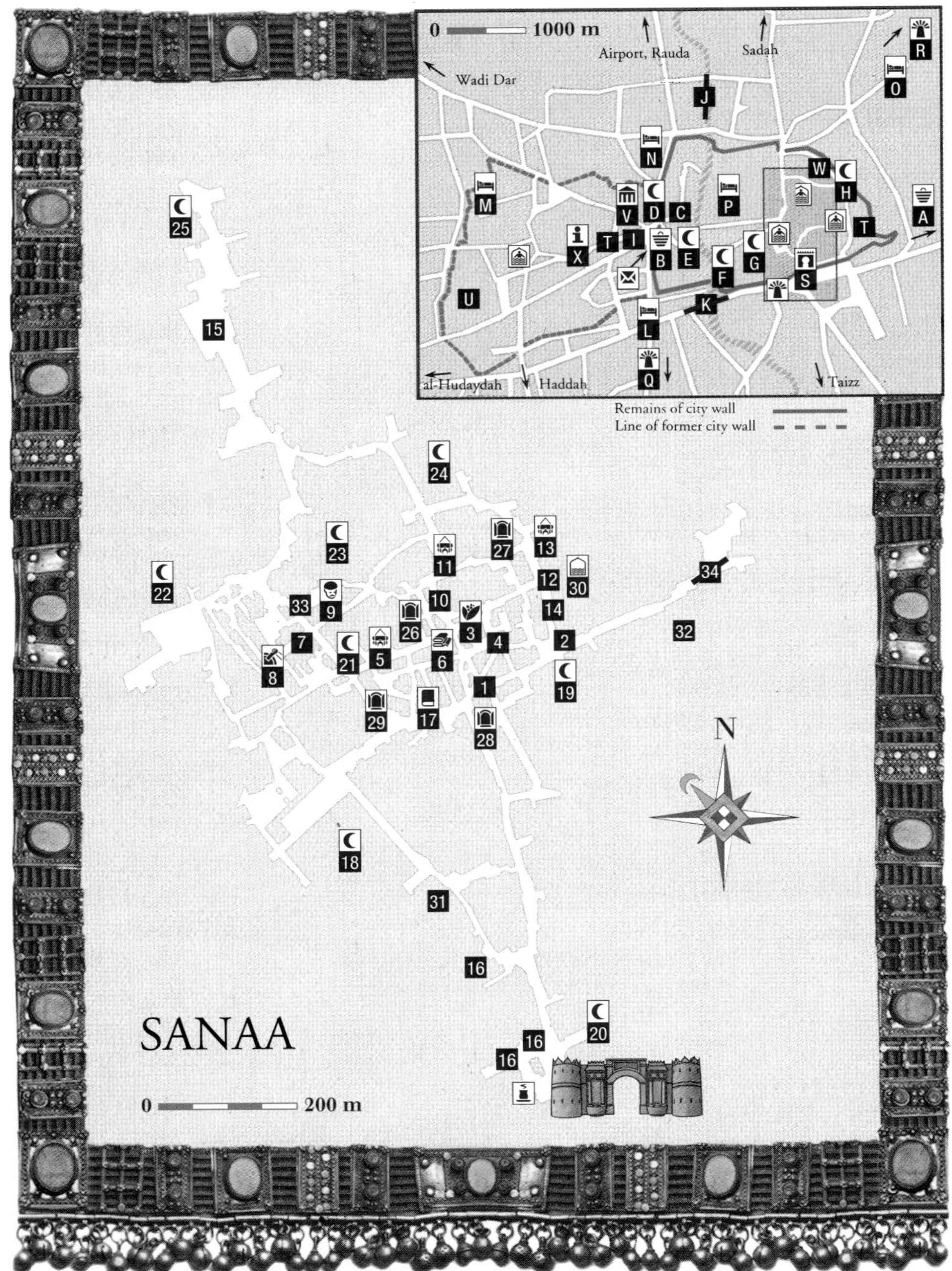

Sanaa – general view
BAZAARS AND MARKETS: ***A*** *Suq Nuqum (qat, food),* ***B*** *Vegetable market,* ***C*** *Fish market. MOSQUES AND MAUSOLEUMS:* ***D*** *Mutawakkil,* ***E*** *Qubbat al-Mahdi Abbas,* ***F*** *Barum,* ***G*** *Abhar,* ***H*** *al-Bakiriya. STREETS:* ***I*** *Maydan at-Tahrir,* ***J*** *as-Saila,* ***K*** *az-Zubayri. HOTELS:* ***L*** *Sheba,* ***M*** *Dar al-Hamd,* ***N*** *Sam City,* ***O*** *Sheraton,* ***P*** *al-Gasmy. VIEWPOINTS:* ***Q*** *Chinese Pavilion,* ***R*** *Ring road. OTHER:* ***S*** *Bab al-Yaman (city gate),* ***T*** *al-Qasr (citadel),* ***U*** *al-Qaal-Ulufi (former Jewish quarter),* ***V*** *National Museum (Dar as-Saada),* ***W*** *Draw wells (back of al-Bakiriya Mosque),* ***X*** *Logo-Info Tourist Corporation (tourist office).*

Market district
SEPARATE MARKETS: ***1*** *Suq al-Milh (miscellaneous goods, formerly the salt market),* ***2*** *al-Khobs (food),* ***3*** *al-Helbeh w al-Milh (spice market),* ***4*** *al-Habb (grain market),* ***5*** *al-Janabi (curved daggers),* ***6*** *al-Bezz (fabrics),* ***7*** *an-Naggarin (carpenters),* ***8*** *al-Haddadin (ironsmiths),* ***9*** *al-Qavafi (cap makers),* ***10*** *al-Qasib (water pipes),* ***11*** *al-Mubsata (clocks, radios, curved daggers),* ***12*** *al-Misbaga (*plangi *[veil] dyers),* ***13*** *al-Fidda (silversmiths),* ***14*** *al-Qat (*qat*),* ***15*** *az-Zumr (miscellaneous shops). SPECIALIST WORKSHOPS AND SHOPS:* ***16*** *Sesame mills,* ***17*** *Bookbinders. MOSQUES:* ***18*** *Jame al-Kabir (Great Friday Mosque),* ***19*** *al-Madhab,* ***20*** *ar-Radwan,* ***21*** *Ali,* ***22*** *Mahmud,* ***23*** *Shahidayn,* ***24*** *al-Akil,* ***25*** *az-Zumur. CARAVANSERAIS:* ***26*** *Samsarah Mohammed bin Hassan (formerly the money depository),* ***27*** *al-Mizzan,* ***28*** *an-Nahas (craft centre),* ***29*** *al-Mansuriyah (artists' studios). WELLS AND BATHS:* ***30*** *Bayt as-Serbeh (drinking water). OTHER:* ***31*** *House of Manuscripts,* ***32*** *(Foundations of) al-Qaliz cathedral,* ***33*** *'Limping Donkey' Square. STREET:* ***34*** *Maydan al-Laqiya.*

BORDER: Woman's silver belt from the Sanaa area.
ILLUSTRATION: Bab al-Yaman.

For general key see page 146.

blind camels turn the heavy millstones of sesame mills in cobwebbed vaults. The food stalls in the Suq al-Khobs serve sheep's-head soup in earthenware bowls and *jerras*, roast grasshoppers. Next door, in the Suq al-Qat, people argue vociferously over the choicest bundles of freshly delivered *qat*, the leaves which Yemenis chew every afternoon for their intoxicating effect. In the chemists' market (right next to the spice market) incense is heaped up amongst thousands of other exotic substances. In the silver market the traders squat in their dim shops, their cheeks bulging with *qat*, behind mountains of curved daggers, belts, rings, chains and the Maria Theresa thalers which smugglers in the north use to pay for refrigerators, video recorders and cassettes from Saudi Arabia. In the shadow of the tall houses herds of sheep and goats wander about next to the ubiquitous little Toyotas. Many shops are not locked at night and the *harasahs*, the watchmen, sit up on the roofs of the shops as they have always done, making sure that no one breaks the law against entering the market area between the evening prayers and dawn.

Even so, anyone who remembers Sanaa before 1962, when the civil war broke out, has good reason to deplore the changes. Before then the arch-conservative imams feared and reviled the rest of the world and the country was kept in isolation. After the victory of the republicans (1970), the old values began to decline and with them the buildings. The capital became a modern administrative centre, attracting more and more people from the provinces. Soon it had a population of 500,000, ten times as many as before the war. As cheap imported goods and heavy traffic flooded the city, the streets were blocked by discarded plastic and wrecked cars. Many families built themselves new concrete houses on the outskirts of town with money from their relatives working in the Gulf States. The splendid but inconvenient houses in the old town increasingly stood empty. The few that were modernized were undermined by water from leaking PVC pipes and collapsed.

However, Sanaa's decline seems to have been halted. The guilds have lost their influence since the national chamber of commerce replaced the ancient assembly of traders in 1963 and the system of self-

government in the residential districts has become less important. Even so, the locals still prefer to do their shopping in the bazaar rather than in the shiny chrome shops in the newer part of town. Men still wear their status symbol, the richly decorated curved dagger (*jambiya*) just as proudly. The old social hierarchy has not changed. At its head is the *sadah* class, the judges, legal experts and officials who claim descent from the Prophet and always wear white. At the bottom is the small group of *ahdams*, who have few rights and usually work as road sweepers. Between them are the two classes of craftsmen – the *manasibs*, nominal members of free tribes, and the rather less privileged *bani humis*.

Most important, though, is the fact that Sanaa's population appears to be constant at around 500,000 – less than 5 per cent of the total population of 11 million – and there appears to be no serious risk of large slums developing.

The prognosis for the buildings in the old quarter is optimistic too. A few years ago property prices suddenly increased. Living in a traditional tower house now has kudos again; parties in the *mafraj*, the sitting room for the master of the house on the top floor, are fashionable. The joint efforts by UNESCO and the government to make living in the centre more attractive and the work more lucrative are now paying off. Many of the little streets and squares have been surfaced and a modern drainage system installed. A stone base has been built for the ruins of the clay city wall. A number of the 28 remaining *samsarahs*, the historic customs, storage and finance houses, have been restored with foreign help. The Samsarah al-Mansuriyah, which now houses workshops for local artists, and the Samsarah an-Nahas, a training centre for traditional crafts, are particularly impressive. There is a line in an old Arabic verse which says that the Pearl of Arabia must be seen, 'however long the journey takes'. There is every chance that this will continue to remain true long into the future.

Yemen's noblemen spend the afternoon chewing the mildly intoxicating leaves of qat.

دبي

Dubai

If it were not for the Creek with its unmistakable meander in the middle, you might think that the views were of two completely different cities. An aerial photograph taken in the 1960s shows flimsily built single-storey houses on each bank with a couple of wind towers and, on the outskirts, bare plots marked out with palm fronds and windowless huts. There are no asphalt roads or cars to be seen. A sandbank covers most of the inlet. Today, in total contrast, the view that opens up is of a metropolis out of an American dream. Huge glass and concrete buildings have sprung up on both sides of the water (which can now be crossed by bridge or tunnel). Expensive cars drive along multi-lane highways. On the coast a forest of cranes juts into the sky. In the last twenty years Dubai has been hurtling towards the future at top speed

The majority of Dubai's population are immigrant workers from the Indian subcontinent and Europe. Workers in the dhow shipyards (opposite) in al-Hamriya harbour are mainly Indian and Pakistani. Many refugees from the war in Afghanistan specialize in making fish traps (below).

The old-fashioned dhows can still compete with modern freighters on the routes to Karachi, Zanzibar, Bombay (Mumbai) and Bandar Abbas. Opposite below: traditional Bedouin stick dance at a wedding.

and, judging by its appearance, it seems to have lost sight of its past.

But when you take an *abra*, a water taxi, from the Ber Dubai district to Deira, you get a different picture. On the east bank dozens of dhows – sailing boats with the characteristic raised stern which the Arabs have used to transport freight for hundreds of years – still bob up and down on the waves between tugs and smart cabin cruisers.

Next to their moorings are small boards with the destination of the next voyage chalked on them – legendary ports like Aden, Bombay, Bandar Abbas, Bahrein, Karachi and Zanzibar. This is where the cargo is loaded and unloaded, with bales and crates heaped up everywhere; it is noisy and bustling and reeks of sweat, salt, refuse and diesel oil. But sometimes an aroma of nutmeg, coriander or cinnamon wafts across the quay. If you follow your nose you will soon find yourself in an atmosphere that is completely unexpected in the ultra-modern surroundings: a traditional covered bazaar whose picturesque little shops entice curious passers-by with all manner of medicinal herbs and spices, water pipes, fabrics and antiques.

It is difficult to get lost in the Deira souqs. With their four parallel streets and a couple of intersecting alleyways they are hardly a labyrinth. The old Dubai souq on the opposite bank of the Creek consists of just a single shopping street 300 metres (330 yards) long and a couple of offices. This is where many foreign goods were transhipped up to the Second World War, but it is now mainly occupied by Indian and Pakistani workshops and wholesale warehouses.

DUBAI

Jumeirah
Sharjah
Abu Dhabi, Jebel Ali
Airport
0 1000 m
0 100 m

Dubai
*DISTRICTS: **1** Ber Dubai, **2** Deira, **3** Bastakiya, **4** al-Shandagah. MARKETS: **5** Dubai Old Souq, **6** Deira Old Souq, **7** Gold souq, **8** Fish, meat and vegetable market, **9** Central vegetable market. MOSQUE: **10** Great Friday Mosque. MUSEUM: **11** al-Fahidi Fort and Dubai Museum. HOTELS: **12** Hilton, **13** Intercontinental, **14** Sheraton. SHOPPING CENTRES: **15** al-Ghurair, **16** Hamarain. STREETS: **17** al-Khaleej Road, **18** Khalid Bin al-Waleed Road, **19** Shandagha Tunnel. OTHER: **20** Port Rashid, **21** Ferry (abra), **22** Tourism Promotion Board, **23** Trade Centre, **24** British Embassy, **25** Dubai Municipality, **26** Dubai Creek.*

***A** Dubai Old Souq*
***B** Deira Old Souq*

BORDER: Stone façade decoration in the old city.
ILLUSTRATION: Deira and Dubai towers on al-Nasr Square.

For general key see page 146.

Falconry is one of the main hobbies of the Dubai sheikhs. They import the birds or rear them themselves and have them trained by experts on an estate outside the city. The ruffed bustard, the birds' natural prey, is becoming rare and nowadays they often have to make do with doves brought along in cages. Alternatively they load everything – falcons, cross-country vehicles and servants – on to a jumbo jet and fly off to the rich hunting grounds of Pakistan.

The two bazaars are no match for most of their competitors, either in size or in age. From excavations in nearby al-Qusais, archaeologists believe that the area around the Creek was already a trading centre for desert caravans and seafarers 3,000 years ago. In al-Jumeirah, now a residential district, they discovered the foundations of a souq and a few houses from the early

Camel racing is equally popular in the Gulf States. Every week during the season the cream of male society meets on the stands under a concrete Bedouin tent to follow the races live as they are transmitted all over the country on television. Some of the valuable and highly strung animals are brought in from the neighbouring states by articulated lorry. A few dozen expensive cars are usually awarded as prizes.

Islamic period. But only a few ruined fortresses and rusty canons have survived even from the 16th and 17th centuries, when the Portuguese had settled temporarily in the Gulf region. Few of the existing buildings date back more than 100 years.

It was not until the 1930s that Dubai became politically significant. Under the leadership of a member of the Maktoum family, which is still in power, 800 men from neighbouring Abu Dhabi settled in the tiny fishing village and set up an independent sheikhdom. Soon afterwards the English, who for a long time had controlled shipping between Basra and the Strait of Hormuz and were constantly at the mercy of Bedouin attack, agreed a ceasefire with the tribal princes, and later on a treaty was signed. The notorious Pirate Coast became the Trucial Coast, the coast pacified by treaty.

With the situation now reasonably secure, traders from India, Iran and Baluchistan moved into the country and built the first coral-limestone houses and wind towers. The Bastakiya and Shandagah districts developed. At that time the main source of income was pearl exports. In the summer more than 20,000 men would arrive on the Gulf coast, equipped with bone nose clamps and wax earplugs, lead weights to take them to the bottom more quickly, baskets for collecting the pearls and leather finger shields to protect them against the sharp shells. On the shores of Dubai alone more than 7,000 local divers risked their health in up to 20 metres (65 feet) of water at peak times.

The British historian J.C. Lorimer was not quite correct in his prediction that the coasts would be depopulated as soon as the supplies of pearls dried up. There was certainly a wave of emigration from the Trucial Coast when Japanese cultured pearls

At the edge of the small souq in Dubai is the al-Fahidi Fort, built in the early 19th century and believed to be the oldest building in the city. Since 1971 it has housed the Dubai Museum. Above: a reconstruction of a Bedouin kitchen made of reeds.
Below: one of the few original shops in the Deira souq on the east bank of the Creek.
Opposite: the new mosque in the residential district of al-Jumeirah.

destroyed the market in the late 1920s. But Dubai had thought ahead. In 1902 a large number of Iranian and Indian traders moved there from the Persian port of Lingah, which was no longer so attractive since the Tehran government's sudden introduction of stricter customs regulations. The following year Sheikh Maktoum secured assurances from the British that in future their freight steamers would stop only in Dubai. The city became the main depot in the eastern Gulf. At the time it had a population of at least 10,000 and the Deira bazaar, with its 350 shops, was the biggest in the region.

Soon after the collapse of the pearl market, traders on the Creek discovered a new and even more profitable source of income: gold smuggling, euphemistically referred to as re-export. The gold, imported from Europe, is cast into 10-*tola* bars (an Indian unit of weight, making each bar about 4 ounces) and shipped to the coast of the subcontinent by the ton in dhows at night. A rather different business, slave trading, is now finally dying out. The great explorer Wilfred Thesiger was one of the last – in 1949! – to write of his own experience with an unscrupulous profiteer travelling across the desert with 48 slaves in tow.

The late sixties saw the start of the oil boom. Modernization began in earnest. In 1971 the British left and the rulers of Abu Dhabi, Sharjah, Ras al-Khaimah, Fujairah, Ajman, Umm al-Qaiwain and Dubai entered into a marriage of convenience, setting up the United Arab Emirates. Even in the new alliances, however, Dubai has remained true to its traditions. Instead of relying on its oil reserves, which in any case are limited compared with Abu Dhabi's, the government is developing the goods transport infrastructure. The shipping channel of the Creek is being made deeper. A free-trade zone is being developed in Jebel Ali, with the largest artificial harbour in the world. The airport is becoming the main transit point for the Middle East. The whole city is being turned into a consumer paradise which is attracting a growing number of tourists with its import duties of 4 per cent or less and its ultra-modern shopping centres.

A small covered souq – the gold traders' souq in the old part of Deira – still plays a key role in the economic structure of this boom town. Dubai imports no less than 10 per cent of the world's gold jewelry every year. Between 25 and 30 tons a year are sold in the 700 shops in this small street alone.

قيروان

Kairouan

It is a long time since Kairouan was a major foreign trade and commercial city. That is obvious from the Rue Ali Belhouane, the main street of the medina. The goods on sale along the 500-metre (550 yard) route between the Bab ech-Chouhada and Bab et-Tounes city gates are mostly designed to appeal to the day trippers from the nearby resorts on the Gulf of Hammamet: copper and leather, silver jewelry, embroidered fabrics, basketwork made from the esparto grass which grows abundantly in the area and, of course, the famous carpets – all quite attractive and traditional souvenirs, but not of the high quality one would expect from the city's reputation and historic status. The souqs in the side streets sell fabrics, clothes and shoes, household goods, food and prepared dishes, mainly to the local people. The

The carpet museum (below) contains some of the most magnificent examples of the traditional carpet-making for which Kairouan is renowned all over the world, the older ones in colourful Berber patterns, the newer ones in the baroque Turkish style. Women bring their new carpets to the official market next door to obtain the recognized government quality mark.

atmosphere there is like that of a provincial town, which is what Kairouan, with its population of 100,000 or so, actually is now. It is hard to imagine that this was once a powerful economic centre. Only the local carpet trade still gives some idea of how the place used to be. It employs more than 8,000 women and girls, working at home or in the workshops in the weavers' district. Carpets marked with the quality seal of the ONAT (Tunisian National Handicrafts Office) are exported all over the world on a huge scale by about two dozen firms. The Souk des Tapis, the carpet market, where the public auctions of the colourful, mostly geometrically patterned *kilim*, *alloucha* and *megoum* carpets are held, is always a hive of activity.

Kairouan's economic importance has declined, but its spiritual importance is as great as ever. It is considered one of the holiest sites in Islam – in the absence of a clear hierarchy, it shares equal fourth place with Damascus. If Maghrebis make seven pilgrimages here, they are exempted from the major pilgrimage to Mecca. According to legend, there are always 500 saints living within its walls. In fact, over a hundred are buried here in *zaouias*, mausoleums. more than 60 of the original 280 mosques have survived, including such fine examples as the Mosque of the Barber, whose elaborate frieze patterns provide inspiration for the carpet weavers, or the Mosque of the Sabres, the burial place of an armourer revered for his piety.

The camel-driven Bir Barouta well (below) is a tourist attraction, venerated by traditional Muslims because its water is said to come straight from the holy Zemzem well in Mecca. A companion of the Prophet who is believed to have carried hairs from his master's beard is buried in the Mosque of the Barber (above: the entrance door).

The city owes its status as a religious centre to a man by the name of Oqba ibn-Nafi, appointed army commander and governor of Ifriqiyya, a province in north-west Africa, in 670 by the Omayyad caliphs. A year later Oqba set up a permanent garrison camp in the middle of a flat landscape which, although dry and very hot, was in a highly strategic position between the coast (still Byzantine) and the mountains where the Berbers lived. To justify his decision, he invented a legend that, when digging a well at this exact spot, he had found a valuable cup which he once lost in Mecca. The well, Bir Barouta, still attracts many pilgrims. Its water, brought up with a wooden scoop system operated by a camel on the top floor of an old house, is believed to work miracles. The well is said to have a direct underground connection with the holy well of Zemzem in Mecca.

Soon after it was founded, Kairouan was sacked several times by Kharijite Berbers. But in the early 9th century, under the local Aghlabid dynasty and later the Fatimids, it became the undisputed capital of the Maghreb, a stronghold of intellectual and religious life and the centre of trade between Egypt, the Mediterranean ports and the Sudan. Symbols of its wealth and power included a 3.5-kilometre (2-mile) city wall, numerous Koranic schools, a state research library (Arabic: Bait el-Hikma, the house of wisdom), a complicated system of wells supplied via long aqueducts (two huge basins can still be seen on the northern edge of the town) and a *tiraz*, a court-financed weaving mill making heavy luxury fabrics. The only other mills of this kind were in Baghdad, Palermo, Córdoba and Tinnis on the eastern Nile delta. The rulers built themselves magnificent residences outside the city, the Aghlabids el-Abbasiya and Raqqada, the Fatimids the fortress of Mahdia and, as a counterpart to Baghdad and symbolic 'navel of the world', Sabra Mansuriya.

However, the golden age did not last long. By 969 the Fatimids, now self-appointed caliphs, were building their new capital el-Qahira (Cairo) in Egypt. They handed Ifriqiyya over to the local governors who, about a century later, declared independence and sparked off a catastrophe. The former rulers, feeling that they had been duped, set Bedouin from Arabia, the Beni Hillal, on the city. Kairouan never fully recovered from the destruction and plunder. Although rebuilt at the end of the 13th century by the Hafsids and much later by the Husseinites, politically and economically it has always been overshadowed by Tunis, which was favoured from then on.

Titus Burckhardt talked about the 'alchemy of light', when the fabric of buildings is transformed just as lead may be turned into gold. In Kairouan the combination of pastel colours and the African light creates a magical atmosphere.

Kairouan – the old city
SEPARATE MARKETS: ***1*** *Souk er-Rab,* ***2*** *Bab el-Kada (clothing),* ***3*** *des Tapis (carpets),* ***4*** *des Sandales (shoes),* ***5*** *Blajia (shoes),* ***6*** *Marché Haddadine (vegetables),* ***7*** *Grand Marché. SPECIALIST WORKSHOPS AND SHOPS:* ***8*** *Tunisian National Handicrafts Office (ONAT) and carpet museum,* ***9*** *Magasin Général,* ***10*** *Patisserie Seguni (Makroudh bakery),* ***11*** *Palais du Tapis (carpets),* ***12*** *Weavers' district. MOSQUES AND MAUSOLEUMS:* ***13*** *Great Mosque (Sidi Oqba),* ***14*** *Mosque of the Barber (Zaouia Sidi Sahab),* ***15*** *Mosque of the Sabres (Djamaa Amor Abbada),* ***16*** *Mosque of the Three Doors,* ***17*** *Zaouia Sidi Abid el-Ghariani,* ***18*** *el-Bey Mosque. BATHS, WELLS AND WATER RESERVOIRS:* ***19*** *Bir Barouta,* ***20*** *Hammam el-Bey,* ***21*** *Aghlabid basins. COFFEE HOUSES:* ***22*** *Café er-Rashid.* ***23*** *Café Hassnat,* ***24*** *Café Taktak. HOTELS:* ***25*** *Marhala,* ***26*** *Splendid,* ***27*** *Continental,* ***28*** *Sabra,* ***29*** *des Aghlabides. STREETS:* ***30*** *Rue Ali Belhouane,* ***31*** *Boulevard Habib Bourguiba. CITY GATES:* ***32*** *Bab ech-Chouhada,* ***33*** *et-Tounes,* ***34*** *el-Djedid,* ***35*** *el-Khouhka. OTHER:* ***36*** *Steps to city wall,* ***37*** *Cemeteries,* ***38*** *Kasbah,* ***39*** *Tunisian National Tourism Office (ONTT).*

BORDER: Mosaic frieze from the Mosque of the Barber. ILLUSTRATION: Minaret of the Great Mosque.

For general key see page 146.

Architecturally, very little remains of the golden age. Most of the present buildings, including the central bazaar, date from around 1700. Its precursor, founded by the governor Yazid in 772, was located on the central north–south axis, the 2-kilometre ($1\frac{1}{4}$-mile) Simat, further to the east. But the city centre gradually moved south-west and with it the centre of business. Eventually the Souk er-Rab was built about 300 years ago. This was a small, completely covered shopping centre whose layout, with the narrow streets at right angles and the impressive stone barrel vaults, is somewhat reminiscent of the Kapali Carsi in Istanbul.

Kairouan has preserved its old historic atmosphere very successfully. The medina in particular, which until only a generation ago non-Muslims could not visit without

Above: the Souk des Sandales in the old city. Below: Kairouan's religious status is evident from the many saints' graves visible from the minaret of the Great Mosque.

قيروان

special permission, still delights visitors with its unusual pastel colours, the soft green, red and blue shades of its windows and artistically nail-patterned doors, and the ochre of its walls and towers. The painter Paul Klee enthused about the colours on his famous Tunisian journey in 1914. The cemeteries with their simple whitewashed gravestones also contribute to the overall atmosphere of the place. The 10-metre (33-foot) high city walls, built in the 18th century on 11th-century foundations, give an air of inviolability, although they were partly broken up in the Second World War to provide filling for runways.

The most impressive structure, however, is the Great Mosque. Named after Sidi Oqba, the conqueror and 'apostle of North Africa', it is the oldest place of worship in the Maghreb (begun in 672). A decree was issued in 1972 prohibiting non-believers from entering any prayer rooms in Tunisia. But even if you just look into the innermost shrine from the courtyard and see the *mihrab*, the *maqsura* and the *minbar* through the pillars, it is obvious why the Sidi Oqba is regarded as the most fascinating mosque in the whole of the Islamic world.

The Great Mosque (left: the outer wall and the minaret) is one of the most famous places of worship in Islam. It was begun in 672 and completed in its present form in 836. Thousands of believers are buried nearby, hoping to benefit from its aura. Below: the façade of the Mosque of the Three Doors.

تونس

Tunis

What better place to get an idea of Tunis's history than the Café Mrabet – a relic of the old days where the waiters still wear baggy trousers and the *farmela*, the long-sleeved waistcoat? The air is scented with jasmine and the only sound comes from the canaries in their little wooden cages. Then on to the heart of the medina, the Souk et-Trouk. Walk through the red-and-green-striped gate, sit down on a stone platform covered with a raffia mat, have a cup of tea and take a quick trip into the city's past.

It started with a settlement called Tunas, probably built by the Berbers, which had existed in the shadow of mighty Phoenician Carthage since at least the 9th century BC. It was destroyed by the Romans in 146 BC and rebuilt in early Christian times. It was not until after the Arab invasion that it became historically important. It then developed into a busy port, mainly as a result of the conquest of Sicily (827), and later, at the time of the Khorassanids and Almohads (11th and 12th centuries), replaced Kairouan as the capital of Ifriqiyya province after Kairouan had been attacked by Bedouin.

Tunis's heyday was under the local dynasty of the Hafsids (1229–1574), originating from the governors of the Almohad central government in Marrakesh. They proved to be extremely cosmopolitan and far-sighted, establishing economic links with the Italian city-states and the Mediterranean ports in France and Spain and building new fortifications and many of the covered bazaar streets which still survive today. They added a university to the Djamaa ez-Zitouna, the Mosque of the Olive Tree, founded in 732. This soon became one of the most important centres of learning in the Islamic world, not least because the legendary ibn-Khaldun worked there. Its intellectual reputation equalled that of the el-Azhar in Cairo or the Qaraouiyine in Fez. During the power struggle between the Ottomans and the Western emperors Tunis went into decline. For 40 years (1535–1574) it was occupied by Spanish Hapsburg troops. When it subsequently came under Ottoman rule it underwent a marked revival. Muslim immigrants from Andalusia, many of them skilled craftsmen and builders, brought new life to the city. By the end of the 18th century the old part of the city looked more or less as it does today. The French demolished large parts of the city walls during the colonial period (1883–1954), but the souqs and most of the residential districts remained untouched.

The Djamaa ez-Zitouna (Mosque of the Olive Tree) is the oldest and most important university in the Islamic world after el-Azhar in Cairo and the Qaraouiyine in Fez, although its minaret (opposite: detail; above: from the roof terrace of the Palais d'Orient) was actually built in the 19th century. Below: the Café Mrabet in the Souk et-Trouk, an ideal place to have a glass of mint tea in a civilized atmosphere.

You can only properly appreciate the architecture of the medina – and the old suburbs of Bab Souika and Bab el-Jazira – when you see it from a height, for instance from the roof terrace of one of the city's palaces. A network of houses with courtyards, cul-de-sacs and narrow streets lies spread out around you. Very few places in the Islamic world are so closed and untouched. It covers 270 hectares (667 acres), has virtually no motor traffic and no ugly new buildings to disfigure it. UNESCO designated it a 'world heritage site' in 1981, partly for that reason and perhaps also because the traditional division into different trades has largely been preserved. The 'luxury' shops selling books and wedding dresses, jewelry, perfumes, spices and antiques and the cap makers' workshops are around the ez-Zitouna Mosque. The area is mostly covered and can be closed off with gates. Further from the centre are the shops selling household goods, food, leather and brass.

Tourbet el-Bey, built 1758–1782, was fully restored a few years ago. Above: the room with the men's tombs, recognizable by the turbans on top of the pillars. Each burial place has a recess in which the dead person's family place grains. The birds that come and pick them up symbolize the ascent to Heaven. Opposite: a scene in the Souk el-Blaghija, the shoe market.

The dyers, smiths and leather embroiderers are near the city gates, although nowadays their numbers are declining.

Although it looks idyllic, there is no denying that in the last few years social changes have had a drastic effect on the medina. In the first half of the 20th century the population of the city almost tripled, to over half a million. After independence in 1956 impoverished farmers really began to pour into the city. Some lived in makeshift *bidonvilles* (shantytowns) on the outskirts, the rest flocked to the medina. Many of the more prosperous inhabitants of the old town moved out to the former European quarter. Their houses were turned into *oukalas* for multiple occupation. Standards of living declined and the buildings became run-down. At the same time there were plans to build modern boulevards across the city centre in the style created by Baron Haussmann in Paris.

In 1967 the city authorities set up the Association de Sauvegarde de la Médina, the Association for the Preservation of the Old Town. Its aim was to conserve the buildings in the medina and make it more of a living city centre. In collaboration with other organizations and national government, and with financial help from the World Bank and the Gulf States, the Association achieved impressive results. For instance, 400 new homes were built in Hafsia, the former Jewish quarter, blending harmoniously with the old buildings. The area around Bab Souika, which used to be the place of execution, was made into a pedestrian zone and redeveloped. Both projects were awarded the Aga Khan prize for architecture.

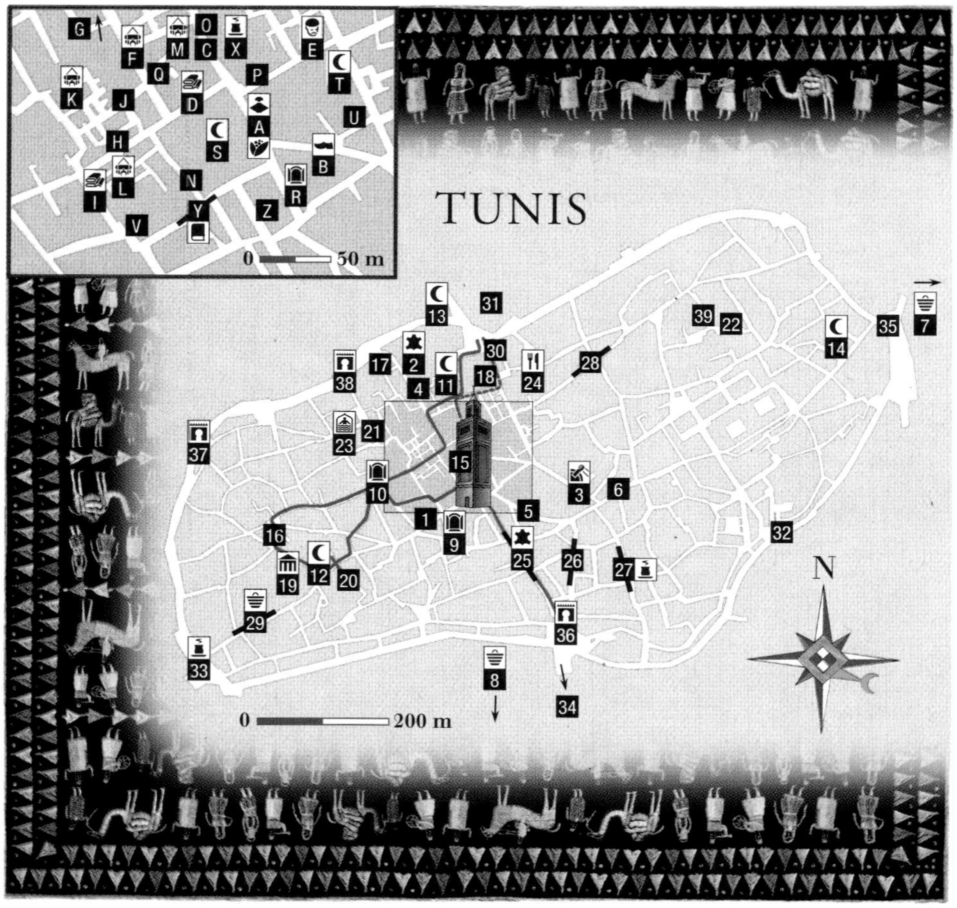

TUNIS

Tunis – the old city
*SEPARATE MARKETS: **1** Souk el-Belat (miscellaneous goods), **2** Sekkajine (leather), **3** du Cuivre (brass), **4** ed-Dziria (clothing), **5** el-Ouzar, **6** el-Grana (both miscellaneous cheap goods), **7** Halfaouine (food), **8** Fondouk el-Ghalla (central food market). CARAVANSERAIS: **9** Fondouk en-Nayar, **10** el-Yasmina. MOSQUES: **11** Youssef Dey, **12** des Teinturiers (Dyers' Mosque), **13** Kasbah Mosque, **14** Sidi Mahrez, **15** Djamaa ez-Zitouna (Mosque of the Olive Tree). MAUSOLEUMS: **16** Tourbet el-Bey, **17** Sidi Boukhrissan. PALACES: **18** Dar el-Bey, **19** Dar Ben Abdallah (folklore museum), **20** Dar Othman, **21** Dar Hussein (National Archaeological and Art Institute), **22** Dar Lasram (old city local authority). BATHS AND WELLS: **23** Hammam Daouletli. RESTAURANT: **24** Dar el-Jeld. STREETS: **25** Rue Djamaa ez-Zitouna, **26** Rue de la Kasbah, **27** Rue Zarkoun, **28** Rue Sidi Ben Arous, **29** Rue des Teinturiers, **30** Place du Gouvernement, **31** Place de la Kasbah, **32** Place Bab Carthajna, **33** Place Bab el-Djazira, **34** Avenue Habib Bourguiba, **35** Place Bab Souika. CITY GATES: **36** Bab el-Bhar (Porte de France), **37** Bab Djedid, **38** Bab Menara. OTHER: **39** Club Culturel Tahar Haddad.*

Central souqs
*SEPARATE MARKETS: **A** Souk el-Attarine (perfume and spices), **B** el-Blaghija (shoes), **C** et-Trouk (souvenirs), **D** des Etoffes (clothing), **E** des Chéchias (cap makers), **F** el-Berka (former slave market, jewelry), **G** el-Leffa, **H** des Femmes (women's market), **I** el-Cachachine (all clothing), **J** el-Kouafi (wedding dresses), **K** des Orfèvres (goldsmiths), **L** de Coton (cotton), **M** Kababjia (jewelry), **N** de la Laine (wool). SPECIALIST WORKSHOPS AND SHOPS: **O** Musée des Turcs, **P** ed-Dar, **Q** Palais d'Orient (antiques and souvenirs). CARAVANSERAI: **R** Fondouk el-Attarine. MOSQUES: **S** Djamaa ez-Zitouna, **T** Hammouda Pacha. MAUSOLEUM: **U** Tourbet Aziza Othmana. KORANIC SCHOOL: **V** Medersa es-Slimaniya. BATHS: **W** Hammam Cachachine. COFFEE HOUSE: **X** Café Mrabet. STREET: **Y** Rue des Libraires. OTHER: **Z** National Library.*

BORDER: Traditional embroidery from the suburb of Sidi-Bou-Saïd. ILLUSTRATION: Minaret of ez-Zitouna Mosque.

For general key see page 146.

The Dar Lasram in the Rue du Tribunal (left: the inner courtyard) was impressively restored in the late 1960s. Since then it has housed the Association for the Preservation of the Old Town, which saved many of the old buildings and helped restore the medina as a centre of city life. Far left: scene in the Rue des Teinturiers. Below: jewelry shop in the Souk el-Bey.

Many mosques, Koranic schools and palaces were restored, providing employment for large numbers of craftsmen, particularly stonemasons, frieze makers and the makers of *naqsh hadid*, the finely carved decorative stucco. Plans were drawn up to demolish dozens of run-down *oukalas* and replace them with new buildings in authentic traditional style. A week-long festival was organized, a craft school was

The Souk des Etoffes with its whitewashed arches and arcades. This souq on the north side of the ez-Zitouna Mosque sells clothing and fabrics. Immediately next door to it is the small Souk el-Berka square where the slave market used to be held.

set up, the retail trade was promoted and a start was made on reviving the old guild system. A special route was devised to encourage tourists to explore Tunis instead of just passing through on their way to the beach resorts as they usually do.

This *'circuit culturel'* starts where European Tunis ends and Arab Tunis begins, at Bab el-Bhar, the Porte de France, and follows a meandering route as far as the government palace, Dar el-Bey. It takes in all the most important sights: the folklore museum in the Dar Ben Abdallah, the Djamaa ez-Zitouna, the Dyers' Mosque and Youssef Dey mosque, and Tourbet el-Bey, the newly renovated monument to the Husseinite beys, only recently reopened to the public after Habib Bourguiba, the father and first

unusually broad and lofty Souk et-Trouk, once the Turkish market.

Even so, the tour only gives a superficial impression and, if you really want to get to know the medina, you would do better to throw away the map and wander at random into its more remote corners. Look into the workshops where the *babouches* (slippers) and *chechias* (caps) are made and into the basements of caravanserais where you can still sometimes hear the whirring of silk-weaving looms. Have a coffee in the shade of a centuries-old olive tree and stroll through the most traditional market of all, the Souk Halfaouine. If you are lucky, you could meet a procession of pilgrims on their way to the mosque of Sidi Mahrez, the city's patron, or come across the entrance to the Tahar Haddad cultural society, which might well be holding one of its regular debates on feminism or student politics.

Reminders of the city's past can also be found in the suburbs: the national museum in Bardo, the palace of the Husseinite beys (Dar el-Bey) with its collection of Roman mosaics, the Charles V fort at La Goulette, the ruins of Carthage and the picturesque village of Sidi-Bou-Saïd, which August Macke painted in 1914.

If you then go on to a bath house like the old Hammam Cachachine or an old-fashioned restaurant like the Dar el-Jeld, you will at least begin to appreciate how the medina, with all its ups and downs, has still succeeded in preserving much of its old way of life.

A salesman in the Rue de la Kasbah proudly shows off a fresh batch of goods. The shop's owner, Mohammed el-Abassi, is the amin *(head) of the cap makers. His workshops are just around the corner in the Souk des Chéchias.*

The Souk des Femmes after the shops have closed. Although it no longer has its own gates, it is still watched over at night by a security guard. Ibn-Khaldun's house is nearby, in the Rue Tourbet el-Bey.

president of the republic, kept it closed for thirty years. The route also goes along the main streets of the bazaar, the Rue Djamaa ez-Zitouna with its rows of 'genuine' daggers and rifles, leather bags, pouffes and stuffed camels, the Souk el-Attarine with its elegant green and gold perfume shops, the jewelry and leather souq, through the former slave market quarter, the Souk el-Berka, and the

مراكش

Marrakesh

The famous Djamaa el-Fna is one of the most magical places in the Islamic world and the greatest of the many attractions that Marrakesh has in store for visitors. A trapezoidal area at the entrance to the bazaar, it covers 5 hectares (12 acres). From early morning to late at night it is swarming with people. Most of them are tourists or farmers from villages at the edge of the Sahara, the High Atlas and the Sous, the area behind Agadir, who come into the city to sell their produce, go shopping and enjoy themselves. As befits such a magical place, the meaning of the name is a mystery even to linguistic experts. It could mean 'mosque of the ruins' or 'meeting place of the nobodies' or, the most popular theory, 'the square of the hanged'. It is a fact that criminals were still executed there in the early part of the 20th

Where Arabia and Africa meet. The legendary Djamaa el-Fna (below) has lost none of its magic. In the background are the Kutubiya minaret and the palms of the Club Méditerranée. Opposite: an elderly dyer in the Souk des Teinturiers.

century and their skulls left on show as a deterrent until the vultures had picked them clean.

The best time to see the Djamaa el-Fna is before sunset on a summer's day, when the worst of the heat has died down – it can sometimes reach 50°C (122°F). There is a constant stream of curious onlookers and idle strollers. The travelling hawkers are setting up their stands. Fires are being lit at the food stalls and the aroma of baked fish and couscous and *harira* soup is beginning to spread across the square. More and more men are drawing their *halga* on the ground, the imaginary circle which a holy man has blessed for them for the regular evening performance.

After sunset the square is a place of total enchantment. In the flickering light of carbide lamps the public crowd around the clowns, monkey trainers, fire eaters, fortune tellers, snake charmers, and faith healers. The story tellers are still significantly the biggest attraction for local people (in Morocco half the men and three out of four women are illiterate). Tourists are more fascinated by the *gnawas*, dark-skinned musicians and acrobatic dancers in white robes whose ancestors are believed to have come from Guinea. The rhythms of their heavy drums, *darbukas*, their tambourines and *gembris*, a kind of banjo, are an evocative reminder of how close Morocco is to black Africa.

From early in the morning to late at night the Djamaa el-Fna is a panorama of humanity: magicians and charlatans, quacks and faith healers, snake charmers, proud owners of a falcon. With the hundreds of performers (all hoping for a little bakshish*), spectators cannot fail to be thoroughly entertained.*

Winston Churchill once described Marrakesh as the most beautiful city in the world. Fifty years on, you can still understand his enthusiasm. Stroll through the Menara, the olive grove in the Sultan's garden, late in the afternoon and enjoy the view across the pool and the summerhouse reflected in it up to the snow-covered peaks of the Atlas. Take a ride on a horse-drawn carriage through the Palmeraie, its 150,000 date palms irrigated by a system of underground canals and springs more than 800 years old. Or wander through the souqs and along the Route des Remparts with its red-clay fortress wall. You realize how untouched and medieval the medina

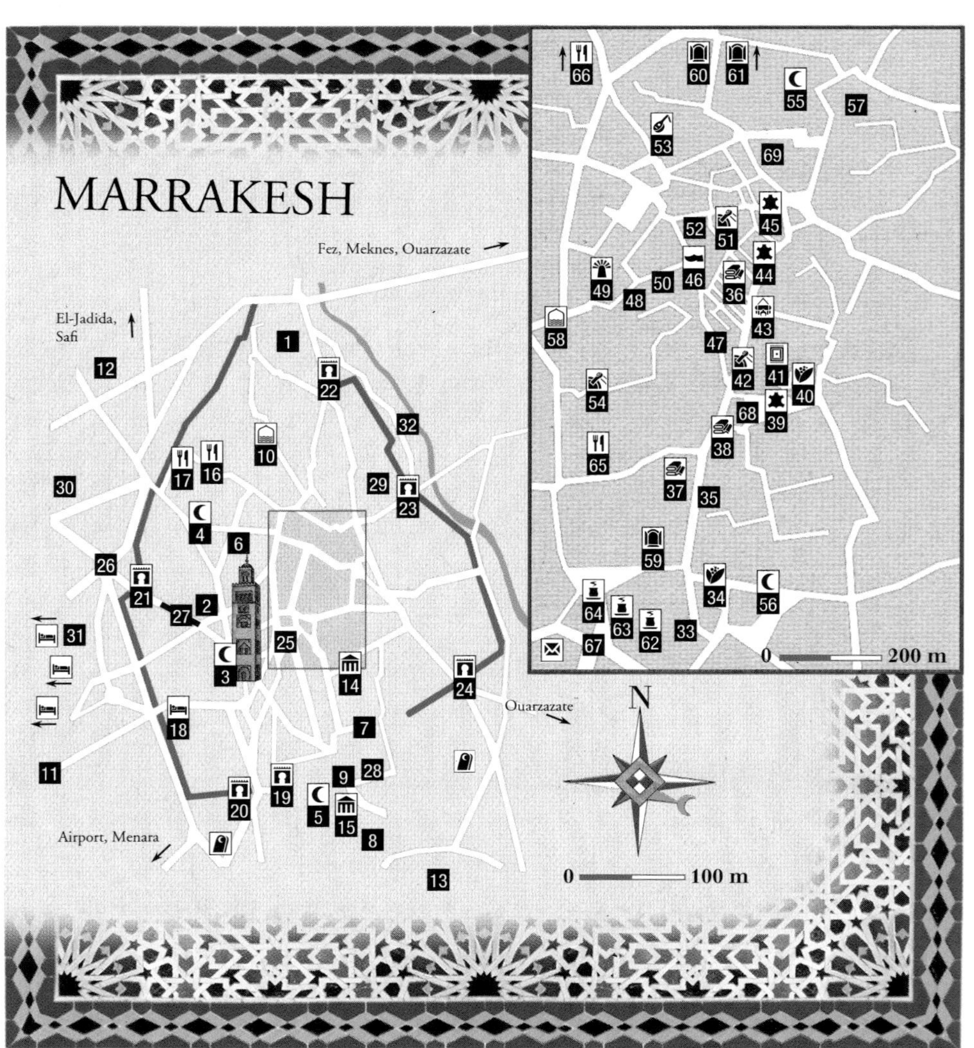

Marrakesh – souqs
SEPARATE MARKETS: ***1*** *Potiers (potters),* ***2*** *Quessabine (dried fruits, spices),* ***3*** *Smarine,* ***4*** *Old Kissariya,* ***5*** *New Kissariya (textiles),* ***6*** *Larzal (wool, secondhand clothes),* ***7*** *el-Maazi and el-Btana (goat- and sheepskin),* ***8*** *Former slave market (spices),* ***9*** *La Crie Berbère (carpets),* ***10*** *Fagharine (smiths),* ***11*** *Bijoutiers (jewelry),* ***12*** *el-Kebir,* ***13*** *Cherratine (leather),* ***14*** *Babouchiers (shoes),* ***15*** *Attarine (secondhand auctions),* ***16*** *Lebadines (felt makers),* ***17*** *Teinturiers (dyers),* ***18*** *Chouari (wood carvers),* ***19*** *des Cuivres (brass),* ***20*** *Haddadine (smiths),* ***21*** *Kenakhine (musical instruments),* ***22*** *Forgerons (coppersmiths). MOSQUES:* ***23*** *Ben Youssef,* ***24*** *Quessabine. KORANIC SCHOOL:* ***25*** *Ben Youssef. WELL:* ***26*** *el-Mouassine. CARAVANSERAIS* (funduqs)*:* ***27*** *Chidimi,* ***28*** *Lamry,* ***29*** *el-Misan. COFFEE HOUSES AND RESTAURANTS:* ***30*** *Café de France,* ***31*** *Café Glacis,* ***32*** *Café Argana,* ***33*** *Stylia,* ***34*** *Dar Merchant. STREETS AND SQUARES:* ***35*** *Djamaa el-Fna,* ***36*** *Rahba Kedima. OTHER:* ***37*** *Qoubba.*

The old city
SEPARATE MARKETS: ***38*** *Souk el-Khemis (cattle),* ***39*** *Handicrafts centre. MOSQUES:* ***40*** *Kutubiya,* ***41*** *Bab Doukkala,* ***42*** *Kasbah. PALACES:* ***43*** *Dar el-Glaoui,* ***44*** *el-Bahia,* ***45*** *Royal Palace,* ***46*** *el-Badi. WELL:* ***47*** *Echroub ou-Chouf. GARDENS:* ***48*** *Menara,* ***49*** *Majorelle,* ***50*** *Agdal. MUSEUM:* ***51*** *Dar si-Said (folk art museum),* ***52*** *Saadian tombs. RESTAURANTS:* ***53*** *Dar Fes,* ***54*** *Dar Yacout. HOTEL:* ***55*** *Mamounia. CITY GATES:* ***56*** *Bab Agnaou,* ***57*** *er-Robb,* ***58*** *Larissa,* ***59*** *el-Khemis,* ***60*** *ed-Debbach,* ***61*** *Rhemat. STREETS AND SQUARES:* ***62*** *Djamaa el-Fna,* ***63*** *Place de la Liberté,* ***64*** *Avenue Mohammed V. OTHER:* ***65*** *Mellah (Jewish quarter),* ***66*** *Tanners' district,* ***67*** *Gueliz,* ***68*** *Hivernage,* ***69*** *Oued/River Issil.*

BORDER: Typical rosettes from zeligs, multicoloured ceramic friezes.
ILLUSTRATION: Minaret of the Kutubiya Mosque.

For general key see page 146.

still is. Its symbol, the 77-metre (250-foot) high minaret of the Kutubiya mosque, soars above all the other buildings. Part of the city's charm comes from its people – many of its one and a half million inhabitants are Berbers from the countryside who still speak *shleuh*, the broad dialect of the Atlas Berbers, and they are delightfully provincial in their attitudes. Unlike the other three royal cities – Fez, Meknes and Rabat – Marrakesh never had a traditional middle class. The simple piety of its people is in sharp contrast to the strict orthodoxy found, for example, in Fez. The Marrakeshis have a strong sense of humour and a calm and relaxed attitude to life.

It is certainly no accident that it is here, in the residential districts of Gueliz and Hivernage with their orange and jacaranda trees, that the international jet-setters have their luxury winter retreats. The beauty of the oasis and its strategic position were recognized as long ago as 1060 by the desert prince abu-Bekr when he advanced to the Hauz plain with his mighty army and built a stone fortress. With the help of Andalusian craftsmen, his Almoravid successor Yusuf ibn-Tashfin and his son Ali developed this into a full-sized city with a mosque, new palace and many other buildings. Except for the ramparts, these have all now long since disappeared.

A caravanserai in the Bab el-Khemis district (below). The day's work over, traders from out of town go to the Djamaa el-Fna for entertainment (above) or smoke a pipe of kif *together in their upstairs rooms.*

Under the Almohads (from 1147) Mraksh, as contemporary historians named the new city, soon became the centre of a kingdom extending from the Atlantic to Tunisia and across a large part of the Iberian peninsula. Its inhabitants traded actively with Spain and the Bilad as-Sudan, the region on the other side of the Sahara. Their main exports to the north were leather, sugar and ceramics. Their main import was gold from the south. The colossal horseshoe-shaped city gates, such as the Bab er-Robb and the Bab Agnaou, the extensive Menara and Agdal gardens, the hospital where famous doctors like Averroes and Avenzoar taught and the Kutubiya, the mosque whose name refers to the adjoining book market, the

Conversation in the courtyard of a funduq. *There are still caravanserais in Marrakesh like the one described by Titus Burckhardt: 'If you enter their courtyards, you find the people and sounds of the villages and Bedouin camps in the centre of the city and depending on the goods that are being unloaded you can smell fruits and grains or skins and earth. If you spend the night on a mat in one of the little limestone-washed rooms, you can hear the animals moving about underneath you and in the morning you are woken by the sound of the* muezzin *even before the cock crows.'*

Koranic schools like this are found all over the medina. Children of all ages learn the verses of the Koran by heart, which is good memory training and familiarizes them with the Arabic language. It is only later that they are taught what the words mean. The illiteracy rate in Morocco is over 50 per cent. The portrait hanging above the blackboard is of King Hassan II.

Souk el-Kotbiye, were all built at that time. There were three bazaars in all: the one south of the Ben Youssef mosque which still exists today, the one below the Kutubiya and a *qaiseriya*, which burnt down a hundred years later but is said to have been magnificent. The city covered a total area of 630 hectares (1,560 acres), compared with Cairo's then 140 hectares (345 acres).

In 1269 the Merinids came to power. They transferred the seat of government to Fez and at the same time the route of the big trans-Saharan caravans shifted further to the east. Instead of going from Marrakesh southwards to Timbuktu, they now went from Fez to Gao via Sijilmassa. The glory of the 'pearl of the south thrown over the Atlas', as an Arabic poet described Marrakesh, soon faded. The population was decimated by famine. The

N° 25
PORTEUR D'EAU
MARRAKECH

flow of gold dried up and chickens were kept in the legendary Almohad library.

The Saadians changed all this in 1524. Shortly before reuniting the kingdom, they brought back the royal court and the city once again had the atmosphere of a capital city. Mulay Abdallah developed the Medersa Ben Youssef into the biggest Koranic school in the Maghreb. He assigned the Jews their own district, the Mellah, in which they could practise their faith and carry on their business, salt trading in particular (*mellah* is the Arabic word for salt). For the Christians he had a community centre and their own trading house built on the edge of the Djamaa el-Fna where the Club Méditerranée now stands. His successor, Ahmed el-Mansur 'the victorious' (1578–1603), extended the medina considerably after defeating the Portuguese and sacking Timbuktu. The most impressive buildings dating from that time (paid for with the booty from his wars and with the proceeds from sugar and leather exports to Europe) were the el-Badi palace and the Saadian necropolis, now in ruins.

In the 17th and 18th centuries the city was again ravaged by wars, poverty and famine. It was not to enjoy another long phase of prosperity until the Alawis (the dynasty to which the present monarch, Hassan II, belongs). They built the el-Bahia Palace and the Dar si-Said (a folk art museum since 1912), now open to the public. At the time of the French advance into southern Morocco in the late 19th century, Marrakesh was the centre of the sultans' resistance. When the French proclaimed Morocco a protectorate in 1912, it was finally relegated to the status of a provincial city. The pasha of the Glaoui tribe, who unscrupulously collaborated with the new rulers, remained powerful until the 1950s.

Marrakesh had already lost its remaining importance as an international trade centre in the previous century, when the Atlantic ports were developed and France conquered West Africa. On the other hand, it has remained important to this day as a centre for crafts. The corporations have lost many of their powers under pressure from the *machzen*, the royal power structure. But officially they still have 10,000 master craftsmen (the total number of traders is considerably higher). Craftsmen still exert considerable influence in the community through the religious brotherhoods to which most corporations are affiliated.

The picturesque costume of the gerrab, *or water seller (opposite). He carries brass cups for Muslims, a white-metal cup for people of other religions, a goatskin for the water and a copper bell which he rings to announce his arrival. Above: scene in the Souk Larzal, the secondhand clothes market.*

Among the most important guilds are the tanners with 430 members, the cloth merchants (237), the silk merchants (100) and in particular the *babouche* makers (1,500). But many other craftsmen in more obscure and exotic trades eke out an existence in the maze of streets in the medina. Right next to the famous dyers' market, for instance, are a couple of felt makers who still work on *lebdas*, prayer mats, coloured with black soap. In the Funduq Tetlaoui they still use the old technique of *brichla*, covering ceramic with silver wire. *Shmes*, the coloured candles for the processions to the seven holiest tombs in the city, are still made and sold in the brass market. At a curious auction held every day in a narrow passage called La Crie men try to sell off their old carpets and their *galabiyyas* and burnouses. Also nearby is the Souk Larzal, where women rummage through piles of secondhand clothes looking for what they want. Between La Crie and Souk Larzal is the Place Rahba Kedima, a smaller version of the Djamaa el-Fna, where wool is sold in the mornings and leather in the afternoons. Until 1912 slaves from sub-Saharan Africa were sold there. Snail soup is served from mobile stalls. In the surrounding shops experts offer for sale a remarkable and bizarre hotch-potch of magic substances and protective objects for *silhacen*, black magic.

فيس

Fez

Thirty years ago Titus Burckhardt compared Fez in the evening light to a rock cavity filled with thousands of crystals. Even today the description could not be more appropriate. The view from the surrounding hills down into the valleys in which the old town nestles looks exactly like an enormous mineral deposit – a dense mass of onyx-brown and amethyst-coloured square buildings with dozens of prisms, the light quartz-coloured minarets, projecting from them. The city is a gem bordered with white stones – the steles in the cemetery – and the terracotta strip of the city wall, which is over 12 kilometres (7½ miles) long. In its centre is a huge gleaming cut emerald. A green glazed brick roof always denotes a holy site in the Maghreb. The green-roofed buildings in the centre of Fez house the famous university mosque, el-Qaraouiyine, founded in 862 by Fatma bent-Mohammed el-Feheri, daughter of an immigrant from Kairouan. Until recently it was the intellectual centre of Morocco. Even older than el-Azhar in Cairo and the Zitouna school in Tunis, it has always attracted the best minds. Ibn-Battuta, Leo Africanus, el-Bitruji (Alpetragius) and ibn-Khaldun, the most eminent Islamic historian, are said to have studied and taught there. It

There is an old saying that every inch of the ground in Fez is occupied by a saint. Opposite: the entrance door of the burial mosque of Idris II. The interior, reserved for Muslims, has wooden cross-beams around it which mark it out as a sacrosanct area. With its white filigree walls and the dark, richly carved cedarwood beams, the Medersa Attarine (left), built around 1324, is regarded as a masterpiece of Merinid architecture. There are dozens of fine faïence-covered wells all over the medina where passers-by can quench their thirst (right). Nearly all are owned by religious foundations and are renovated regularly.

In the Middle Ages, Fez was culturally far in advance of European cities. Now, with its timelessness and unchanging character, it carries the visitor back into that era. The 40-kilometre (25-mile) city wall (opposite top) is completely intact. The citizens preserve their traditions – opposite centre: a wedding procession. Even the old trades such as wool dyeing (opposite bottom) have mostly survived.

was there too that, at the turn of the first millennium, Gerbert of Aurillac learnt the decimal system with Arabic numbers, including the nought, which he would later introduce into Europe after he became Pope Sylvester II.

The complex covers an area of 16,000 square metres (4 acres) overall. It has 14 massive gates, a magnificent library and a 16-aisle prayer hall with 270 columns, which, together with the inner courtyard, can readily accommodate more than 22,000 worshippers. Even the huge wash-houses and latrines next to it have carved and painted cedarwood ceilings.

No one knows exactly when Fez's history began. A settlement called Madinat el-Faz, built by Idris I and inhabited mainly by Berbers, is believed to have existed on the right bank of the Wadi Fez in 789, but most historians believe that the city was actually founded in 808. On 22 December of that year, on the advice of astrologers, Moulay Idris II (who was only 16 years old at the time) laid the foundation stone for the future capital of his kingdom on the opposite bank, where his burial mosque now stands.

In the 9th century, thousands of families flocked in from Kairouan and Córdoba. Their craftsmanship and learning helped build the foundations for the city's future prosperity. At first the immigrants lived in two strictly segregated areas – el-Andalus on the eastern side of the river and el-Qaraouiyine to the west. Their rivalry, a microcosm of the conflict between the Spanish Omayyads and the Fatimids from Ifriqiyya (Tunisia), was a major obstacle to the city's development for 200 years. In 1069 the Almoravid conquerors began to tear down the dividing walls, build bridges between the two halves and surround the resulting city, Fez el-Bali, with new fortified walls.

It was only then that the advantages of the site became clear. The numerous wells in the city were cased, the river regulated and

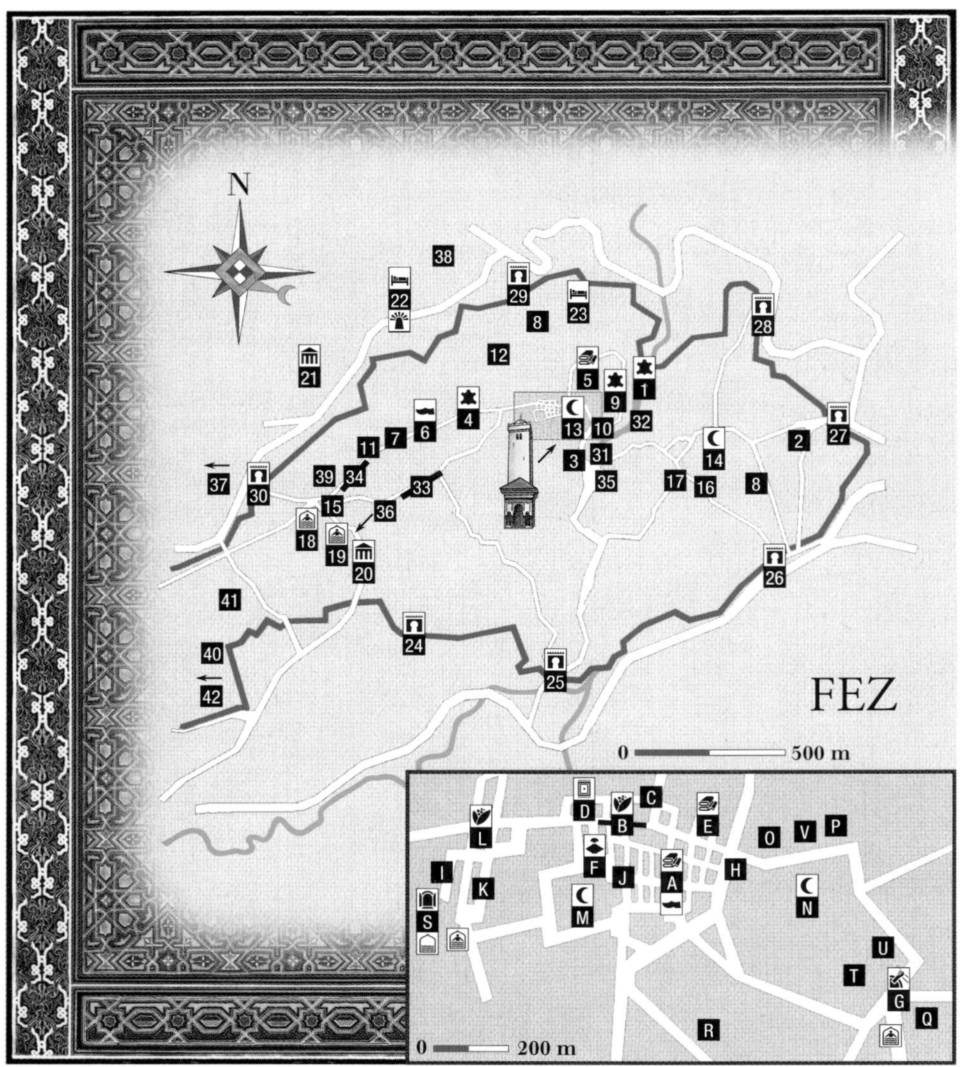

Fez el-Bali – the old city
*SEPARATE MARKETS AND COMMERCIAL DISTRICTS: **1** Madabigh Chouara (tanneries), **2** el-Fakharine (potters), **3** Souk Sebaghine (dyers), **4** Labatine (sheepskin), **5** Sidi Ahmed Tijani (fabric market), **6** Cherrabliyne (shoe repairs), **7** Assal and Melh (salt and honey), **8** Zitoun and Ghlal (olives and snails), **9** Eljald Sinnat Starem (leather pouffes), **10** Mechatine (horn combs), **11** Maharite (ploughs), **12** Elhamam (birds; Fridays only). MOSQUES: **13** Qaraouiyine (and university), **14** des Andalous. KORANIC SCHOOLS: **15** Medersa Bou Inania, **16** es-Sehrij, **17** el-Oued. BATHS: **18** Bildi (new), **19** Bildi (old). MUSEUMS: **20** des Arts marocains/Dar Batha (arts and crafts), **21** Musée des Armes/Borj Nord (weapons). HOTELS: **22** Les Mérinides, **23** Palais Jamai. CITY GATES: **24** Bab el-Hadid, **25** Jdid, **26** Ftouh, **27** el-Khoukha, **28** Sidi Boujida, **29** Guissa, **30** el-Mahrouk. BRIDGES: **31** Gzam ben Skoum, **32** Beine Mdoun. STREETS AND SQUARES: **33** Talaa Seghira, **34** Talaa Kebira, **35** Place Rsif, **36** Place de l'Istiqlal. OTHER: **37** Cherarda Kasbah, **38** Merinid necropolis, **39** House of the Water Clock, **40** Fez Jdid, **41** Boujeloud garden, **42** Royal Palace.*

Central souqs
*SEPARATE MARKETS: **A** Qaissariya (fabrics, shoes), **B** Souk el-Attarine (spices), **C** el-Haik (tailors/*jellabas*), **D** Tillis (carpets), **E** el-Bali (wool, weavers), **F** Elaotour (perfumes), **G** Enhaissi (brass smiths), **H** Smat Laadoul (notaries), **I** en-Nejjarine (carpenters), **J** Elmaaden Labyad (white metal/nickel silver), **K** Essarraj (saddlers), **L** el-Hinna (henna). MOSQUES: **M** Burial mosque of Moulay Idris, **N** Qaraouiyine. KORANIC SCHOOLS: **O** Medersa Attarine, **P** Mesbahia, **Q** Seffarine, **R** Cherratine. CARAVANSERAI: **S** en-Nejjarine (and well). OTHER: **T** University Library, **U** Former* kadi*'s house, **V** Wash-house and latrines.*

BORDER: Painted wooden doors in the Royal Palace. ILLUSTRATION: Minaret of the Qaraouiyine Mosque.

For general key see page 146.

a complex double network of canals built to supply fresh water to mosques, houses and workplaces. Large-scale olive, fruit and grain cultivation was started on the fertile hills of the region and they were also used as grazing land. The cedar and oak forests of the Central Atlas and the many nearby quarries proved a virtually inexhaustible source of building materials. But most important was the realization of the city's strategic advantages for trade. It was at the intersection between the main routes from the Atlantic to the eastern Maghreb and from the Mediterranean to the mountain passes leading to the Sahara. Soon the merchants of Fez were trading all over the world. They travelled to Persia and India, China, East and West Africa. Under the Almohads (1146–1248) the tax register listed 89,000 households, 20,000 warehouses, 9,000 shops, 785 mosques, nearly 500 *funduqs* and the same number of mills. In addition, there were thousands of workshops: weavers, dyers, tanners, paper and silk makers, smiths and kilns for firing ceramics.

The next rulers, the Merinids, elevated Fez to a royal seat for two centuries. They established an administrative and garrison district called Fez Jdid, new Fez, on the plateau to the west of the city. It contained spacious gardens, a sultan's palace (Dar el-Makhzen) and a Jewish quarter, the Mellah. A number of architectural gems were built in the old part of the city, mainly by Moorish artists from Spain. The most notable were the famous Koranic schools such as Bou Inania, Attarine, Mesbahia and Seffarine. Their stucco, carvings and friezes are nearly as impressive as those in the Alhambra. Fez was the most splendid city in the Maghreb, on a par with Cairo and Granada.

Its decline began in the late 15th century with political unrest, epidemics and famine. Marrakesh and later Meknes replaced Fez as the capital. But even then it still retained its national religious and commercial importance. Under the Alawis, who had their seat in Fez from 1727, European influence gradually increased, culminating in the Treaty of Fez under which Morocco formally became a French protectorate on 30 March 1912. The Ville Nouvelle (New Town), a modern quarter in the European style, was built in the next few years. Marshal

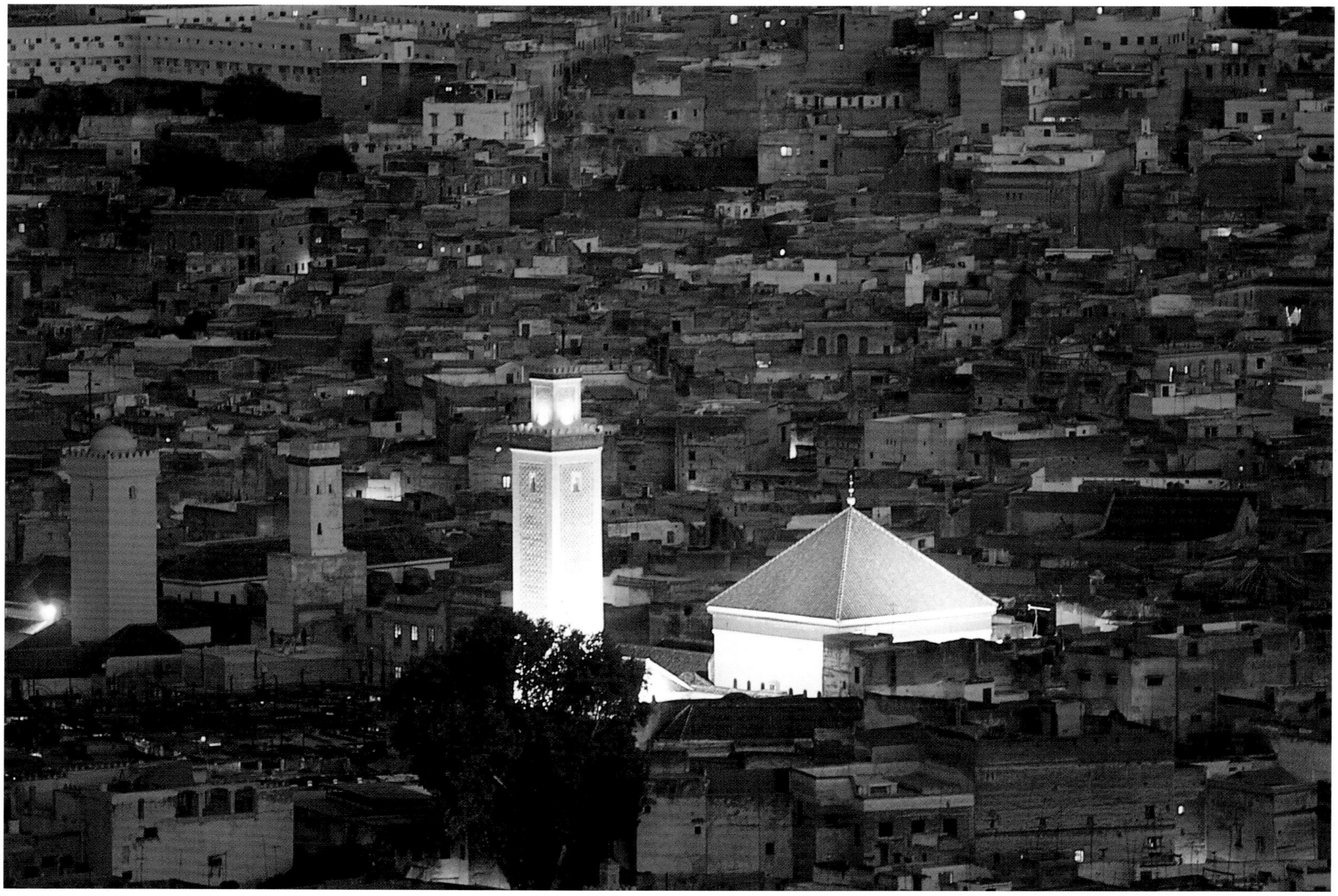

Lyautey, the first French resident-general, declared Fez el-Bali and Fez Jdid historic monuments.

Sanaa with its wedding-cake façades might seem more exotic to a European visitor at first sight, Damascus more steeped in history, Cairo more enormous in scale, but no other city in the Islamic world gives such an authentic impression of how the Orient was in the Middle Ages. There are few cities in which the visitor has such a feeling of being in a complex and strange world whose mysteries would take years to fathom.

In many ways Fez has preserved its religious, intellectual, political and economic traditions. In the streets around Moulay Idris's tomb there are still head-high wooden crossbeams which keep out riding animals (considered unclean), force passers-by to bow down and remind everyone that this is a holy area. Although Morocco's most modern university is in Rabat, el-Qaraouiyine still enjoys an outstanding reputation, especially for theology. The monarch moved his seat to the capital some time ago, but for a couple of weeks a year he still takes up residence in the Dar el-Makhzen in Fez, the most ancient royal city. Casablanca might be the country's economic centre, but the Fassi, the old-established citizens of Fez, are still regarded in the rest of Morocco as an elite. A handful of local aristocratic families, such as the Tazis and Charuits, Mokris, Hadshauis and Hababus, still control textile industries and trade all over the country and like to show off their status at lavish weddings or circumcision ceremonies.

The future of the craftsmen in the souq is threatened, as it is in every other souq, but crafts are still relatively important in Fez. 30,000 master craftsmen belong to corporations. More than half the 300,000 inhabitants of the old quarter earn their living from crafts, covering 780 different trades. There are the comb makers, who remove the horns from dead oxen, split them open,

The 13 remarkable wooden brackets protruding from the front of a house in the western part of the Talaa Kebira, the higher of the two main streets, are the remains of a 600-year-old water clock (below). Nobody knows now how it worked, except that it rang bells when it was time for prayers. Above: the burial mosque of Idris II.

unroll them over a fire and, with enormous patience, saw each tooth by hand; the ember makers, who hand out glowing pieces of wood to locksmiths and smiths, cooks and pot menders early in the morning so that they can light their fires; cutlers and knife grinders; public scribes with antiquated typewriters; women who paint hands and feet with *harqus* (henna patterns); and community bakers, to whom families take their individually marked flat loaves every morning. There are special markets for such goods as keys, ploughs and leather saddles, olives and snails, honey and salt. Unfortunately the friendly little office in which boys who lost their pennies when they were fetching tea could get new ones (to avoid a beating when they got home) closed down many years ago.

The idyllic impression is to some extent deceptive. It disguises the fact that Fez's future is under threat. For decades, especially since independence in 1956, more and more people have been flocking into the city

The tanners' district in the Quartier Chouara is one of the most unwholesome parts of the city, especially with the stench of the animal hides and tanning materials. The location was chosen deliberately; this is where the river, the Wadi Fez (Oued Fès), flows out of the city, carrying all the toxic waste with it.

from the rural areas. In only thirty years the population has quadrupled to a million. Inside the medina there are now nearly a thousand people to every hectare (400 to the acre). Many upper-class people have moved to the new part of the city. Most of their old palaces are overflowing with new arrivals. The buildings have deteriorated and, with them, the whole infrastructure. The once extolled 'river of pearls' is ecologically dead where it flows eastwards out of the city. In the early 1980s UNESCO took the old town under its wing and a comprehensive rescue plan was drawn up. One of the shorter-term measures is for about 70,000 people to be moved to new buildings on the outskirts in the next few years. This operation alone will cost several hundred million dollars. Will it ever be completed?

شيراز

Shiraz

A city of learning and poetry, gardens, roses and wine. It might sound like a flattering cliché, but it was not far from the truth – at least up to two or three generations ago.

The capital of Fars province in southern Iran has been a great centre of learning for centuries. An unusually high proportion of its inhabitants have been doctors, lawyers, alchemists, astronomers and mathematicians. It is where the two most important Persian poets, Hafiz and Saadi, were born, worked and are buried. Isfahan is famous for its roses, symbols of perfection to the Sufis, believed to have grown from the Prophet's sweat when he ascended to heaven. Shiraz grapes are appreciated by wine connoisseurs all over the world. Shiraz lies 1,500 metres (5,000 feet) above sea level and has been happily endowed by nature with a protective ring

In Islam, as in antiquity and Christianity, the rose is a symbol of eroticism. Throughout history its scent and its power as a symbol of paradise and love have inspired mystics and poets in Shiraz, a rose-growing centre. Opposite top: the mausoleum of the poet Hafiz, who died in 1390.

of mountains, a surplus of water and an exceptionally mild climate, especially in the spring – hence its magnificent gardens.

Settlers discovered its advantages in the Achaemenid period, back in 600 BC. Under the Sassanians, Shiraz became an important regional centre and around the beginning of the 11th century it was so splendid and prosperous that it even rivalled Baghdad. Spared from the Mongol hordes of Genghis Khan and Tamerlane through the political astuteness of its provincial governor, Atabeg, in the next few centuries it blossomed into one of the leading Islamic centres for literature, calligraphy, painting and architecture, and remained so in the Safavid period, despite strong competition from Isfahan. It was not until the early 18th century that Shiraz went into a period of decline when it suffered a series of earthquakes and epidemics, was invaded by the Afghans and besieged by Nadir Shah. However, from 1751, when Karim Khan, founder of the Zand dynasty, made Shiraz the national capital, it had another brief but glorious heyday.

The symmetry of the bazaar in Shiraz makes it one of the most beautiful markets in Iran. Its main axis (below), consisting of the Bazaar-e-Vakil and the Bazaar-e-Nou, is over 500 metres (550 yards) long and 20 metres (65 feet) wide and reminiscent of the nave of a huge church. Even today its six gates are locked and guarded after the shops shut and on public holidays.

The new ruler, who modestly called himself *vakil*, governor, proved a wise and benevolent patron. He fortified the city with trenches and walls, laid out gardens and plantations with a complex canal system and encouraged art of all kinds. He invited 12,000 craftsmen and artists from all over the country to build a royal quarter for him outside the old town. They built a mighty citadel, the Ark (Arg-e-Karim Khani), a mosque, the Masjed-e-Vakil, baths, the Hammam-e-Vakil, and two water reservoirs. Between them were avenues, the Bagh-e-Nasar garden, a place for riding and polo-playing – and a bazaar.

Obviously, Shiraz already had its large bazaars (the only one that has survived is the Bazaar-e-Ordu), but none of them could compare with the new buildings. The mere fact that they were near the Istachr gate, the way out of the city on the road to Isfahan, meant that they became the chief centre for trade. The main sections, Bazaar-e-Vakil and Bazaar-e-Nou, are over 500 metres (550

The roof vault of the Bazaar-e-Vakil has two ceilings. The 60-cm (2-foot) space between them protects people passing below against the outside temperatures, which can be extreme. The inner ceiling is artistically decorated with bricks. Thanks to skilful structural engineering it has never been damaged in an earthquake since it was built 200 years ago.

yards) long and are lined with innumerable caravanserais. All the shopping streets have a double vault insulating them against heat and cold. At the point where the central axis (Persian: *rasteh*) crosses the two main side streets there is a 20-metre (65-foot) high *charsu* with an octagonal dome. In the time of Karim Khan this housed the bazaar administrators and a pool fed by underground canals which controlled the bazaar's micro-climate. The bazaar was so splendid that the city often chose to entertain important visitors and official envoys there.

In 1794 Lutf Ali Khan, the last ruler of the Zand dynasty, was murdered. His successors, the Kajars, moved their seat to Tehran, 700 kilometres (435 miles) to the north. Shiraz retained some of its prosperity thanks to its special sovereign rights and its key position on the main trade route to Bushehr on the Gulf, but politically it declined into a provincial town. In the 20th century Shiraz has shared the fate of other Iranian cities. The impoverished rural population, attracted by the new jobs in industry, flocked to the provincial capitals, which soon became full to overflowing.

Between 1960 and 1979, the year of the revolution, Shiraz's population rose from 120,000 to 460,000. In 1993 the official figure was 1.4 million, but the true figure was probably twice that. The appearance of the city is being marred by haphazard and tasteless development. Many of the gardens and open spaces of the royal quarter have been concreted over. Drinking water is scarce. As the old inhabitants moved to modern houses on the outskirts, many districts in the old part of the city became hives of petty crime. Shiraz had already lost its importance as a transit point when the

Shiraz – the bazaar district

SEPARATE MARKETS: ***1*** *Hat makers' bazaar,* ***2*** *Former textile bazaar,* ***3*** *Former quiver makers' bazaar,* ***4*** *Former sword makers' bazaar,* ***5*** *Former trimmings bazaar,* ***6*** *Bazaar-e-Nou,* ***7*** *Bazaar-e-Ordu,* ***8*** *Bazaar-e-Mesgari (coppersmiths),* ***9*** *Bazaar-e-Moshir,* ***10*** *Bazaar-e-Haj. MOSQUES:* ***11*** *Masjed-e-Vakil,* ***12*** *Masjed-e-Nou,* ***13*** *Masjed-e-Jame (Friday Mosque),* ***14*** *Haj-Ghani. MAUSOLEUMS:* ***15*** *Baghe-ye-Sayyed Mir Mohammad. KORANIC SCHOOLS:* ***16*** *Madrese-ye-Akhabada Khan,* ***17*** *Madrese Khan. CARAVANSERAIS:* ***18*** *Karavansarai-ye-Rezasadeh,* ***19*** *Mehdieh,* ***20*** *Sukhteh,* ***21*** *Gomrok,* ***22*** *Ahmadi,* ***23*** *Rohani,* ***24*** *Phil (carpets),* ***25*** *Moshir (arts and crafts). BATHS:* ***26*** *Hammam-e-Vakil,* ***27*** *Hammam-e-Nakhshak. OTHER:* ***28*** *Arg-e-Karim Khani (Ark/citadel),* ***29*** *Muze-ye-Pars (Parsi museum). STREETS: Bolvar-e-Karim Khan-e-Zand,* ***31*** *Kheyabun-e-Lotf Ali Khan-e-Zand.*

BORDER: Shiraz carpet.
ILLUSTRATION: Hafiz mausoleum.

For general key see page 146.

trans-Iranian railway was built in the thirties and had consequently forfeited much of its trade.

Time did not stand still for the bazaar either. In an act of urban vandalism in 1936, the Bolvar-e-Karim Khan-e-Zand was built through the hat makers' bazaar. Soon afterwards the pool was filled in and the level of the central strip was raised by a metre (3 feet), affecting the air circulation. In the meantime, most of the caravanserais were turned into car parks, emergency housing for new arrivals or – at best – into carpet stores, their appearance disfigured by aluminium and corrugated iron. The goods were no longer arranged in separate sections. Many of the shops were split into smaller units. Their merchandise is mostly mass-produced and the only traditional products of the region still available in quantity are carpets.

With all its shortcomings, however, the bazaar has a uniformity and a harmonious design unequalled anywhere else in Iran.

The Khoda Khane, the house of God, in the courtyard of the old Friday Mosque (top), was built more than 600 years ago and has no equal in Islamic architecture. It was based on the Kaaba in Mecca and is a shrine for valuable copies of the Koran. The mausoleum of Shah Kheragh (centre) is an important place of pilgrimage for the Shiites. Sayyed Mir Ahmad, brother of Reza, the highly revered eighth imam, is buried under its striking dome. The 130-year-old Sarai Moshir (bottom) was originally used by the people of the bazaar as a financial institution. Today the caravanserai has been impressively restored and houses craft and souvenir shops.

اصفهان

Isfahan

At the entrance to the bazaar is an open space measuring 500 by 150 metres (18½ acres) – seven times the size of the Piazza San Marco in Venice. It has flowers, trees and a huge pool with fountains in the centre. On all four sides are the imposing façades of two-storey buildings with balconies, housing souvenir and craft shops. To the north is the magnificent gate to the Qaiseriye, the emperor's bazaar. To the west, the Ali Qapu royal palace with its baldachin supported by 18 enormous wooden pillars, visible for some distance around. To the east and south are two mosques which are among the finest in the Islamic world, the Masjed-e-Sheykh Lotfollah and the Masjed-e-Imam (or Shah Mosque).

The first, the smaller and older of the two (built 1602–1618) has probably the most perfect faïence dome in the world. The second, built between 1612 and 1630, has for some years been officially known as the Imam Khomeini mosque. Its beauty and size are breathtaking.

But even the imposing setting and the recent ambitious renovation work cannot conceal the fact that the Meydan-e-Shah, the Imam Square as it is now called, is only a pale reflection of its former splendour. Soon after it was built in the 17th century, all kinds of entertainments were put on there in the king's presence on feast days: lion fights, bullfights, wrestling matches, jousting and polo matches (the goal posts can still be seen on the two transverse sides). On special occasions there were legendary firework displays and brass lanterns were hung on the balconies to illuminate the festivities. On working days, by contrast, the square was full of traders. The goods were laid out on carpets, protected by awnings. Dozens of moneychangers sat on square bedsteads with small leather bags or metal cash-boxes beside them. Camels and horses were sold outside the gate of the Shah Mosque in the mornings. In the afternoon carpenters, wood and bird dealers put up their stands there. Twice a day a special court ceremony was held on the balcony above the bazaar door, still known as *Naqqarehane*, the drum house.

'Esfahan nesf-e-jahan', 'Ishahan is half the world'. The Isfahanis' pride in their city is not to be wondered at, considering its glorious and majestic past.

The Masjed-e-Sheykh Lotfollah (opposite: the entrance) and the Masjed-e-Imam or Shah Mosque (below: front iwan *and dome). The two were built on the orders of Shah Abbas as part of his magnificent emperor's square complex and are a prime example of Persian faïence art. The names of the architects, Ali Riza Abbasi and Ostad Ali Akbar-e-Isfahani, were commemorated in documents, which was very unusual.*

The desert settlement at an altitude of 1,600 metres (5,250 feet) on the banks of the Zayandeh-Rud so impressed the Achaemenid kings about 2,500 years ago that they made it their seat. The Sassanians (AD 224–651) used Sephhahane (Persian for army rallying point) as a garrison and provincial centre. But it was not until the year 1000 that it acquired greater cultural importance, first under the Shiite Emir Ala ad-Daula, who brought the great Avicenna to his court, and later under the Seljuk prince Togril-Beg, who made it the capital of his kingdom. At the time there were two centres, the older Gayy near the Sharestan bridge and al-Yahudiya around the Great Mosque 3 kilometres (almost 2 miles) north-west, named after the large Jewish community whose members claimed descent from Jews taken to Babylon by Nebuchadnezzar and later carried off to Persia by Cyrus.

However, Isfahan really owes its world-famous reputation as a complete work of art to one man, the Safavid Shah Abbas I, who did not come to the throne until the late

اصفهان

Si-o-Se Pol, the Bridge of 33 Arches (also known as Pol-e-Allahverdikhan) links the southern and northern sections of Chahar Bagh Boulevard. In the interests of conservation, it was recently closed to traffic. Since then it has been a popular place to stroll and meet friends.

16th century (it had in the meantime been attacked by the Mongols in 1240 and by Tamerlane's hordes in 1387). In 1598 Shah Abbas chose the city as his seat. A cosmopolitan polymath, he established contact with the ruling dynasties in the West and encouraged the first European traders, English and Dutch, to settle in Persia. On the south bank of the river he settled Armenian Christians (who had a reputation as gifted entrepreneurs) from the north Persian city of Jolfa. Even today the part of Isfahan known by the same name houses a large Christian community. At the same time he invited countless builders and artists to renovate the city. They came from all over the country and also from China and India, Europe and the Levant.

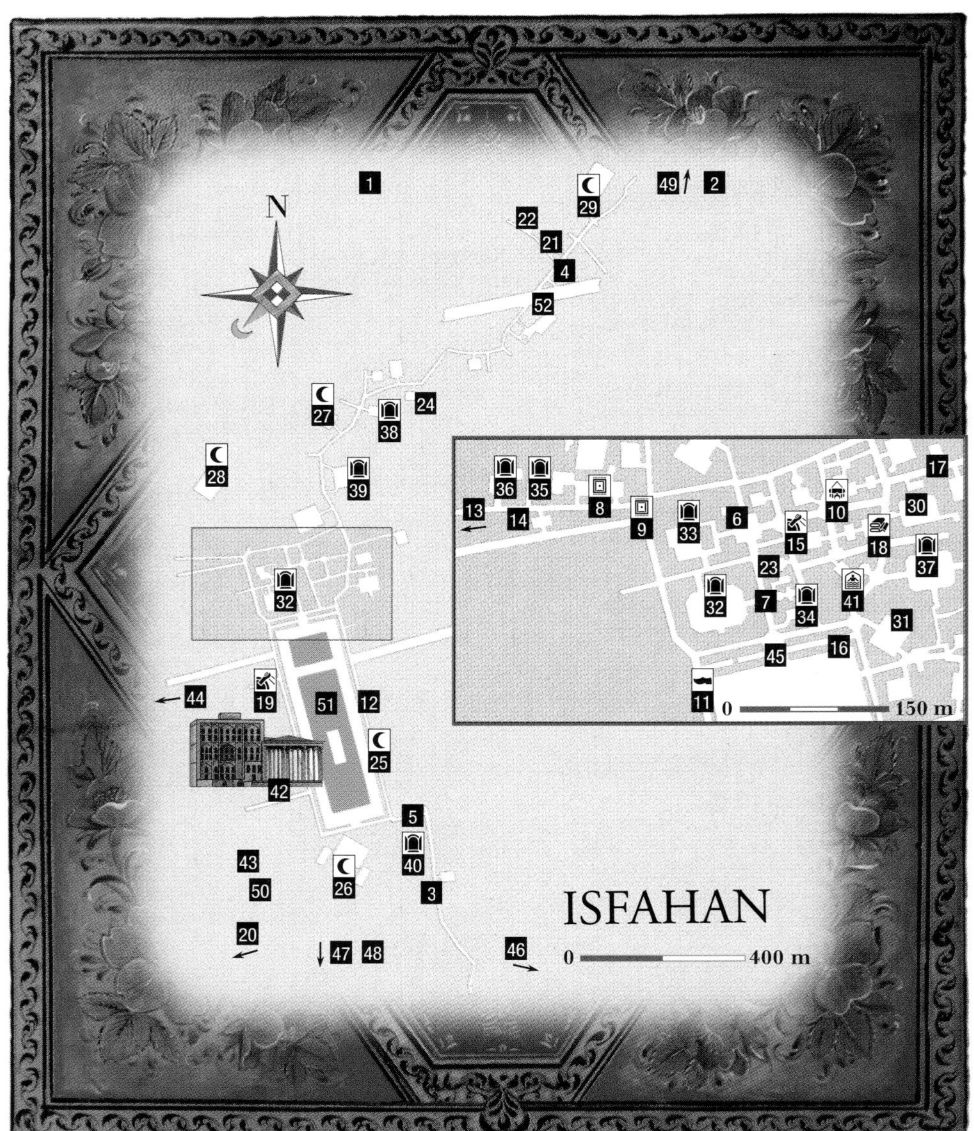

Isfahan – The bazaar district

SEPARATE MARKETS: ***1*** *Bazaar Dar-Dasht,* ***2*** *Bazaar Majlesi,* ***3*** *Hasan-Abad,* ***4*** *Bazaar-e-Bozorg,* ***5*** *Maqsud,* ***6*** *Jitsazha,* ***7*** *Qaiseriye (arts and crafts, antiques, souvenirs),* ***8*** *Farsh Forushha (carpets),* ***9*** *Rangrazan (dyers and carpets),* ***10*** *Zargarha-e-Tala,* ***11*** *Kaffashha (shoemakers),* ***12*** *Ahnagaran (ironsmiths),* ***13*** *Ghanadi (sugar),* ***14*** *Kashisazi (tile makers),* ***15*** *Karbasforushha/Samarvasazha (samovar makers),* ***16*** *Sarrafan (formerly moneychangers, old coins),* ***17*** *Monaggem-Bashi (wool, silk, carpet repair materials),* ***18*** *Mohles (textiles),* ***19*** *Mesgaran (coppersmiths),* ***20*** *Bazaar-e-Boland/Honar Bazaar (crafts). SPECIALIST WORKSHOPS AND SHOPS:* ***21*** *Asri (oil presses),* ***22*** *Koy Shamaleh (oil presses),* ***23*** *Gas production,* ***24*** *Dyers (in the former Hammam Goud). MOSQUES:* ***25*** *Masjed-e-Sheykh Lotfollah,* ***26*** *Masjed-e-Imam (Shah Mosque),* ***27*** *Masjed-e-Nou,* ***28*** *Masjed-e-Hakim,* ***29*** *Masjed-e-Jame (Great Mosque). KORANIC SCHOOLS (MADRESE):* ***30*** *Jadde-Bozorg,* ***31*** *Molla-Abdollah. CARAVANSERAIS AND HALLS (SARAI AND TIMCE):* ***32*** *Shah Sarai,* ***33*** *Jitsazha,* ***34*** *Shelle (fabric printers/*qalamkar*),* ***35*** *Linj,* ***36*** *Borujeniha,* ***37*** *Mohles,* ***38*** *Hajji Karim,* ***39*** *Arbab,* ***40*** *Abbas Yavari. BATHS (HAMMAM):* ***41*** *Shah. PALACES:* ***42*** *Ali Qapu (royal palace),* ***43*** *Hasht Behesht,* ***44*** *Chehel Sotoun. OTHER:* ***45*** *Naqqarehane (drum house = bazaar entrance),* ***46*** *Sharestan bridge,* ***47*** *Si-o-Se Pol (Bridge of 33 Arches),* ***48*** *Jolfa (Armenian quarter),* ***49*** *Jowbareh (Jewish quarter),* ***50*** *Chahar Bagh. SQUARES:* ***51*** *Meydan-e-Shah (e-Imam),* ***52*** *Old square.*

BORDER: Parchment painting from the Kajar period.
ILLUSTRATION: Ali Qapu (royal palace).

For general key see page 146.

With its pavilions, arcades and terraces between the drainage canals, the Pol-e-Khajou bridge (above) is primarily a place for relaxation and only secondarily a traffic route and a weir for the waters of the Zayandeh-Rud. The picture was taken on the lowest level.

Previous page above: the dome of the Masjed-e-Sheykh Lotfollah, a transcendentally symbolic carpet of faïence. Below: the view from the terrace of the Chehel Sotoun, the Pavilion of the Forty Columns, is the same view that its builder, Shah Abbas, would have enjoyed.

traffic. The centrepiece was the 4-kilometre (2 1/2-mile) boulevard which is still the main north–south axis, bisected by the river.

More than 150 new mosques were built at the beginning of the brief but glorious Safavid period in the early 18th century, together with 50 Koranic schools, dozens of caravanserais and more than 200 public baths. The centre of government activity shifted from the medieval site near the Great mosque to the area around the Meydan-e-Shah, and with it the centre of the bazaar.

By the 11th century, the old square (*meydan*) had become the centre of the city. It had a castle, a drum house, a *qaiseriya* and shops selling silk, brocade, materials, precious stones, ivory and many other goods. There were markets along the main streets radiating out from the *meydan* from at least

Hundreds of these huge dove towers (above) are scattered around the streets of Isfahan and the surrounding fields, although now only a couple of dozen are still in use. The birds' droppings were at one time used as fertilizer for the famous melons. Left: the 500,000 tiles, mainly yellow, cobalt blue and turquoise, with their flower patterns, kufi *script or the medallions and tendrils of a prayer-mat pattern merge into a perfect whole in the Masjed-e-Imam (Shah Mosque).*

They created the strictly geometrical palace quarter, the Chahar Bagh, with pleasure gardens full of promenades and watercourses, massive administrative buildings, court factories, summerhouses like the Palace of the Eight Paradises (Hasht Behesht) or the Pavilion of the Forty Columns (Chehel Sotoun) and the Bridge of 33 Arches (Si-o-Se Pol), recently closed to

that time. Some, like the Bazaar Dar-Dasht and the Bazaar Majlesi, are still used as local markets. The 1.5 kilometre (1,650-yard) shopping street leading to the western gates of the city is still the main street in the bazaar, the longest vaulted bazaar street in the world. The embankment of building rubble and refuse accumulated over the ages raises it about 2 metres (6 1/2 feet) above the level

Overleaf: the Ali Qapu Palace was also the gateway to the imperial parks. Its terrace room with a flat roof supported on 18 slender columns is one of the landmarks of the Meydan-e-Shah. Shah Abbas used it as a kind of royal box from which he watched parades and polo games in the square. The music room on the upper floor (seen in the photograph) shows the level of sophistication at the court. Its walls and alcoves are covered with a wood and plaster membrane with artistic shapes cut out of it to improve the acoustics.

Although mass-produced goods are flooding the market in Isfahan, there is still an astonishing range of craft work. Qalamkar *– hand-printed fabric – is one example (above: a shop in the Qaiseriye). The smiths' guild takes great pride in the* allamat *(below), the metal tree of life festooned with bells, carried at the front of the procession at the Ashura festival.*

of the adjoining courtyards, which shows how old it is.

Shah Abbas redeveloped the city extensively and had a number of new bazaars built: the buildings surrounding the Meydan-e-Shah (originally including a large number of coffee houses), both the Hasan-Abad and Maqsud bazaars to the south-east and the large bazaar to the north. The old *meydan* soon deteriorated into a wood and vegetable market, but the high-class retail businesses established themselves where they could expect a good turnover from the courtiers, soldiers and visitors from the nearby Chahar Bagh. The area to the east of the main axis, the Qaiseriye and its extension, the Jitsazha (fabric printers' bazaar), became the most sought-after site. It had brokers and coin minters, moneychangers and goldsmiths, coffee dealers, rifle and samovar makers. The less busy western part on the other hand, around the Jitsazha and Shah Sarai, housed the more basic craftsmen such as dyers, shoemakers and smiths, and the cotton and muslin printers.

A great deal has changed since then. Carpet dealers with their shops and stores, offices and repair workshops have taken over the narrow streets and courtyards of the north-western bazaar district. In the Qaiseriye, miniature painters, souvenir and antique sellers replaced the traditional craftsmen when large numbers of tourists flocked in between the Second World War and the late 1960s. Many import-export firms transferred to Tehran and wholesalers have moved out to the arterial roads which are more convenient for traffic. The shops selling western consumer goods aimed at customers with money to spend have for some time now been based in the modern business quarter on Chahar Bagh boulevard. The Bazaar Shah near the old *meydan* has been brutally bisected by a wide street – something that Iranian town planners seem fond of doing.

Even so, compared with the disastrous developments in other large cities, the historic centre of Isfahan (which is also the stronghold of the fundamentalist Hizbollah party) has so far stood up to the onslaught of modernity remarkably well. It still has its traditional low clay houses, its avenues and green spaces and its riverside promenades.

The bazaar has been lucky too, on the whole. It has never suffered any serious earthquakes and, even when it was sacked by the Afghans (1722) and the troops of the Persian despot Nadir Shah (1732), its buildings remained largely intact. As a result it contains a representative selection of Islamic secular architecture over the last 500 years. It has about 5 kilometres (3 miles) of shopping streets, some with brick arches, some with poplar beams, well over a hundred caravanserais (*sarai*), innumerable covered halls (*timce*) and connecting wings (*dehliz*). Although there are some modern concrete, steel and glass buildings, these blend in fairly well with the whole. In addition, it has two domed buildings (*chaharsu*) otherwise found only in Central Asia and several strange, windowless pillared halls half set into the ground, built some time in the early 19th century and probably used originally either as warehouses or as stables for camels.

Many of the local crafts have also been preserved. Obviously the days are gone when the coral from Yemen, musk from Tibet and squeaky toys (*sic!*) from Aleppo (mentioned in an early guide to Isfahan for foreign businessmen) were to be found, when sheep's-head cooks and camel-hide knackers practised their trade and Georgian maidservants and elephants were for sale. But living relics of the pre-industrial age can still be found in many corners: brocade weavers, fabric printers and samovar makers, tile and carpet pattern painters, dyers, pea roasters, sugar-loaf moulders, not forgetting the specialists who make the scourges with which, every year at Ashura, the feast in honour of the martyr Hussein, devout Shiites whip themselves like medieval flagellants until they bleed.

Ancient oil presses and grain mills (above) can still be found in the side alleys around the 900-year-old Great Mosque. In Isfahan, as elsewhere in Iran, restoration work has been going on for many years on artistic monuments like the Naqqarehane or drum house (below), the massive gateway to the bazaar.

سمرقند بخاری جیوا

Samarkand, Bukhara and Khiva

If you take a map of Asia and draw a line from China to the Mediterranean and another from Moscow to India, the two intersect in a region which in recent years has been somewhat isolated from world events, but in earlier times was more than once at their centre. The ancient Greeks called this region Transoxiana, the Arabs Mawarannahr, while the Russian occupiers in the 19th century called it Turkestan because of its large Turkic population. Few regions are more full of contrasts.

At its heart are two vast deserts, the Kyzyl Kum and the Kara Kum, swept by sand- and snowstorms and with temperatures ranging from minus to plus 50°C (–58° to +122°F). They are bordered by endless steppes, the massive Pamir and Tien Shan mountain ranges and the Aral Sea, the fourth largest inland body of water in the world. The arid

The Registan in Samarkand is the most magnificent square in Central Asia. Below: the Medressa Tilla-Kari, one of three theological colleges around the enormous square, illuminated for the nightly son et lumière *show. Its façade is a massive tapestry of faïence decoration. Its interior (opposite below) is covered with gold leaf and lapis lazuli.*

landscape is bisected by two long rivers, the Syr Darya and the Amu Darya, both edged with fertile oases, in which the climate is relatively mild and life is easy. From primeval times to the beginning of the 20th century, the inhabitants of the oases, settled farmers, were in constant conflict with the nomads living in the inhospitable empty region beyond the narrow fertile areas. If they were strong enough, they protected their territory with ramparts. If they showed any signs of weakness, they were attacked and their irrigation canals, the lifelines of their civilization, were destroyed.

Even more terrible than these local wars were the foreign invasions. Alexander the Great, Genghis Khan and Tamerlane, Huns, Turks, Arabs and Russians – the conquerors came from every side. Their barbarity has never been equalled in the whole course of history. Time and time again, cities and even entire civilizations were wiped out, although some came back to life again and flourished as they had before.

The words of Samarkand's founder, Tamerlane, on one of the city gates, 'If you doubt our power, look at our buildings', are particularly true of the Friday Mosque, Bibi-Khanym (above: a side dome). Even though its 43-metre (140-foot) high prayer hall collapsed soon after it was completed, the megalomania of its builders is evident from the ruins. It is currently being rebuilt with UNESCO help.

The town of Kunya Urgench, on the lower reaches of the Amu Darya, is a particularly dramatic example of the region's turbulent history. In the pre-Islamic period it was an important trading centre. Under the Arabs it became the capital of the Khorezm oases and for a short time – after the destruction of Baghdad and before the rise of Cairo – was even a glittering centre of the Islamic world. It had magnificent palaces, mosques and mausoleums and a population of several hundred thousand. In 1221 it was conquered by Genghis Khan. The Mongols had its inhabitants slaughtered or deported, they demolished its dams and turned it into 'a place where jackals and crows live', as the Persian historian Juwaini wrote. Soon afterwards it underwent a renaissance under the local Sufi dynasty. But in 1379 Tamerlane besieged the city and nine years later he razed it to the ground. Kunya Urgench was not rebuilt until the 19th century.

Artistically too, Central Asia has always been a region of contrasts, but in this case

سمرقند بخاری جیوا

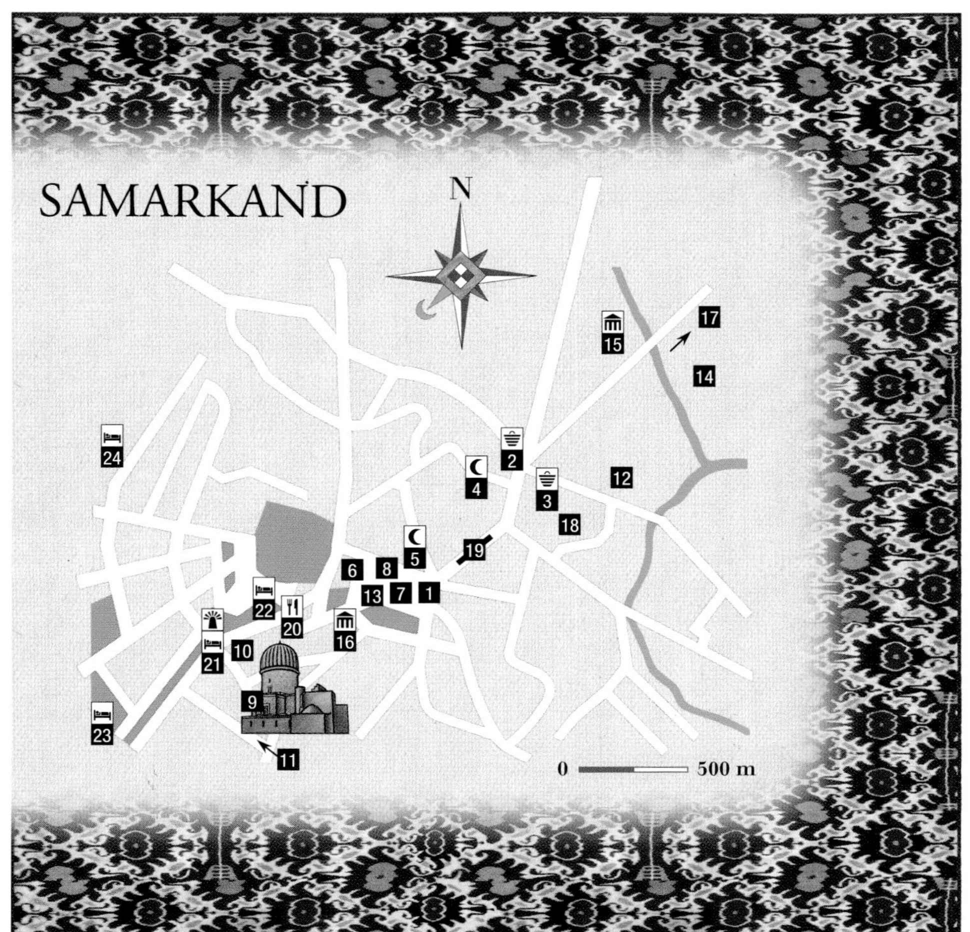

Samarkand
BAZAARS AND MARKET BUILDINGS: ***1*** *Charsu,* ***2*** *Siab (collective farm) market,* ***3*** *Sunday market. MOSQUES:* ***4*** *Bibi-Khanym,* ***5*** *Jubilee Mosque (for Samarkand's 2,500 years). KORANIC SCHOOLS (MEDRESSA):* ***6*** *Ulughbek,* ***7*** *Sher-Dor,* ***8*** *Tilla-Kari (souvenir market). MAUSOLEUMS:* ***9*** *Guri Amir (Tamerlane's tomb),* ***10*** *Rukhobod,* ***11*** *Ak-Saray,* ***12*** *Shah-i Zinda (necropolis). OTHER:* ***13*** *Registan,* ***14*** *Ulughbek Observatory,* ***15*** *Archaeological Museum/Afrasiab,* ***16*** *Museum of Local History, Art and Culture,* ***17*** *Old Zeravshan bridge,* ***18*** *Jungut Makhalla (Jewish quarter),* ***19*** *Tashkent Street. RESTAURANT:* ***20*** *Kafe Sogd. HOTELS:* ***21*** *Samarkand (+ restaurant),* ***22*** *Kuksaray (+ restaurant),* ***23*** *Zeravshan,* ***24*** *Registan.*

BORDER: Silk Parda wall-hanging, c. 1900.
ILLUSTRATION: Tamerlane's tomb (Guri Amir).

For general key see page 146.

Bukhara
BAZAARS AND MARKET BUILDINGS: ***1*** *Taqi Zargaron (former jewellers' bazaar),* ***2*** *Taqi Telpak Furushon (former cap makers' bazaar),* ***3*** *Taqi Sarafon (former moneychangers' bazaar),* ***4*** *Tim Abdullah Khan (former fabric bazaar),* ***5*** *Central bazaar,* ***6*** *New bazaar. MOSQUES:* ***7*** *Bolo-hauz,* ***8*** *Kalan (+ minaret),* ***9*** *Maghoki-Attar,* ***10*** *Baland,* ***11*** *Namozgokh,* ***12*** *Hoja Zaynuddin. KORANIC SCHOOLS (MEDRESSA):* ***13*** *Mir-i-Arab,* ***14*** *Ulughbek,* ***15*** *Abdul Aziz Khan,* ***16*** *Kukeldash,* ***17*** *Nadir Divanbegi,* ***18*** *Modari Khan,* ***19*** *Abdullah Khan* ***20*** *Char Minar. WELLS, BATHS, BASINS:* ***21*** *Chashma-Ayub,* ***22*** *Labi-hauz,* ***23*** *Hammam Sarafon (under restoration),* ***24*** *Hammam Furushon (men only),* ***25*** *Hammam Kalan (women only). OTHER:* ***26*** *Citadel (Ark + Registan),* ***27*** *Samanid mausoleum,* ***28*** *Nadir Divanbegi Khanaka (formerly pilgrims' lodgings),* ***29*** *Faisabad Khanaka (formerly pilgrims' lodgings). RESTAURANTS:* ***30*** *Gorsin (oriental),* ***31*** *Baht (Korean). VIEWPOINTS:* ***32*** *Water tower,* ***33*** *Big wheel. HOTEL:* ***34*** *Bukhoro.*

BORDER: Silk Parda wall-hanging, c. 1900.
ILLUSTRATION: Samanid mausoleum.

For general key see page 146.

their effect was inspirational. Greek, Indian and Persian, Chinese and especially Arab-Islamic elements blended with the local traditions of the steppe dwellers and new, independent forms of expression developed, particularly in fabrics, jewelry, ceramics and metal engraving. Architecture also developed its own style, for instance, in the magnificent decorations made of fired and glazed tiles, alabaster, carving and terracotta, as well as in the perfection of vault construction. For the bazaar buildings in particular, the local architects devised a form unique in the Islamic world: the *tak*, *tim* or *charsu*. They consist of a number of large interlocking rooms and domes, usually over a crossroads. Despite the frequent military incursions, cities such as Bukhara, Khiva and Samarkand developed into religious and commercial centres whose influence extended widely into all corners of the known world. Men like the mathematician al-Khorezmi, the astronomer and geographer al-Biruni and the most important scholar the Middle East has ever produced, abu-Ali ibn-Sina (known in the West as Avicenna), studied and taught in their libraries and Koranic schools. Their workshops produced goods much sought after in Europe: silk and cotton yarns, carpets, miniature paintings, weapons and the prized Turkestan ceramics. Chinese prisoners of war taught them to make the famous rag paper.

The necropolis of Shahi-Zinda, the Living King, in Afrosiab, old Samarkand. The group of mausoleums and mosques built by Tamerlane for relatives and loyal friends is still a place of pilgrimage. Kussam ibn-Abbas, who brought Islam to Central Asia, is believed to have lived in a cave there, fasting and praying. Above: Restoration work in a dome niche.

The temporary prosperity of the cities was also partly due to their position on the central section of the Silk Road. They were intermediate storage points for all the goods carried between Eastern Asia and the Middle East, India, Russia and North Africa. For the traders the shady oases were a welcome respite from the stresses of a journey that could often last several years.

With the exception of Khiva, however, their heyday was several centuries ago. Now the region is struggling to catch up with the modern world. Sea and air transport have long since taken over all the major long-

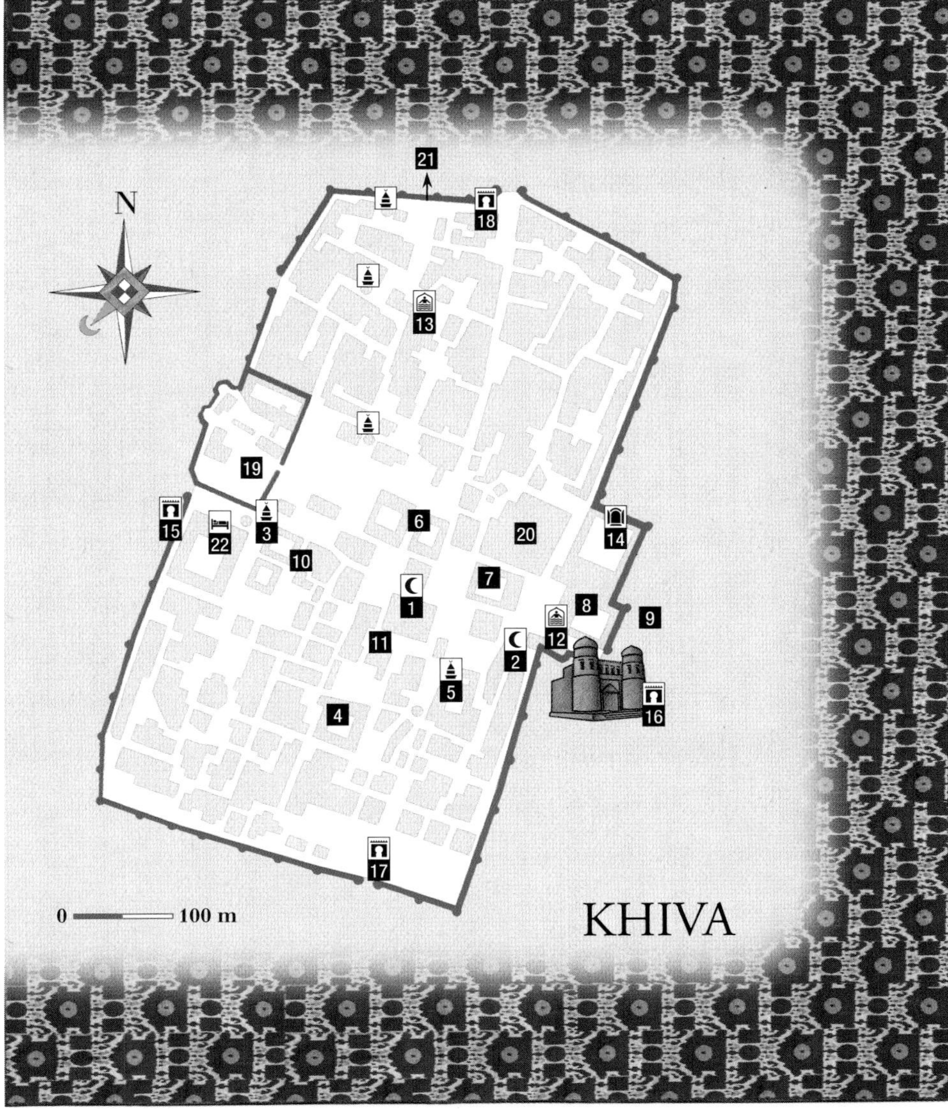

Khiva – Ichon-Qala – the old city
*MOSQUES: **1** Juma (Friday) Mosque, **2** Aq. MINARET: **3** Kalta Minor. KORANIC SCHOOLS (MEDRESSA): **4** Sherghozi Khan, **5** Islom-Huja (+ minaret), **6** Arabhana, **7** Kutlimurodinok, **8** Alloquli Khan, **9** Bazaar. MAUSOLEUMS: **10** Sayid Alauddin, **11** Pahlavon Mahmud. WELLS AND BATHS: **12** Anusha Khan bath house, **13** Kheivak well. CARAVANSERAI: **14** Tim Alloquli Khan. CITY GATES: **15** Ota-darvoza, **16** Polvon-darvoza, **17** Tosh-darvoza, **18** Buhoro-darvoza. OTHER: **19** Citadel (Kukhna Ark), **20** Tosh-Khovli palace, **21** Nurulla-Bay palace. HOTEL: **22** Medressa Amin Khan (souvenir shops).*

BORDER: Silk Parda wall-hanging, c. 1900.
ILLUSTRATION: Ota-darvoza city gate.

For general key see page 146.

The strongest testimony to Samarkand's role as a religious centre is the famous 15th-century observatory. Built on the orders of Tamerlane's grandson Ulug Beg (Ulughbek), a noted astronomer, it was at the time considered the most modern astronomical research establishment in the world. Generations of archaeologists have puzzled over the location of the original domed three-storey building. It was not until 1908 that the Russians discovered its heart – the massive sextants, some driven into the rocks, which once determined the exact positions of more than a thousand stars without a telescope.

distance routes. In the meantime, Joseph Stalin and his successors managed, in just seventy years, to strip the country of most of its resources.

A large part of the agricultural population and intelligentsia and the whole of the Islamic clergy fell victim to Stalin's reign of terror. He divided the country up arbitrarily, sowing the seeds of future discord between the Uzbeks, Tajiks and Tatars. He built linked factories all over the region to increase its economic dependence and diverted the profits from the huge gas and oil deposits to Moscow in true colonial fashion. He turned mosques into cinemas and storehouses and destroyed caravanserais and markets. In short, he did his best to eradicate 2,500 years of history. It must be said that some of his innovations were positive; for instance, increased literacy and the abolition of the *paranja*, the woven horsehair veil with which women used to have to cover their bodies and faces. Khrushchev and Brezhnev turned the country into the biggest cotton monoculture in the world, with the result that the water became totally polluted by artificial fertilizers and pesticides and the excessive water consumption gradually dried up the Aral Sea.

Despite these setbacks, the people did not lose all their zest for life. You can still see them sitting in the courtyards and gardens on the traditional *chipoys*, flat wooden beds, eating *plov*, the national dish made of lamb, rice and carrots. The old men still have their quail fighting in dark corners of the tea houses and if strangers come by, as they do very occasionally, they welcome them with a friendly '*Sog boling*', 'Cheers' and offer them apricot kernels boiled in salt water and the obligatory green tea.

Since the Republic of Uzbekistan declared independence in the summer of 1991, the country has in some respects returned to its roots. Hundreds of prayer houses have been reopened. Once again there is public and communal prayer at the tombs of the great mystics, for instance, the founder of the Sufi brotherhood of the Naqshabandi buried near Bukhara. Monuments to Tamerlane and the national poet, Alisher Navoi, now stand on squares that used to carry Lenin's name. In the autumn of 1993 the Uzbeks decided that in future they would adopt the Roman rather than Cyrillic alphabet, reviving their

Opposite: view of the walls and the eastern tower of the citadel (Ark) from the water tower next to the Bolo-hauz Mosque in Bukhara. The present fortress dates from the 18th century. Its predecessor was completely destroyed by Genghis Khan. Until a hundred years ago, a large market was held daily on the Registan, the broad open square underneath it.

Turkish heritage. At the same time, private enterprise is flourishing all over the country. On the long avenues of mulberry trees, Marlboro cigarettes, vodka, champagne, Bounty, Mars and Snickers bars are sold from makeshift stalls. In the private sections of the collective-farm markets, the farmers seem to take more care setting out their surplus fruit and vegetables than they used to. Meat is for sale on barrows at street corners, although at exorbitant prices. Many of the streets have almost the atmosphere of a bazaar.

In the large Friday market in the south of Samarkand, the poison sellers (above) have something to laugh about: they obviously have a sure-fire way of getting rid of rats. The little boy in the colourful hat (below), on the other hand, looks out at the world with mixed feelings during his circumcision ceremony.

Take **Samarkand** for example. Nowhere else in Central Asia has inspired Europeans with more romantic ideas over the centuries. Its size and splendour were renowned. In the time of Alexander the Great, when it was still called Maracanda or Afrosiab, the city on the river Zeravshan was already a thriving centre of trade. But it also owes its legendary reputation to Tamerlane, a distant relative of Genghis Khan, who rebuilt it after the Mongol invasion. Tamerlane was a despot who was capable of anything: indescribable cruelty – he had walls and towers built from the skulls of his brutally killed enemies – and the most magnificent artistic creations – the mosques, mausoleums, Koranic schools and palaces he had built in his capital in the late 14th century were at the time unsurpassed.

It is estimated that 17 million people died in Tamerlane's campaigns, which took him as far afield as Damascus, Delhi and almost to Moscow. But anyone who was talented escaped death. In all the provinces of his huge empire – Fars, Azerbaijan, Syria and Iraq, India, Khorezm and Khorassan – the tyrant spared the master craftsmen and carried them off to his 'city of cities'. Ruy Gonzalez de Clavijo, the envoy of Henry III of Castile, reported that he had thousands of them imprisoned in his castle 'to make weapons and helmets, bows and arrows for him for the rest of their lives'.

In just twenty days, without any regard for the existing buildings, he had a covered market street built through Samarkand with shops on both sides. He ordered a huge domed bazaar to be built at the point where it met the other main roads leading out from the gates of the new city wall to the centre.

Around this Tamerlane's grandson, the famous astronomer Ulug Beg (Ulughbek), later built the Registan, the 'sandy square', where orders were promulgated, military parades held, criminals executed and their severed heads displayed to the public on high poles – a practice which continued

Although the bazaar sells carpets (above), there is no chance of finding high-quality Bukharas like those made by nomads. The carpets now sold in Uzbekistan have nothing in common with them apart from the name. Below: a woman from the collective farm shows off her wealth: mulberries, natural silk and gold-plated false teeth.

until 1868. Ulug Beg also built the first of the three Koranic schools around the Registan which still survive today. The other two, Sher-Dor and Tilla-Kari, were only built in the mid-17th century after the older mosques and caravanserais had been razed.

Rauf Klishev, director of the government department which has for some time been rebuilding the Medressa Ulughbek from scratch, keeps stacks of historic photographs in his office on the Registan. They show what the square looked like at the end of the 19th century: the façades, domes and minarets of the three Koranic schools have been damaged by the ravages of time and a series of earthquakes, but underneath them, in contrast to today, can be seen the bustle of an oriental market. Here are turbaned traders squatting in wooden huts or under simple awnings with their wares piled up beside them, a water cistern, donkeys and horse-drawn carts. Crowds of people are thronging around the travelling entertainers, food stalls and story tellers.

Today the only relics of the old commercial activity are a single *charsu* (north-east of the square) and a rusty caravan monument (to the east). To see a living market you have to go to the other end of Tashkent Street, the city's central shopping and pedestrian zone, to the Siab market in the shadow of the colossal ruins of Tamerlane's Friday Mosque, Bibi-Khanym. The market mainly sells basic provisions, but specialities such as *han atlas*, the colourfully dyed natural silk from the Fergana valley, *susane*, the woven material used for carpets and the 'Samarkand' local brandy are also available. The Sunday market immediately opposite meets the local demand for cheap imported goods from Turkey.

By far the most poignant market is the one in the Jungut Makhalla, the Jewish quarter, where three times a week thousands of men and women wanting to emigrate to join their relatives in Brooklyn or Tel Aviv wait for buyers for their pathetic household goods, pots and blankets, clothes and shoes. The most important, however, is the Juma or Friday bazaar. It takes place 20 kilometres (12 miles) to the south of the city on the road to Tajikistan in Urgut province, which is famous for its tobacco. As one of the five big Friday markets of Uzbekistan – which incidentally have been held on Saturdays since the Soviet period – it regularly attracts a fascinating collection of people. War veterans with the red Soviet star on their lapels, proudly telling tales of their battles against the Germans. Dervishes begging for alms and blessing donors by rubbing banknotes over their heads, murmuring religious phrases. Peasant women in their splendidly colourful costumes, mutely and patiently holding out hand-crocheted objects to passers-by. Cooks in the typical steppe coat, the *chopan*, loudly singing the praises of their chick-peas with mutton and their fried fish. Not forgetting the *nasorachi*, the official bazaar controller, very conscious of the dignity of his office, carrying out random checks and making the private traders produce their receipts to prove they have paid the fee for the stall.

The most impressive examples of old bazaar architecture, however, are in **Bukhara**, Samarkand's perennial rival, about 300 kilometres (185 miles) to the west. Three magnificent 16th-century *charsus* have withstood countless earthquakes and now, after exemplary renovation, they once again house shops and workshops. They might only be a tiny remnant of the domed bazaar street that used to run through the Shakristan, the historic city centre, but they give a very good idea of what it must have been like here when Bukhara still depended on the Silk Road for its livelihood.

In the Taqi Telpak Furushon, the cap makers' bazaar, for instance, there must have been a constant bustle. This elegantly asymmetrical hexagonal building with its massive domes was considered the best place for felt caps, *tyubeteyka* caps embroidered with gold thread or glass beads and the skilfully wrapped turbans up to 20 metres (65 feet) long which become a shroud for the wearer when he dies. The Taqi Zargaron, the jewellers' dome, built to replace the old Charsu Bukhari, once had more than thirty workshops with their anvils, bellows and furnaces. The Taqi Sarafon, in which the moneychangers, mostly Indians, dealt with foreign currency, must have been busy too. The baths of the same name next door were said to be the finest in the whole country. Both are on the banks of a narrow, neatly tiled canal, the Sharirud or Gold Canal, through which, in the 19th century, the city's reservoirs were filled with water

The Zoroastrians called a source of wisdom 'bukhar'. In its heyday Bukhara had 180 Koranic schools with more than 30,000 students. All but one were closed down under the Soviets, but since independence in 1991 the city is well on the way to living up to its name again. Several hundred budding theologists have now enrolled. Opposite: Koran students outside the Kalan Mosque. Below: the Kalan Mosque with its minaret, the death tower from which, up to the early years of the 20th century, condemned criminals used to be thrown. Above: the Medressa Char Minar, built in 1807.

Pages 242–43: the domes of the Taqi Sarafon in Bukhara, formerly the moneychangers' market. The building is a classic example of the distinctive bazaar architecture of Central Asia.

جيوا

from the Zeravshan twice a month by means of a complicated system of sluices.

However, the Mogh or Mond bazaar, at which images of local deities were sold in the presence of the ruler on certain feast days in pre-Islamic times, has now gone. In its place is the oldest house of prayer in Central Asia, the extensively restored Maghoki-Attar Mosque. The Indian caravanserai between the jewellers' dome and the Tim Abdullah Khan, where silk fabrics are still sold, has also gone. It is still possible to drink wonderful tea at the other side of the old town, by the Labi-haus on the shady bank of a small artificial lake, but the bazaar where you could buy it has long since disappeared.

All the life has gone from the Registan, like its counterpart in Samarkand. No weapon and slave markets, no hospital, no arsenal and no guild mosques. Only the massive lattice gate leading to the Ark, the citadel, still reflects the square's former splendour. The modern 'central bazaar' is busy, especially on market days (Sundays and Thursdays) when rope dancers and other acrobats show off their tricks to the customers and musicians accompany them on the *surnai*, an ancient kind of clarinet, and the *karnai* (trumpet).

Khiva, far to the north-west, is both a historical and an architectural curiosity. For most of its 2,500 years this oasis town on the banks of the Amu Darya was an unimportant stopping point on an offshoot of the Silk Road, from which the traders continued southwards to Merv and northwards towards Astrakhan on the Caspian Sea. It was not until Kunya Urgench was destroyed in 1592 that Khiva replaced it as the seat of the Khorezm khans. Its real heyday was in the mid-19th century (it had in the meantime been almost completely destroyed by the Persian conqueror Nadir Shah). This late (and relatively short-lived) prosperity came from a somewhat ignoble source, namely slave trading. From Persia alone around a million slaves were taken into (mainly Russian) captivity via Khiva in the space of a few decades. The khan forced about 60,000 of them to beautify his fortified town with monumental buildings. At that time Europeans believed Khiva to be one of the most dangerous places in the world. Thousands of foreigners languished in dungeons there and many travellers had already paid for their innocent curiosity with their lives.

When Khiva eventually became part of the Soviet Union in 1924 and was made a prohibited area, it faded into obscurity. It was opened up again in 1968, to general amazement: although the new town, Dishon-Qala, had been partly torn down and rebuilt in Moscow concrete-slab style, the historical Ichon-Qala was a completely preserved feudal city from the Islamic Middle Ages. For the foreign tourists it was like a story from *A Thousand and One Nights* brought to life. Tosh-Khovli and Kukhna Ark, the two large palace complexes, have been faithfully restored. So too have the dozens of *medressas* and mausoleums with their typical floral blue and brown majolica. The thousand-year-old wooden pillars of the Friday Mosque, the best-known examples of Khorezmic carving, are undamaged. The magnificently decorated minarets, Kalta-Minor and Islom-Huja, newly glazed, shine out in their original splendour. Even the old bazaar in the Alloquli Khan caravanserai is still in use, although it is much smaller now that there are only about 2,000 people living within the city walls.

Although most of present-day Khiva was only built just under 200 years ago by Persian slaves, it is regarded as a typical example of a feudal Islamic city. One of its landmarks is the Islom-Huja minaret (opposite above) built in 1910, with its decoration of ceramic bands; another is the Juma (Friday) Mosque, some of whose wooden pillars are a thousand years old (opposite below). The mausoleum of the national saint Pahlavon Mahmud (above) was a holy site until 1960, after which it became a museum for thirty years. Since the collapse of the USSR it has reverted to its original purpose. The palace of the Khan Tosh-Khovli (below: a detail from the harem courtyard) is an outstanding example of Khorezmic architecture.

The light of the bazaars

Whether in the moonlight or the sunlight, between the Atlas mountains, in endless deserts, in the Levant or on the steppes at the foot of the Pamirs, the bazaar is the heart of a city: a resting place and meeting place, trading centre and workplace for people of many tribes and countries with different ideas and skills, a refuge, a reflection of various periods of history and political developments, an amalgam of old and new. The common factor that brings order to this cosmopolitan chaos is the sense of a shared religion.

Not only is the diversity of the colours, perfumes and arts a sensual experience, it is also a microcosm of society.

The light of the bazaars is different from the light of the south, of Greece, the polar regions or Tuscany. It has more in common with the subdued light of cosy living rooms or a single beam of light from below. It is more the shadow that brings out the light.

My own adventures and encounters have made more impression on me than any book. By experiencing 'normal' everyday life in a strange environment, I began to understand the culture. The openness, hospitality and tolerance extended to me personally came from a sympathy and serenity rarely found anywhere else. That was why, when I pointed my camera, I decided to focus on the people. The people of the bazaars are the real light, the photographer is just passing through. He disrupts the atmosphere of the bazaar rather than enhancing it. The more discreet he is, the better the result. It helps to use a small, quiet camera and fast film, but the way the photographer behaves is far more important than the technical side if the pictures are to be 'authentic'.

Before I went back to the world of the shopkeepers and craftsmen with a specific commission, I followed my instincts and only photographed people after I had spent some time with them and we had developed a relationship of trust so that we both felt at ease. Mutual understanding is only possible between equals.

Having now made thirty-five trips to more than twenty Islamic countries, I still try to remain true to that principle. I am not interested in sensationalism or a dry historical record. What interests me is other people's lives. I try to see and discover something new all the time and involve myself in it. That is one part; the other is to communicate it, to record it as it looks at that moment, to photograph it. A photo is always a record of time and place. It does not matter whether or not it is art; in any case, there are no rules.

My first exhibition in 1977, which I called 'Encounters', was a record of my travels and of the fascination of the Orient. It attracted a surprising amount of interest when it was shown in German and Austrian museums and galleries.

I want to thank everyone for their help and tolerance while I was working in the bazaars illustrated here. I hope my photographs will show that the bazaar is still very much alive.

Kurt-Michael Westermann

A rare find: a photographic studio in the bazaar, Niamey, Niger.

Glossary

amin: master of a guild (also: *arif, rais* or *sheikh*)
ark: normal term in Central Asia for city fortification, citadel, seat of a ruler
azan: call to prayer

bab: (city) gate, entrance
bagh: court garden or pleasure pavilion
bait: house; literally also: family
bakshish: small charitable donation not requiring any service in return
baraka: blessing, favour
basilica: hall in Roman city for public use
basmala: abbreviated form of the set phrase *'bismi llahi r-rahmani r-rahim'* – 'in the name of Allah, the compassionate, the merciful' preceding each verse of the Koran and also many actions
bazaar: Persian name for a market (Arabic: *suq*); traditional economic, trade and production centre of any Islamic city
bedesten: covered market hall for particularly valuable goods in the centre of the bazaar, originally a treasure-house
bir: well
burnous: light-coloured hooded wool coat, mostly worn by men in the Maghreb

caliph: spiritual head of Islam, literally Mohammed's representative
camii (Turkish): Friday mosque
caravanserai: rest house for overland caravans
carsi (Turkish): market (also: market street or building)
chador (Persian: tent): black cloak covering the head and body
charsu: domed bazaar above a street intersection
chechia: traditional felt cap made in Tunisia, usually red

dar: house
darwasa: gate, door of a house in Central Asia
dervish: Islamic mystic of Sufi origin, usually belonging to a brotherhood

emir: originally high-ranking administrator, later also a princely title
esunduq: communal funds of a brotherhood or guild

fatwa: expert opinion by a mufti on matters of religious law
fez: cylindrical felt hat, usually red, worn in North Africa
fityan: members of Islamic men's associations
funduq: literally 'hotel'; Maghrebi name for lodgings for traders (= *khan*)
futuwwa: literally 'youth'; ideal embracing virtues such as piety, selflessness and bravery adhered to by many esoteric men's associations in classical Islam, e.g., the dervish orders

galabiyya (*jellaba*): cotton garment worn mainly in Egypt
ghusl: greater ritual ablution in which the whole body, including the head, must be cleansed or immersed

Hadith: sayings and deeds of the Prophet Mohammed
hadjam: barber, who also provides dentistry, tattooing, circumcision and cupping services
hafiz: literally 'the keeper'; epithet for someone who has learned the Koran by heart
hajj: pilgrimage to Mecca
hajji: one who has made the pilgrimage to Mecca
hakawati: formerly a story teller in the coffee house; nowadays rare, except during Ramadan
hakim: in the wider sense 'philosopher', 'guide'; in the narrower sense 'doctor'
hammal: porter
hammam: (warm) baths
hanut: shop or workshop, stall in a bazaar
hara: literally 'spouse'; living accommodation
haramlik: women's or private quarters in an Islamic house or palace (see also: *harem*)
harem: literally 'consecrated', 'protected' or 'forbidden' place; used for women's or private quarters in an Islamic house or palace
harqus: tattooing with henna or other dyes mixed with oil, mainly worn by women in the Maghreb as a magic symbol on the face, hands and feet
hijra: the Prophet's secret flight from Mecca to Medina/Yathrib in 622; beginning of the Islamic calendar

id al-fitr (Turkish: *seker bayrami*): 'feast of the breaking of the fast' at the end of Ramadan
ihram: state of devotion of a pilgrim in Mecca
imam: originally a synonym for caliph, the leader of the community; for Sunnis a prayer leader; for Shiites also the head and senior teacher of the community of believers
Ismaili: member of a Shiite sect which considers Ismail, son of the sixth imam, the lawful leader of the community and awaits his return as the *'mahdi'* (messiah)
iwan: vaulted hall in mosques and Arab houses opening on to the courtyard

jamal: camel
jambiya: Arab curved dagger, especially in Yemen
jar: client relationship between 'patron' and 'protégé', between patricians and their less privileged neighbours
jdid: new
jellaba: see *galabiyya*
jemaa (*djamaa, jame*): mosque
jebel: mountain
jimmi: literally 'protected person'; a person of another religion under Islamic rule
jinn: spirit created from fire
jiwar: verbal solidarity agreement between individual neighbours
jubba (also *gandura*): sleeveless tunic tied with a sash, worn by Maghrebi women

Kaaba: the central shrine of Islam – a cube-shaped structure draped in a black brocade cover in the Great Mosque in Mecca, housing the 'black stone', a meteorite
kadi: judge appointed by the ruler, whose functions included the supervision of foundations, inheritances, etc.
kaftan: long-sleeved coat opening down the front, originally Turkish
kalam (Turkish: *divit*): reed quill used by calligraphers
kasbah: fortress; in North Africa also Arab quarter of town
khamsa: literally 'five'; also the name for the 'hand of Fatima', a popular amulet against the evil eye
khan (Turkish: *han*): lodgings for traders and travellers, usually in the town centre; in the Turkic/Mongolian regions also a name for the ruler
khutba: Friday sermon
kismet: fate preordained by God
Koran: the holy book in Arabic, believed by Muslims to be God's last message to mankind which has existed for eternity, revealed by Mohammed between 610 and 632
kufi: ancient form of Arabic script

madrasa (*madrese, medersa, medressa*): higher theological college
mafraj: reception room of the head of the household on the top floor of a Yemeni house
Maghreb: the Islamic west, now Tunisia, Algeria and Morocco
mahalle (Turkish): part of a town
mahriya: dowry for married women, formerly jewelry but now often money
makhzen: the power structure of the monarch
maqsura: ruler's enclosed box in a mosque
marabout: Islamic holy man or his tomb
maristan (*bimaristan*): hospital

mashrabiya: turned wood latticework screen or grill in windows of old houses
masjed (Turkish: *mecset*): small everyday mosque
mastaba: stone bench that used to stand outside every bazaar
maydan (*maidan, meydan*): square
mazalim: court directly answerable to the ruler and his representatives
medina: Arab town, now mainly used of the old quarter
mellah: Jewish quarter
mihrab: empty niche inside a mosque indicating the direction of Mecca for prayers
minaret: tower on every Friday mosque from which people are called to prayer
minbar: pulpit for Friday sermon in the mosque, originally the caliph's seat as ruler and judge
mosque: Islamic religious building for public and private prayer by Muslims
muezzin: person who summons the faithful to prayer
mufti: legal scholar appointed by the authorities; advises the faithful on matters of pious living and gives binding legal opinions
muhtasib: market overseer with various public functions, including price and quality control and supervision of public morality
mulid: religious festival to honour a saint

narghile (also: *shisha*): water pipe
naskhi: cursive form of Arabic script
nazar (Turkish: *göz boncugu*): evil eye

oud: lute
oued (also: *wad*): river, wadi

pasha: title of a general or provincial governor

qahwa: coffee, originally believed to mean 'wine'
qaiseriya: literally 'emperor's hall'; in bazaars in the Maghreb, a central network of narrow streets which can be closed on all sides, where valuable goods (especially fabrics) are sold; in the Levant: small *khan*
qamiz: collarless knee-length shirt
qanat (also: *khettara* or *foggara*): system of drains and tunnels found particularly in the Sahara and the Iranian mountains through which spring water is carried long distances underground
qibla: direction of Mecca for prayers

rasteh (Persian): central axis of the main bazaar
ribat: fortified monastery, originating in the Maghreb in the 9th century

sabil: literally 'way' refers mainly to public; fountains donated by private individuals
sadaqa: the voluntary giving of alms
salamlik: public area of a house also accessible to male visitors
samsarah: special type of *khan* up to seven storeys high, found only in Yemeni towns
saray (*sarai*): Turkish for 'palace'; in Persian also: group of *khan* buildings
sharia: Islamic law, which Muslims believe contains the rules laid down by God and valid for the whole world
sharif (pl. *shurfa*): descendant of the Prophet Mohammed, regarded as a nobleman
sheikh: honorary title with many meanings for a person in authority; to the Bedouin it usually means a freely elected tribal chief; in villages, a local leader; in a religious context, an important theologian or mystic
sheikh al-masheykh (also: *shahbander* or *kethuda*): head of a guild elected from all the guild masters
Shiites: members of one of the two main branches of Islam (see also *Sunnis*), who recognize only Ali and his descendants from the marriage with Fatima as the legitimate leaders of the whole community
souq (*souk, suq*): market
Sufism: Islamic mysticism; named after the penitent's robe worn by its adherents, made of wool, *'suf'*
sultan: title given to a ruler under the Seljuks and Ottomans
Sunna: oral tradition of the life, works and sayings of the Prophet Mohammed; for the Sunnis, who take their name from it, the second source of their faith after the Koran
Sunnis: believers in orthodox Sunna
sura: one of the 114 chapters of the Koran
suwwaqa: market people

tak (also: *tim*): domed bazaar
taqiya: small embroidered cap, usually of white cotton
tarbush: cylindrical red felt hat worn in Egypt
tekke: Dervish monastery
tughra: artistically decorated name of the sultan

ulema: higher clergy, community of legal scholars
umma: community of all Muslims

wakalat: special type of *khan* with several storeys, found only in Cairo
wala: protection and loyalty pact which a trader or craftsman enters into with his trade association
waqf: religious foundation
wazir: high-ranking government official, vizier; grand vizier: 'prime minister' in the Ottoman Empire
wudu: lesser ritual ablution in which the face, hands, forearms and feet have to be washed and the head wiped with the wet hand

yali: summer residences on the Bosporus or lakeside

zakat: charity tax
zaviya: mystic brotherhood or its monastery

SPELLING

The transliteration of terms and names from the Arabic, Persian, old Turkish or Central Asian languages using the Cyrillic alphabet is always problematic. Many sounds and characters have no precise equivalent in the Roman alphabet and any solution is inevitably a compromise.

It might be academically correct to include all the diacritical marks denoting Arabic guttural sounds, 'emphatic' consonants, long vowels or vocalizations, but that would rather defeat the object of this book, which is to make the Islamic world more accessible and understandable. Most such marks have therefore been omitted.

Furthermore, different conventions have arisen locally in the transliteration of Arabic, largely as a result of whether the main European influence has historically been, for example, British or French. As an aid to the traveller, therefore, the form of spelling most likely to be encountered on local signs, maps and guides has been adopted for each place individually. This, it is believed, will be more useful than any attempt at imposing a uniform style purely in the interests of scholarly consistency.

CHRONOLOGICAL TABLE

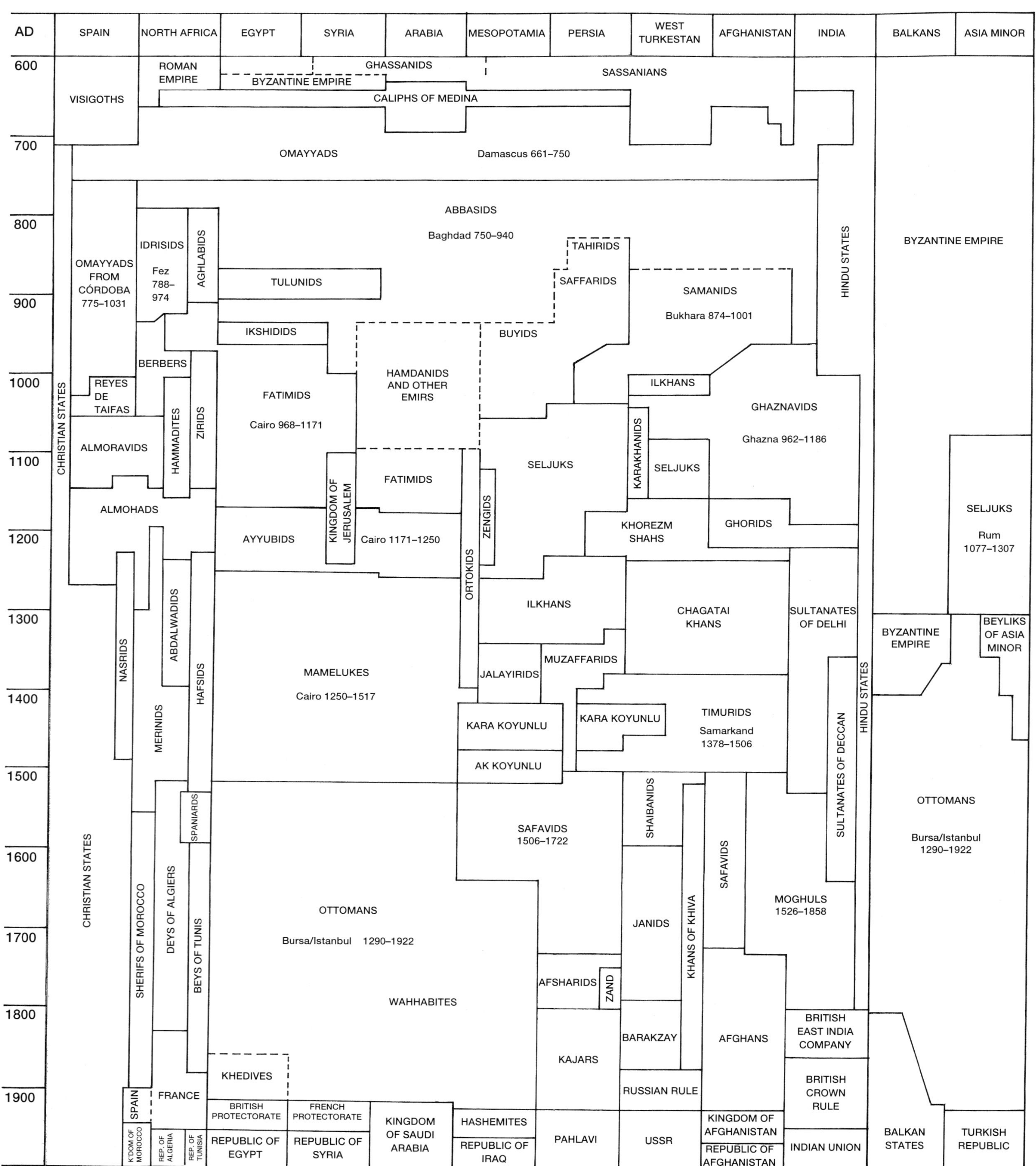

Bibliography

GENERAL ART AND ART HISTORY

Asad, Muhammad: *Der Weg nach Mekka.* Luchterhand, Hamburg 1992
Bianca, Stefano: *Hofhaus und Paradiesgarten – Architektur und Lebensformen in der islamischen Welt.* C.H. Beck, Munich 1991
Boorstin, Daniel J.: *The Discoverers.* Vintage, New York 1985
Brandenburg, Dietrich: *Die Ärzte des Propheten – Islam und Medizin.* Edition q, Berlin 1992
Croutier, Alev Lytle: *Harem – Die Welt hinter dem Schleier.* Heyne, Munich 1989
Dermenghem, Emile: *Mohammed.* Rowohlt, Reinbek bei Hamburg 1960
Donini, Pier Giovanni: *Arab Travelers and Geographers.* Immel, London 1991
Duri, Abdalaziz: *Arabische Wirtschaftsgeschichte.* Artemis, Zurich 1979
Durou, Jean-Marc: *In der Tiefe der Sahara.* Bucher, Munich and Marseilles 1993
Faroqhi, Suraiya: *Herrscher über Mekka – Die Geschichte der Pilgerfahrt.* Artemis, Munich 1990
Fernea, Elizabeth W. and Robert A.: *The Arab World – Personal Encounters.* Anchor, New York 1985
Garcia, Michèle Maurin: *Le Henné – Plante du Paradis.* Eddif, Geneva 1992
Gosciniak, Hans-Thomas (ed.): *Kleine Geschichte der islamischen Kunst.* DuMont, Cologne 1991
Göttler, Gerhard: *Die Tuareg – Kulturelle Einheit und regionale Vielfalt eines Hirtenvolkes.* DuMont, Cologne 1989
Grunebaum, Gustave Edmund von (ed.): *Der Islam I und II.* Fischer, Frankfurt/Main 1971
Heller, Erdmute, and Mosbahi, Hassouna: *Hinter den Schleiern des Islam – Erotik und Sexualität in der arabischen Kultur.* C.H. Beck, Munich 1993
Hillenbrand, Robert, *Islamic Art and Architecture.* Thames and Hudson, London 1997
Khuri, Fuad I.: *Tents and Pyramids.* Saqi, London 1990
Kreiser, Klaus, and Wielandt, Rotraud (ed.): *Lexikon der Islamischen Welt.* Kohlhammer, Stuttgart 1992
Kühnel, Ernst: *Islamische Kleinkunst.* Klinkhardt & Biermann, Brunswick 1963
Lewis, Bernard: *The World of Islam – Faith, People, Culture.* Thames and Hudson, London 1976
Michell, George (ed.): *Architecture of the Islamic World.* Thames and Hudson, London 1978
Nippa, Annegret: *Haus und Familie in arabischen Ländern, vom Mittelalter bis zur Gegenwart.* C.H. Beck, Munich 1991
Raymond, André: *The Great Arab Cities in the 16th–18th Centuries.* New York University Press, New York 1984
Reisch, Max: *Karawanenstrassen Asiens.* Welsermühl, Wels 1974
Renz, Alfred: *Geschichte und Stätten des Islam von Spanien bis Indien.* Prestel, Munich 1977
Riazuddin, Akhtar: *History of Handicrafts, Pakistan – India.* National Hijra Council, Islamabad 1988
Ricketts, Howard: *Splendeur des Armes Orientales.* ACTE-EXPO, Paris 1988
Salahdine, Mohamed: *Les Petits Métiers clandestins.* Eddif Maroc, Casablanca 1988
Scharabi, Mohamed: *Der Bazar – Das traditionelle Stadtzentrum im Nahen Osten und seine Handelseinrichtungen.* Wasmuth, Tübingen 1985
Secret, Edmond: *Les Sept Printemps de Fès.* Amiens 1990
Shah, Idries: *Die Sufis – Botschaft der Derwische, Weisheit der Magier.* Diederichs, Munich 1976
Simon, Karl Günter: *Islam – Und alles in Allahs Namen.* Gruner & Jahr/GEO, Hamburg 1988
Taeschner, Franz: *Zünfte und Bruderschaften im Islam: Texte zur Geschichte der Futuwwa.* Artemis, Zurich 1979
Thesiger, Wilfred: *Arabian Sands.* Penguin, London 1959
Wirth, Eugen: 'Zum Problem des Basars', in *Der Islam*, Berlin 1975
Zaman, Hasanuz: *Economic Functions of an Islamic State.* The Islamic Foundation, Karachi 1981

CITIES, COUNTRIES AND REGIONS

Adnan, Ethel, and Nachef, Michel: *Maroc – l'artisanat créateur.* Almadariss, Paris/Casablanca, 1983
Akhmisse, Mustapha: *Médecine, Magie et Sorcellerie au Maroc.* Casablanca 1985
Barisch, Klaus and Lissi: *Istanbul.* DuMont, Cologne 1976
Bausani, Alessandro, *et al.*: *Iran – The Future on the Plateau.* Giovanni de Agostini, Rome 1976
Bell, Gertrude: *Syria – The Desert and The Sown.* Heinemann, London 1908
Beyer, Ursula (ed.): *Kairo – Die Mutter aller Städte.* Insel, Frankfurt/Main 1983
Binous, Jamila, *et al.*: *Tunis.* Sud Editions, Tunis: 1985
Burckhardt, Titus: *Fes, Stadt des Islam.* Graf-Verlag, Olten 1960
Chwaszcza, Joachim (ed.): *Jemen.* APA, Berlin 1993
Daum, Werner (ed.): *Jemen.* Pinguin, Innsbruck and Frankfurt/Main 1987
Dostal, Walter: *Der Markt in Sanaa.* Akademie der Wissenschaften, Vienna 1979
Freely, John, and Sumner-Boyd, Hilary: *Istanbul.* Prestel, Munich 1972
Gallwitz, Esther (ed.): *Istanbul.* Insel, Frankfurt/Main 1981
Garcin, Jean Paul: *Damaskus.* Librairie Universelle, Tunis 1982
Gaube, Heinz, and Wirth, Eugen: *Der Bazar von Isfahan.* Reichert, Wiesbaden 1978
Gaube, Heinz, and Wirth, Eugen: *Aleppo – historische und geographische Beiträge zur baulichen Gestaltung, zur sozialen Organisation und zur wirtschaftlichen Dynamik einer vorderasiatischen Fernhandelsmetropole.* Reichert, Wiesbaden 1984
Gaudio, Attilio: *Fès – Joyau de la civilisation islamique.* Les Presses de l'UNESCO, Paris 1982
Gippenreiter, Vadim E., and Magowan, Robin: *Fabled Cities of Central Asia.* Abbeville, New York 1989
Glazebrook, Philip: *Journey to Khiva.* HarperCollins, London 1992
Gülersoy, Celik: *Story of the Grand Bazaar (Istanbul).* Kitabligi, Istanbul 1990
Hambly, Gavin (ed.): *Zentralasien.* Fischer, Frankfurt/Main 1966
Heard-Bey, Frauke: *From Trucial States to United Arab Emirates.* London 1982
Helfritz, Hans: *Marokko.* DuMont, Cologne 1980
Herzog, Werner: *Der Maghreb: Marokko, Algerien, Tunesien.* Beck, Munich 1990
Hopkirk, Kathleen: *A Traveller's Companion to Central Asia.* Murray, London 1993
Kalter, Johannes: *The Arts and Crafts of Syria.* Thames and Hudson, London 1992
King, John, *et al.*: *Central Asia.* Lonely Planet Publications, Hawthorn, Vic. 1996
Knobloch, Edgar: *Turkestan – Taschkent, Buchara, Samarkand.* Prestel, Munich 1973
Köhler, Michael: *Tunesien.* DuMont, Cologne 1983
Lawton, John, and Venturi, Francesco: *Samarkand and Bukhara.* Tauris Parke, London 1991
Maheu, René, and Boissel, Jean: *Iran – Rebirth of a Timeless Empire.* Éditions j.a., Paris 1976
Maréchaux, Pascal and Maria, and Champault, Dominique: *Yemen*, Thames and Hudson, London 1998
Neumann, Wolfgang: *Die Berber – Vielfalt und Einheit einer alten nordafrikanischen Kultur.* DuMont, Cologne 1983
Odenthal, Johannes: *Syrien.* DuMont, Cologne 1982
Pander, Klaus: *Sowjetischer Orient – Kunst und Kultur, Geschichte und Gegenwart der Völker Mittelasiens.* DuMont, Cologne 1982
Pope, Arthur Upham: *Persian Architecture.* Oxford University Press, Oxford 1969
Raymond, André, and Wiet, Gaston: *Les Marchés du Caire.* Institut Français d'Archéologie Orientale, Paris 1979
Renz, Alfred: *Marokko.* Prestel, Munich 1984
Renz, Alfred: *Tunesien.* Prestel, Munich 1979
Sack, Dorothée: *Damaskus.* Philipp von Zabern, Mainz/Rhein 1989
Sami, Ali: *Shiraz.* Shiraz 1971
Scheck, Frank Rainer: *Jordanien – Völker und Kulturen zwischen Jordan und Rotem Meer.* DuMont, Cologne 1985
Scholl-Latour, Peter: *Den Gottlosen die Hölle – Der Islam im zerfallenden Sowjetreich.* Bertelsmann, Munich 1991
Schweizer, Gerhard: *Iran – Drehscheibe zwischen Ost und West.* Klett-Cotta, Stuttgart 1991
Semsek, Hans-Günter: *Ägypten – Die klassische Nil-Reise.* DuMont, Cologne 1990
Sözen, Metin: *The Evolution of Turkish Art and Architecture.* Haset, Istanbul 1987
Stevens, Roger: *The Land of the Great Sophy.* Methuen, London 1962
Thubron, Colin: *Mirror to Damascus.* Arrow, London 1967
Wald, Peter: *Der Jemen.* DuMont, Cologne 1980
Wald, Peter: *Kairo.* DuMont, Cologne 1982

Index

Page numbers in *italics* refer to illustrations

ACKNOWLEDGMENTS

The author and photographer wish to thank the following for their advice and practical assistance:

Hanne Egghardt, Peter Gallhofer, Siegfried Haas, Diether Lenhart, Tarek Many, Rashid Hoda, Auguste Kern, Fritz Langauer, Nosratollah Rastegar, Michael Schrott, Alice Weiss (Vienna); Stefan Makowski (Strass im Attergau); Mara Kaselitz (Frankfurt); Alberto Valese (Venice); Brigitte Agstner-Gehring, Mohamed Amer, Anwar Abou Elella, Margarete Hasbani, Ernst Huber (Cairo); Bashir al-Ash, Nashad Sharaf (Damascus); Edip Eroglu, Celik Gülersoy (Istanbul); Yahya al-Haifi (Sanaa); Klaus and Yvonne Gruschwitz, Horst Kauch, Ghazi al-Tajir (Dubai); Abdussalam Sultan (Tripoli); Mohammed el-Abassi, Jamila Binous, Zalia el-Mechat, Zoubeir Mouhli (Tunis); Yousfi Mohsen (Kairouan); Abdellatif Rifi Mbarki (Fez); Mohammed Agouri (Marrakesh); Werner K. Koch (Jeddah); Evelyn and Joachim Brennhausen, Martina Javidnia-Ehlers, Sepehr Sepahrom (Tehran); Ahmad Ghazavi (Isfahan); Sabit Madaliev (Tashkent); Osoad Sabirova, Flora Gataullina (Samarkand); Bella Avanesova (Bukhara); Elena Allajarova (Khiva).

Special thanks to Diane Naar and Elisabeth Vidotto for their suggestions, patience and direct help.